Coventry's First Cathedral

PAUL WATKINS MEDIEVAL STUDIES

General Editor: Shaun Tyas
Consultant Editor: David Roffe

1. ANDERSON, Alan Orr, *Early Sources of Scottish History AD 500-1286*; a new edition with corrections, in 2 vols. (1990).

2. HARMER, Florence, *Anglo-Saxon Writs*; a new edition comprising the original work together with her later essay 'A Bromfield and a Coventry Writ of King Edward the Confessor' (1989).

3. STENTON, Sir Frank Merry, *The Early History of the Abbey of Abingdon*; reprinted for the first time since 1913 (1989).

4. SPITTAL, Jeffrey and FIELD, John, *A Reader's Guide to the Place-names of the United Kingdom* (1990).

5. HILL, Sir Francis, *Medieval Lincoln*; reprinted with an introductory essay by Dorothy Owen (1990).

6. PARSONS, David (ed.), *Eleanor of Castile 1290-1990, Essays to Commemorate the 700th Anniversary of her Death: 28 November 1290* (1991).

7. COATES, Richard, *The Ancient and Modern Names of the Channel Islands, a Linguistic History* (1991).

8. FOULDS, Trevor (ed.), *The Thurgarton Cartulary* (1994).

9. ORMROD, W. M. (ed.), *England in the Thirteenth Century*, Harlaxton Medieval Studies I (1991).

10. ANDERSON, Alan Orr, *Scottish Annals from English Chroniclers, 500-1286 AD*; a new edition with corrections (1991).

11. LINDLEY, Phillip, *Gothic to Renaissance: Essays on Sculpture in England* (forthcoming, 1994).

12. HICKS, Carola (ed.), *England in the Eleventh Century*, Harlaxton Medieval Studies II (1992).

13. ROGERS, Nicholas (ed.), *England in the Fourteenth Century*, Harlaxton Medieval Studies III (1993).

14. STANNCLIFFE, Clare and CAMBRIDGE, Eric (eds), *St Oswald: Northumbrian King to European Saint. Essays from the Durham Conference* (forthcoming).

15. ORMROD, W. M. and LINDLEY, Phillip (eds), *The Black Death* (forthcoming).

16. ROGERS, Nicholas (ed.), *England in the Fifteenth Century*, Harlaxton Medieval Studies IV (1994).

17. DEMIDOWICZ, George (ed.), *Coventry's First Cathedral. The Cathedral and Priory of St Mary. Papers from the 1993 Anniversary Symposium* (1994).

COVENTRY'S FIRST CATHEDRAL

The Cathedral and
Priory of St Mary

Papers from the 1993 Anniversary Symposium

Edited
by
George Demidowicz

Paul Watkins *of* Stamford

© The Contributors, 1994

Published by

PAUL WATKINS
18 Adelaide Street
Stamford, Lincolnshire, PE9 2EN.

ISBN

1 871615 49 6

Printed on long-life paper

Printed and bound by Woolnoughs of Irthlingborough

CONTENTS

CONTRIBUTORS

George Demidowicz	Coventry City Council
M. J. Franklin	Wolfson College, Cambridge
John Hunt	Workers' Educational Association
Robert Jeffery	Worcester Cathedral
Keith Lilley	University of Birmingham
Michael Mayne	Westminster Abbey
Richard K. Morris	University of Warwick
Margaret Rylatt	Coventry City Council
Michael Sadgrove	Coventry Cathedral
J. J. Scarisbrick	University of Warwick
R. Swanson	University of Birmingham
Heather Wallace	Coventry Cathedral

LIST OF ILLUSTRATIONS

Figures

PREFACE

It is not widely realised that in its long history, Coventry has had three cathedrals. The destruction of the second by enemy action in 1940, and the consecration of the third in 1962, put Coventry on the international map. But its first cathedral, the Benedictine Priory Church, founded as St Mary's Abbey in the eleventh century, is little known, even amongst the citizens of Coventry itself. To help put this right, a weekend of celebrations was held in September 1993 to commemorate the 950th anniversary of its foundation. By an unconscious piece of serendipity, the event began on the anniversary of the death of Lady Godiva, wife of the Abbey's founder Leofric, both of whom were said to be buried near the west end of their church.

The event took the form of a symposium, the aim of which was to bring together scholars in a variety of disciplines in order to pool the present state of their knowledge and understanding of Coventry's first cathedral. The fruits of that rich debate are presented in this volume. These papers are of far more than purely local interest. The case-study they offer provides a fascinating perspective on the medieval world and its decline through the eyes, as it were, of a single institution.

But the symposium was more than a survey of the current state of research on St Mary's. It was heartening that so many from the city, the cathedral and beyond were present to contribute to the discussion. The exposure to each other of scholars and the general public was an especially valuable feature of the event. Where knowledge fell short (and the scant remains of the priory are an eloquent symbol of how much we do not know about the church and its community), imagination came into play. Clambering around the ruins, walking the site to gain an impression of its size, delving into the cellars of Priory Row in search of medieval stonework, was as important as listening to the papers.

No less important, the symposium offered the opportunity to reflect more generally on the middle ages and our own contemporary view of a long-vanished world. In its way, the weekend itself offered a model of the Benedictine way of life, combining as it did study, prayer, work and, not least, hospitality. A civic reception ('symposium', literally 'drinking together') in the noble dormitory of the Whitefriars – strictly speaking, a marvellous Carmelite irrelevance in a Benedictine weekend – helped create the medieval atmosphere. The cathedral act of worship reminded us that principles fundamental to the Benedictine life are still lived out by many people today.

If the symposium achieved nothing else, it certainly reawakened awareness of Coventry's medieval past, not least in the media. I should like to express my gratitude to all those – too many to name here – who gave so generously of their time and effort to make the symposium both valuable and enjoyable. Perhaps this event can be seen as a modest dress-rehearsal for the millennium celebrations next century. I hope that the publication of these papers stimulates a new wave of interest and research around one of the nation's greatest lost medieval treasures.

Michael Sadgrove
Chair of the Symposium Planning Committee,
Coventry Cathedral
March 1994

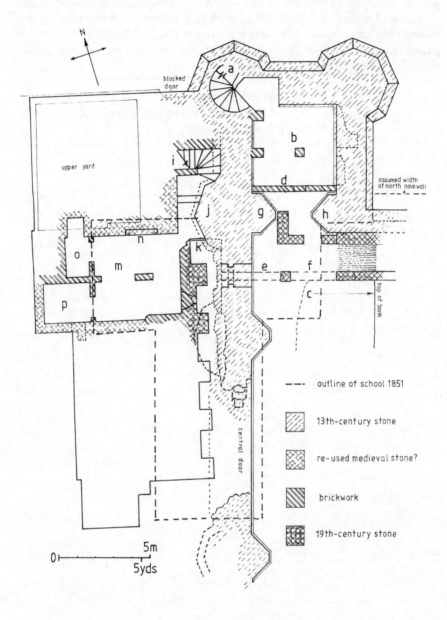

Figure 1. Cellars, Blue Coat School

Coventry - A New Beginning?
GEORGE DEMIDOWICZ

On 10, 11 and 12 September 1993 the 950th anniversary of the founding of the Benedictine monastery of St Mary was commemorated by a symposium held at Coventry Cathedral. This book contains all of the papers that were read over that weekend. This was no ordinary academic conference, however, as the contributions ranged from the new findings of scholarship to the spiritual uplift of the sermon. The long-gone and oft-forgotten priory of St Mary had, in its anniversary year, stimulated a revival of research which, it is hoped, will introduce the building and its history to a wider public, Coventrians first and foremost. But not only that, the same building, symbolic of a distant, complex and profound way of life, was able to inspire the present religious community to seek its relevance to a very different world.

As with many anniversaries with origins far in the past, the supposed foundation date of 1043 did not bear close scrutiny. We were meeting perhaps several years too late (see Hunt, this volume). The symposium was more likely to have been celebrating the dedication of the monastery in 1043, rather than the foundation by Leofric and Godiva, which probably took place in the 1020s or 1030s. This suggestion was typical of the many new ideas presented at the symposium, contributions to which can be divided neatly into three parts: the first, an examination and review of the material evidence – architectural, archaeological and topographical, the second, historical analysis based on written sources, and the third, enquiry into and exposition of the spiritual dimension. Canon Michael Sadgrove's paper on liturgy and worship in St Mary's adeptly links the scholar and priest of parts two and three respectively.

The demolition of the cathedral and priory in the years following 1545 created a large gap in the centre of Coventry. An important place in the physical and economic make-up of the town quickly became a backwater, which was not recolonised until the 18th century, and then only partially. Folk memory lingered on but it was not until the 19th century that serious study began, prompted in particular by the exposure of the west end ruins at the Blue Coat School (c.1856-7). As the cathedral and monastic records had been lost, attention focused on the disputes between the prior and the town, which were preserved in the corporation archive and in the Public Record Office. It was also hoped that archaeology could compensate for the missing documents. Since the 1850s, however, the accidental discovery of the east end chevet during the construction of the new cathedral in 1955 and the 1965-7 Brian Hobley trenches provide the sum of reliable evidence from this discipline. Myth, error and confusion have bedevilled attempts to reconstruct

1

the layout of the priory cathedral and Richard Morris takes on this daunting task in his paper. Its extra length reflects the need to disentangle fact from fiction and, as Dr Morris himself argues, the need to cover the whole of a church comparable in size to Worcester or Gloucester Cathedral. (The oft-quoted figure of 425 feet from west to east end must now be viewed with caution until an accurate measured survey of the whole site has been carried out.) The analysis of the conventual buildings is touched on only in so far as it elucidates the plan and development of the cathedral.

In the first part of his paper Richard Morris carefully sifts and weighs the evidence, much hitherto unpublished, for the plan of the church. He offers a new version, which should stand for some time, given that additional information of any value is only likely to come from further archaeological excavation, of which none is planned or foreseeable at present. He then follows this with an examination of the various architectural styles used in extant and lost building fabric in order to identify the date range of different phases. Somewhere, below the south transept perhaps, is the site of the abbey church established by Leofric and Godiva. Its physical remains may never be found, however, as they were possibly removed entirely in the rebuilding of the priory in Romanesque style during a great part of the twelfth century. This latter phase has implications on the laying out of Coventry's market place (see below). In about 1220 the large Norman Romanesque mass of this church, that is nave, crossing tower, transepts and presbytery, was given an impressive west front in the new fashion of Early English Gothic. There are few indications of any Decorated work, but the Perpendicular is well represented in the chevet east end, which may represent a rebuilding of the then unfashionable Romanesque presbytery and apse in the late 14th and early 15th centuries. Richard Morris offers his paper as a starting point, but it is more than that, for his meticulous analysis provides a working model and a firm foundation for future research.

Margaret Rylatt provides a summary review of the archaeological evidence from the whole of the priory site. She begins her account, however, with the earliest chance finds of any size in the city – an Anglo-Saxon door jamb and a wooden vat, dated c.1000. Found in Palmer Lane and Bishop Street, these may be pointers to the location of the pre-Conquest settlement of Coventry. Most excavation has taken place within the church itself, most notably 1856-7 (west end), 1955 (east end chevet), 1965-7 (nave) and 1989-90 (west end), but only the latter two were carried out with any archaeological rigour.

The Brian Hobley excavations of 1965-7 had as their grand aim the discovery of the Leofric and Godiva church and, it was hoped, even St Osburga's nunnery. This was not to be, but much of the plan of the Benedictine conventual buildings was recovered, along with some artefacts and a considerable quantity of architectural fragments and debris. In these terms the excavation proved to be a great success and Margaret Rylatt provides a résumé of the findings. As is frequently the case, however, the presence of such a massive archaeological site has whetted the appetite for further investigation. Such opportunities in the future are unpredictable, but the pressing need to renovate Blue Coat School and the New Buildings ribbon weaving factory may satisfy our curiosity on these matters sooner rather than later.

Keith Lilley breaks much new ground in his analysis of the topographical development of Coventry and the role of the priory. Documentary sources, poor already, are particularly lacking in information on the management and development of its landed property in town and countryside. However, historical geographers, amongst others, stress that the landscape is itself a document, which can be read in much the same way as an ancient palimpsest written over many times. It is extraordinary that it has taken so long to appreciate that the pattern of streets, plots and buildings, as shown on early Coventry maps, has a meaning which can be interpreted by those with a topographical eye. A great opportunity was lost when the *Atlas of Historic Towns* did not adopt this approach for Coventry.[1] Work has been done on selected areas but an overall systematic analysis has hitherto not been undertaken.[2]

Some time ago it was suggested that the Much Park Street and Little Park Street area was planned in the late medieval period, but even this view has been disputed.[3] Keith Lilley, by contrast, has identified twenty-one separate plan-units and in his paper concerns himself with just two: the priory precinct and the market area. The first has obvious relevance but the second, remarkably, has not hitherto been perceived as a place strongly connected with or influenced by the priory. The boundary of the priory precinct is delineated with variations from the *Atlas of Historic Towns* solution and the west, north and east sides are relatively straight lines enclosing a compact sub-rectangular area. To the south the matter is more difficult and the ward and parish boundaries are not helpful, forming awkward salients not easily followed by a major boundary wall. It is now up to future researchers to test and verify this line.

The precinct is identified by Lilley as abutting the plan unit to the west – the market area. The geographical relationship between the two is crucial in

[1] M. D. Lobel (ed.), *The Atlas of Historic Towns: Coventry* (London, 1975).
[2] See, for example, N. W. Alcock, 'Coventry Streets: West Orchard and the Sherbourne, Development and Topography, 1600 to 1940', *Transactions of the Birmingham and Warwickshire Archaeological Society*, 91 (1981), 83-116.
[3] See discussion, Susan M. Wright, 'Much Park Street, Coventry: the Development of a Medieval Street. Excavations 1970-74', *Transactions of the Birmingham and Warwickshire Archaeological Society*, 92 (1982), 13-14.

understanding the early development of Coventry. The Benedictine monastery here, in common with many others, was responsible for stimulating town growth and the most tangible expression of this policy was the laying out of a market area. The favoured location was 'on the doorstep', overlooked by the monastic buildings and supervised by the community within. The 12th-century nave of St Mary's with its added 13th-century frontage relates closely to the market area, suggesting that the latter was created early in the 12th century, if not before. In front of the west end lay a forecourt enclosed by the precinct wall and entered by a gate directly from the triangular market, which was originally extensive: c.1.3 ha (3.2 acres). In time, and probably by the beginning of the 14th century, the market place was infilled with two large blocks, leaving a circuit of streets, Great Butcher Row, Bull Ring, Ironmonger Row, Cross Cheaping, connected by Little Butcher Row. The loss of this impressive open space, lined with merchant houses and shops and overlooked by the priory gate and lodging house, was an important change to the topography of medieval Coventry.

What is surprising is the length of time it has taken for this major topographical event to be recognised, given the number of scholars who have worked on the early history of Coventry. But perhaps it is not so strange, since much effort over the last few decades has been expended on the forged charters and the great prior's half/earl's half debate. In fact it was Philip B. Chatwin who was the first to suggest the idea of a gradual filling in of the market. In 1928 he wrote: 'In medieval times there was more or less open space in front [of the cathedral west end], extending to the other side of Cross Cheaping... On market-days this open space was filled with stalls. The temporary nature of these must always have been an inconvenience, and gradually they became more permanent; the various stalls first became huts, then houses, and the different rows and streets were known by the nature of the commodities sold there.'[4] These pioneering thoughts were unfortunately lost in the clamour of the 'Great Debate' mentioned above. It was not until 1982 that a triangular market founded by monastic enterprise was written of again, but the area was not defined nor a map produced.[5] More recently my own researches undertaken within the conservation section of the City Planning Department have led inexorably to belief in the existence of a large prior's market place. In 1993 we published the Coventry City Centre Trail, which indicated the extent of the pre-infill market in the Broadgate/ Ironmonger Row area.[6] Keith Lilley's researches now place the market into a

[4] Philip B. Chatwin, 'Early Coventry', Transactions of the Birmingham and Warwickshire Archaeological Society, 53 (1928), 133.

[5] T. R. Slater, 'Urban Genesis and Medieval Town Plans in Warwickshire and Worcestershire', in Field Forest: An Historical Geography of Warwickshire and Worcestershire, ed. by T. R. P. J. Jarvis (Norwich, 1982), 189.

[6] Coventry City Centre Trail, City Planning Services, Development Directorate,

much wider topographical framework, which, it is hoped, will engender a new era of debate on Coventry's origins in which all the sources, archival, archaeological, architectural and topographical, will be brought to bear.

John Hunt's paper, the first in the history section, conveniently begins at the beginning, but, as mentioned above, a little earlier than hitherto thought. (Unfortunately, and not unexpectedly, no more light can be thrown upon the supposed previous foundation of St Osburga's nunnery.) The patronage of Coventry priory by the house of Leofric is examined in the wider context of the family's interests throughout the earldom of Mercia. Leofric and Godiva, in particular, are remembered for their piety, but this was only one aspect of patronage, albeit genuine in some cases. Benefaction and endowment was not without political gain, as through these means prestige and influence could be extended beyond the normal reach of the House of Leofric. John Hunt identifies the Coventry foundation as an essential part of this policy, the more striking as the monastery was also adopted as the family mausoleum. This decision raises the question: why was Coventry chosen? Was it already an important place at this time or was its potential as a replacement of the proto-Coventry at Lunt/Baginton foreseen? John Hunt wisely avoids this knotty issue, as the contemporary Anglo-Saxon sources are not forthcoming. The question, however, remains vital to an understanding of Coventry's origins.

The dissolution of the priory and cathedral in 1539 not only destroyed a community and its buildings, but also the archive which had recorded monastic activities over five hundred years. Had the documents survived, no doubt St Mary's, Coventry, would have a more prominent place in the general corpus of knowledge of medieval monasteries and cathedrals. Historians of the priory are greatly disadvantaged, as there are only scattered fragments of evidence available for study and little prospect of finding a long-lost cartulary. It is to the credit of the historians who took part in the symposium that so much new material has been brought to light, proving that their skill lies as much in their ability to track down previously unknown or unsuspected sources as in their ability to understand and interpret them.

M. J. Franklin's study of the Anglo-Norman bishops of Coventry uses episcopal acta to revise the accepted view that they were non-entities placed in charge of an unimportant diocese. His account enlivens their personalities and enlarges hitherto scant biographies. Dr Franklin stresses that their lives should be viewed against the background of an almost continual conflict with the Benedictine monks of Coventry with whom the bishops, reluctantly it seems, shared the cathedral and whose wealth was regarded as a fair target for appropriation to aid the burden of ecclesiastical administration. Indeed,

Coventry City Council (1993).

according to William of Malmesbury Bishop Robert de Limesey transferred his see from Chester to Coventry in order to seize the wealth of the Coventry monks. The move has moreover been interpreted as part of the Norman policy of locating episcopal sees in larger centres of population.[7] If Coventry was such a centre at the turn of the twelfth century when the transfer of the see took place, then the Domesday Book entry recording only a large agricultural community must have omitted the town. It is a compelling argument which relates directly to the question of Coventry's origins. The Benedictine foundation undoubtedly stimulated urban growth, but was this grafted onto a budding trading centre? Coventry's success as a town in the second half of the eleventh century might have been as much an attraction to the financially strained bishops in despoiled Chester as the conspicuous riches of the monastic establishment. If the Norman bishops have left any mark in Coventry then it is in Bishop Street, which once connected the prior's market with the suburb of St Nicholas over the river Sherbourne. Its bold straight line has the look of a planned street and may reflect a short-lived but successful episcopal encouragement of town expansion in the early twelfth century.

Dr Franklin hands over at the thirteenth century to Dr Robert Swanson, who takes the story to the dissolution in 1539. Focusing on the priory as an organisation, he examines both its internal structure and its external relations, the latter complicated by its function as a cathedral in a diocese with a second seat at Lichfield. Dr Swanson naturally bemoans the loss of the St Mary's archive, which has made life difficult for historians, but from scraps and gleanings he has been able to 'dissolve some of the shadows'. The community was, in fact, remarkably small for such a major house, hovering in size over the centuries between the late teens and the twenties. This meant that each monk usually held some office, such as treasurer, steward, and pittancer, and in these circumstances the rhythms of Benedictine worship had to compete with the affairs of secular administration to a greater extent than in a larger Benedictine community.

The division of rights, privileges and possessions of the pre-Conquest bishopric between the bishop, the priory and the Lichfield canons had not yet been completed in the thirteenth century and hence this was a period of vexatious quarrels. Although the see had been located in Coventry from around 1100, these disputes may have caused the migration of the seat to Lichfield during the following century. The bishops preferred to work with the less disputatious secular canons at Lichfield; they rarely lodged in Coventry and 'in truth... had little need for the second cathedral' (p. 146). This Lichfield perspective does not diminish the status of Coventry cathedral and priory, which from the fragments of evidence assembled by Dr Swanson

[7]   Peter R. Coss, *The Early Records of Coventry* (London, 1986), xv.

was clearly a major institution in medieval England. The presence of two cathedrals in one diocese was, however, a deciding factor in the destruction of St Mary's, Coventry, at the Reformation.

Professor Scarisbrick recounts the political manoeuvring and upheaval surrounding the loss of Coventry's cathedral and priory. It is worth repeating here that no other cathedral was demolished during Henry VIII's reforms. Fortunately, in comparison with the material for the medieval period, the records of the dissolution of St Mary's are relatively copious and are accessible through the 'Letters and Papers' of the reign of Henry VIII published by the Public Record Office. The documents themselves do not necessarily convey the drama of the events but Professor Scarisbrick eloquently communicates the tragedy of the fall of St Mary's, which was played out on the local and national stage. The monastic cathedral was not pulled down immediately on the expulsion of the monks on 15 January 1539, for the monastery and church were apparently still standing six years later, though they had been made uninhabitable. Their despoiled presence provided not only a symbol of the trauma suffered by the monastic communities themselves, but also of the economic dislocation brought about by the destruction of a powerful and wealthy organisation.

The reason that the cathedral stood more or less intact in 1545 was partly a result of the efforts of the corporation to save it, along with Whitefriars church, in order to create two extra parishes. It was claimed that Holy Trinity and St Michael's were overcrowded. But the city fathers' argument failed to convince and the necessary money could not in any case be raised. A stark fact had then to be faced: the cathedral was surplus to requirements. There was already one in the diocese at Lichfield and the cathedral there was already staffed with secular canons, more acceptable to Henry VIII. The creation of a separate Coventry diocese could not be justified. The city had two large and magnificent parish churches, and a third alongside was unnecessary. The time for negotiations and delaying tactics was over and in June 1545 the crown disposed of priory property in Coventry to a value of £1000, including the site of the cathedral. John Hales was the purchaser and it is likely that demolition began in earnest soon after the sale. Fortunately this was not conducted ruthlessly and systematically and the north-west tower survived above ground into the 19th century. Another large fragment near the alley, Hill Top, a wall with blind arcading, part of the conventual buildings, disappeared some time after 1800.

Michael Sadgrove breathes life into the fragments of evidence which hint at the liturgical splendours of Benedictine life. All too often the evidence is missing entirely and he can only draw on parallels from similar or related institutions such as Worcester and Lichfield. Fortunately Canon Sadgrove draws on his insights and experience as an active member of the present religious community at Coventry Cathedral. Scholar and cleric fruitfully combine to reveal a little more deeply the mystery of faith and its expression through worship at the medieval St Mary's: the legendary shrines of St Osburga, and of Leofric and Godiva, the fantastical relics, the celebration of the centrality of the mass, the exotic accoutrements that adorned it – pyxes, censers, paxbreds, the regular punctuation of the monks' day through the interpretation of *The Rule of St Benedict* and the *Regularis Concordia*, the processions on the feast of Corpus Christi and on the holy days of the Virgin Mary. It is no wonder that Michael Sadgrove concludes that this heady mixture of ritual and precious artefact should be seen as 'the theatre of the soul', a performance first and foremost through which faith could literally be absorbed.

I am not qualified to comment on the sermons delivered during the symposium and shall only attempt a brief summary. Canon Heather Wallace sought the relevance of the Rule of St Benedict to modern living and in particular to the need for and notion of community, whose cement is self-discipline, commitment, love and respect. Those in authority over the community should know how to communicate and consult, and although individual members need sufficient privacy and personal space, all newcomers should be made welcome. The Very Rev Michael Mayne also dwelt on the relevance of the Benedictine Rule to religious life today. The medieval edifice of St Mary's was built to enable St Benedict's *Opus Dei*, the work of God, to be carried out within and in turn its buildings can inspire and reveal the spiritual nature of the human condition. The Very Rev Robert Jeffery cast his eye over the medieval world and saw little to commend in its cruel, ordered and introverted life. Christianity in this period had a different form, lacking missionary zeal, but providing through the Church and the Eucharist a direct route to the presence of God. Since then great changes in the Christian Church have taken place and faith has been reinterpreted many times, making use of tradition but in new guises. In this process worship and liturgy have retained a strong pull, the more so when festive, creative and exciting. To celebrate the past alone is insufficient, as today's problems have to be faced through a celebratory, protesting, but simple way of life.

* * *

This introduction gives me an opportunity to reveal some relevant findings made by the Conservation section of the City Planning Department in and about the West End ruins and the old Blue Coat School. This research was prompted by the proposed marketing of the school by the Council and the need to tidy the ruins following the 1989-90 excavation and to rescue and store architectural fragments which lay scattered around the site. The actual work to the ruins was carried out in the spring of 1994 by the Conservation section.

The West End and Blue Coat School.

In 1714 the Blue Coat School for girls was founded and used as part of its premises the north-west tower of the priory church. By 1780 new buildings had been erected at the site and were in use by the school.[8] The 1851 Board of Health map probably shows this phase of buildings at their maximum extent. At this time the west front of the cathedral was not exposed, as one school building immediately south of the tower straddled it and the next building to the south probably used the wall as the base of its eastern elevation. This is not to say that this large piece of priory masonry was not known at the time – it could have been exposed internally in school cellars – but it was not yet a public monument.

In May 1856 it was reported that the school buildings were structurally unsound, particularly the school room.[9] Its walls had been supported on timber, which had decayed leaving a hollow of about a foot in depth. Underpinning was not recommended, since it was likely to cause the collapse of the whole structure. In the previous August the Corporation had served notice on the trustees that 'rebuilding and alterations going on' were in breach of the Public Health Act.[10] The exploratory excavations mentioned by the architect, Murray, in his report may have uncovered the west end wall. It was obvious to all now that new school buildings were necessary and so the opportunity was taken to expose the ruins and lay them out as a formal antiquity. The main schoolroom with an undercroft playground was deliberately set back westwards off the west end ruins. How much this decision was as a result of antiquarian pressure from without or due to the interest of the trustees themselves is not known.

Certainly the topographical artist, Nathaniel Troughton, was party to the conveyance of the school land to its trustees and he had drawn some important sketches of the ruins before the new school was built.[11] Construction took place in two stages, the first in 1856 providing the main schoolroom with its impressive timber-truss roof. The second, a year later, the building of ancillary rooms, such as the matron's accommodation, dormitories and a kitchen, extended northwards into the north-west tower with a new frontage overlooking the ruins to the south. It was originally intended to retain the walls of the tower at their existing height, as the building plans show, but this was not carried out and they were demolished down to the plinth save for a few pinnacles of masonry.[12] It is possible that some of the south-west tower above the plinth had also survived, if the

8   Coventry City Council, Deeds relating to Blue Coat School, File 3843.
9   Coventry Record Office, 1037/93/1, Letter from I. J. Murray to the school trustees, 3 May 1856.
10 Coventry Record Office, 1037/92/1, Notice from Town Clerk, 18 Aug 1855.
11 See note 8 above; CRO, 1/9/22-3,30-2, Troughton sketches.
12 Coventry Record Office, 1490/1, Specification for works to Blue Coat School.

Troughton sketch is to be believed.[13]

There is more of the north-west tower and the cathedral west wall to be seen within the school itself (Fig 1). The spiral staircase (marked (a) on Fig 1) within the tower's north-west octagon leads down into a cellar which takes up the whole of the base of the tower (b). This area formerly opened out into the first bay of the north aisle of the cathedral (c). The walls on three sides of cellar are constructed of sandstone ashlar and are probably original 13th-century fabric, as these correspond to the undisturbed plinth level. A modern brick wall (d) divides the cellar from the area under the two flat Victorian arches (e, f), now secured by grilles, which support the footpath entrance to the main door. Within this covered area the bases and jamb shafts (g, h) of the arch between the north aisle and the tower can be seen, though partially obscured by and incorporated into later Victorian constructions.

A second cellar is approached by a separate dog-leg staircase (i) set against the external face of the west wall of the priory cathedral. As soon as the steps are descended the base and shafts of a polygonal and shafted buttress can be seen (j). This structure marks the position of the north aisle wall within the nave of the cathedral and braces the north-west tower arch mentioned above (g-h). Part of buttress (j) lies on the exterior, separated from the cellar by a narrow pointed arch (k), probably Victorian, and now blocked by brickwork. It was exposed during the 1989-90 excavations, but covered over once more in 1994 by a loose fill to prevent the erosion of the school foundations. Returning to the interior, a narrow gap allows entrance into the main part of the cellar (m) and here you stand only a little above the original level of the cathedral forecourt. There is a niche (n) in the north cellar wall, but it does not look medieval and the two shafts on either side are reused (Morris, this volume, note 164). This cellar, except for small compartments on the west side (o, p), roughly corresponds with the plan of the west half of the pre-1856-7 school building, which was attached to the south side of the north-west tower. The lower half of the cellar wall is composed of sandstone ashlar, the upper part brick, and it is likely that this building reused priory masonry in its construction sometime in the 18th century. If the cellar dates from this period also, then this area of the cathedral frontage was already accessible before the 1856-7 rebuild. When the latter took place the old arrangement of a separate girls' entrance on the west side approached from Great Butcher Row and a staff entrance on the east side from Priory Row was maintained. This segregation provides a clue to a more precise location of the priory gate connecting the market and the cathedral forecourt.

[13]   Coventry Record Office, 1/9/4.

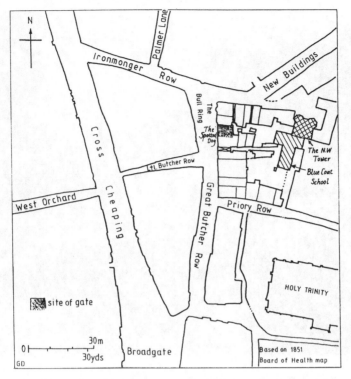

Figure 2. Location of Priory Gate based on 1851 Board of Health map

The Priory Gate

Poole recounted the events which led to the demolition of the priory gate in about the year 1704.[14] In the June of that year the Corporation ordered a Mrs King to rebuild the 'stone arch leading into the Priory court', which her workmen had undermined and thrown down. This had been acquired by the Corporation in 1545 and was described in 1581 as 'a gate howse and waye leading from the Bull Ring unto the ...pryorie and mylne'.[15] The wording implies that the gate led directly off The Bull Ring into the former cathedral forecourt and then leftwards down what was later to become the street called New Buildings, to the remainder of the priory site and its mill.

The Corporation order to reconstruct the gate was never carried out and after some litigation the land was sold in September 1705 to Mrs Cave King for £5, and a public house, known later as 'The Dog' or 'Spotted Dog', erected over the site. The pub, demolished in 1936 to make way for the

---

14 Poole, *A History of Coventry* (London, 1870) p. 11; Coventry Record Office, Borough Minutes, 1 June 1704, 8 August 1704, 29 Sept 1705, BA/H/C/17/4.
15 Coventry Record Office, BA/A/A/2/3, 1581 survey.

Figure 3. Taunton engraving of Great Butcher Row, after Gifford

beginning of Trinity Street, was located on The Bull Ring to the north of the girls' entrance to Blue Coat School (Fig 2). This entrance can be seen on the extreme left-hand side of Taunton's engraving of The Butcher Row, 1850, reproduced in Poole's volume (Fig 3). At about second floor level above the entrance there projects a jetty and to its left, almost out of the picture, is another jetty at a lower level belonging to the neighbouring property.

A 1920s photograph taken lower down in The Bull Ring swings the view further to the left (Plate 1). 'The Spotted Dog' is the two storey stuccoed building with dentilled eaves and a hipped plain tile roof. A first floor window, vertically sliding with an exposed sash box almost flush with the wall, suggests a very early 18th-century date. Adjoining 'The Spotted Dog' to the right (the south) is the single-bay jettied building on the very edge of the Taunton engraving; its gable faces the street. It seems to have been taken over by the pub by this time, as it bears large advertisements for the brewery which owned it. Next to the right is a brick building, or at least a brick facade, the high level jetty visible in the Taunton view having been removed. Much of it is a shop front except for the narrow round-arched passage used by the Blue Coat schoolgirls. Given that 'The Spotted Dog' was

Figure 4. Bull Ring, Coventry, by Edgar W. Pitt, 1934
Courtesy of Herbert Art Gallery and Museum

built over the priory gate after 1705 and the adjoining two jettied buildings, timber-framed structures by definition, can be no later than 17th-century in date, the gate could not have stood further south than the frontage of the early 18th-century 'Spotted Dog' shown in the photograph. This is not opposite the opening of Little Butcher Row nor over the deep plot extending towards the west front of the cathedral, as suggested by Lilley (this volume). The deep plot, in fact, corresponds to the girls' narrow right of way to the Blue Coat School.

'The Spotted Dog' frontage was no wider than that shown in the 1920s photograph, as Pitt's watercolour of 1934 reveals (Fig 4). The building was approximately five metres wide by seven metres deep, a plot sufficient to have accommodated a gate the size of Hill Street Gate or Whitefriars Gate, Much Park Street, for example. The site now lies under the pavement and roadway of Trinity Street opposite Ironmonger Row and immediately fronting the mock timber-framed shops erected in 1939 (Fig 5). When J. B. Shelton excavated in this very area in 1937 and 1938 he believed that he had found the 'west archway pillars' of the gate, most of the remaining

13

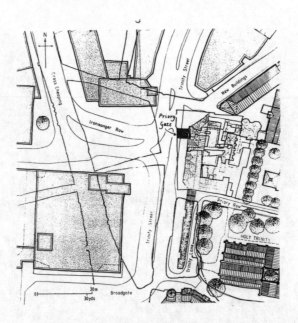

Figure 5. Modern plan of Priory Gate area
with 1851 Board of Health map overlaid

foundations having long since been removed for the pub cellars.[16] The
evidence that these 'pillars' were part of the gate in question is,
unfortunately, not conclusive, as there are no drawings or photographs. The
site, however, needs to be watched in case of potential disturbance.

What of future research? I have already hinted at some of the directions
and some of the questions which need to be tackled. The study of the
Benedictine Priory at Coventry is intertwined with the study of Coventry's
origins. The foundation year of 1043 used to give Coventry its first
documented event. The fact that this has now been put back to the 1020s and
1030s emphasises that the Benedictines were at the historical beginning as we
know it. But the foundation of the Benedictine monastery, whenever it took
place precisely, is not early enough – for why did Leofric and Godiva choose
Coventry? It was supposedly on the edge of their sphere of influence, which
they wanted to extend. So what attracted them to this particular place? The
House of Leofric cannot be seen as the equivalent of the later Cistercians
looking for peace and solitude in the deep forest; the Anglo-Saxon dynasty
had an eye for the main chance. What then were the advantages of Coventry?
Had it begun to grow at the important junction of Arden and the more open

16 See articles by Shelton in *Austin's Monthly Magazine*, Vol. XXIX, no. 359 (May,
    1937), Vol. XXXI, no. 369 (October, 1938).

and anciently settled areas of the Avon valley, displacing a more ancient centre at Baginton/Lunt? The latter was held under the rival lordship of the Earls of Warwick, and Coventry could have been deliberately selected to compete. If this were the case, the decision was clearly successful.

The question of whether Coventry was already a town in the last decades of the Anglo-Saxon period may never be settled. There may be more likelihood, however, of establishing which lord – earl or prior – was the most responsible for the growth of Coventry in the two centuries following the Norman invasion. There is no doubt that the priory and even the bishops wished to see their part of Coventry develop as a commercial centre and the topography of the town in the prior's fee reflects these ambitions, i.e. the market place, Bishop Street. The issue is whether the earls of Chester gave the matter equal attention in the late 11th and early 12th centuries, even taking the initiative or, conversely, whether the earls, mindful of the success that the priors had achieved in boosting town growth, simply followed suit.[17] If this latter question has any validity, the well known east-west axis from Spon Street to Gosford Street, which figures so prominently in the topography of medieval Coventry, may not be such an ancient feature. It may have appeared later and have been subordinate to the north-west to south-east route from the direction of Tamworth, Lichfield and places farther north, via the prior's market in the centre of Coventry, towards London. In this context a review of the relatively plentiful contemporary documentation should be rewarding and at the same time the prior's half/earl's half debate may be advanced towards a consensus. I have already stressed that all the evidence should be considered from now on – topographical, architectural, archaeological and documentary – but place names should also not be forgotten. Before the foundation of the Benedictine monastery there was another known historical event: that is, the naming of Coventry ('Cofa's tree'). Recent thoughts on this matter have concluded that most names of this type are late Anglo-Saxon and indicate a boundary tree given the name of a neighbouring landlord.[18] It is interesting to speculate that the territory of Coventry was already divided at this time.

Acknowledgments
I would like to thank my colleagues in the Conservation and Urban Design section who helped in the preparation of this Introduction; Paul Vyse Widdicombe and Mark Singlehurst for the survey of the cellars at Blue Coat School and the west end remains and for helpful comments on the draft text; and Kevin Wilkins for stimulating discussions and conjectures on the topography of early Coventy.

[17] *op. cit.*, Coss, p. xvii.
[18] Margaret Gelling, *Place-names in the Landscape* (London, 1984), pp. 211-18 and subsequent personal communication.

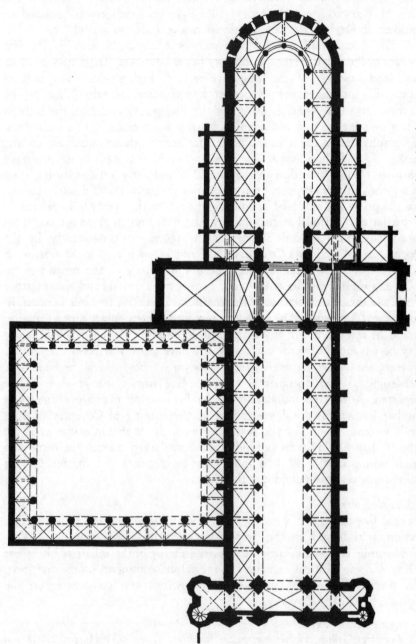

Figure 1. Reconstruction of St Mary's church and cloister, after Tickner (1918).

The Lost Cathedral Priory Church of St Mary, Coventry
RICHARD K. MORRIS

St Mary's, Coventry, was the only English cathedral church to be demolished at the Reformation. So total is its obliteration in the minds of men that virtually all surveys of the cathedrals of England and Wales fail to give it a section,[1] and as recent a work as Pevsner and Metcalf, *The Cathedrals of England*, omits it entirely.[2] Yet its loss as a cathedral is a rather artificial statistic, because numerous other great churches without cathedral status, but of equal interest to the architectural historian, disappeared in the same decades, such as the midland abbeys of Evesham and Winchcombe. St Mary's was as much a monastic church as the seat of a bishop, and episcopal patronage by no means dominated its building history between the twelfth and sixteenth centuries. Bath Abbey, the other example of a cathedral church in a joint-diocese which suffered demotion (but not demolition) at the Reformation, was rebuilt on a smaller scale after 1499 at the instigation of the bishop, Oliver King. In contrast, the priors of St Mary's seem to have been the main promoters of new works on Coventry Cathedral in the later middle ages.

This paper aims to assess the material evidence for the architectural form and style of the cathedral, and to bring some previously unpublished aspects of that evidence to a wider audience. But the overwhelming problem is, of course, the lack of information. No helpful old views exist of the cathedral before its destruction, comparable to the set of Hollar's engravings of Old St Paul's Cathedral in London, lost in the Great Fire in the next century.[3] Moreover, Coventry shares with other sites like Evesham the problems posed by a dearth of substantial standing fabric, in contrast to, say, Tintern Abbey; and a lack of rigorous modern excavation of the whole church site, in contrast to, say, Bordesley Abbey.[4] The Godiva Commemoration Excavation directed by Brian Hobley in 1967 was restricted

---

1   E.g. F. Bond, *The Cathedrals of England and Wales*, rev. ed. (London, 1912); J. H. Harvey, *The Cathedrals of England and Wales*, rev. ed. (London, 1974), St Mary's omitted from the catalogue (pp. 217-45) but passing mention in the main text.

2   N. Pevsner and P. Metcalf, *The Cathedrals of England: Midland, Eastern and Northern England* (Harmondsworth, 1985), 62-70.

3   See R. K. Morris, 'The New Work at Old St Paul's Cathedral', *Medieval Art, Architecture and Archaeology in London* (*BAACT*, issue for 1984, published 1990), 74-100. For abbreviations used in this essay, see the list on pp. 65-66.

4   S. M. Hirst and S. M. Wright, 'Bordesley Abbey Church: a Long-term Research Excavation', in *The Archaeology of Rural Monasteries*, ed. R. Gilchrist and H. Mytum, British Archaeological Reports, British series 203 (Oxford, 1989), 295-311.

to selective trenches in the nave area,[5] and the whole eastern arm of the church remains uncharted territory except for the Gothic chevet. The west front is the only architectural remnant standing to any height today (pl. 13), and the most useful past observations of architectural fabric *in situ* have all been in the area of the church west of the crossing. Even so, it is frustrating to discover how many carved and worked stones sighted by previous generations have disappeared without detailed record. Dr Troughton's drawings of the mid-nineteenth century, though much admired, provide no adequate substitute because most of his subjects are unprovenanced.[6] Some of his drawings almost certainly depict features from the conventual buildings, which are not a major concern here except where an aspect of their planning or style bears on the architectural history of the church.

With the loss of the priory's muniments, very few documentary references exist around which to model an architectural history, and they can be summarised very briefly.[7] The Benedictine abbey church of St Mary was consecrated in 1043, probably having been founded some years earlier by Earl Leofric and the Lady Godiva, perhaps in the 1020s.[8] St Mary's was raised formally to cathedral status in 1102 by Bishop Robert de Limesey, transferring the see from St John's, Chester. In the civil wars of King Stephen's reign, the church and priory buildings were occupied during a siege of the castle in 1143, and may have suffered serious damage. In about 1189, we hear of a church which is unfinished, for Bishop Hugh Nonant had replaced the monks with secular canons and destroyed conventual buildings, re-using the materials for the church. This is the clearest documentary evidence we have for a rebuilding of Leofric and Godiva's church in the twelfth century, as also for a major refurbishment of the conventual buildings when the monks returned after 1198. A royal grant of timber for the church is recorded in the *Calendar of Close Rolls* for 1247-51. In the early years of Prior Henry Irrey (1322-42), indulgences were being granted to contributors to the fabric of the cathedral church. In 1409 mention is made of 'our new work' in connection with the intended consecration of altars. In the following year a double feast was established in honour of St Osburga, and there may have been a translation of her relics in 1462. The monastery was dissolved in 1539, though wholesale destruction of the church and monastic buildings seems not to have commenced until 1545 and after.[9]

---

5   Hobley, 89-90; and see further Rylatt, this volume.
6   'Troughton' in Coventry Public Record Office.
7   Full references may be found in *VCH Warks.*, II, 52-59, and *VCH Warks.*, VIII, 125; and Lambert in Hobley, 46-78.
8   See further Hunt, this volume.
9   See further Scarisbrick, this volume. Small amounts of stone were used as early as 1541 for the new Coventry Cross; *VCH Warks.*, VIII, 143.

THE LOST CATHEDRAL PRIORY CHURCH

The best way to approach the architectural history of the cathedral is to consider the evidence for its plan first of all; and then, in the second half of this paper, to assess the clues for its chronological development and style. Unfortunately no definitive measured plan of the site exists with the surviving fabric and all recorded sightings of stonework *in situ* mapped on it, and a completely new survey is needed in order to draw any really meaningful conclusions about the proportions and dimensions of various parts of the buildings. Modern authors usually cite the length of the cathedral church in its final medieval state as about 425 feet (about 130 m.),[10] which seems to be the distance between the exterior wall surfaces of the east chevet chapel and of the west facade (fig. 5); but the dimension needs to be treated with some tolerance.

Moreover, there is no certainty that the church remained on the same east/west axis for the whole of its length, as assumed implicitly by all commentators. In fact, the topography of the site hints at the possibility of a slight deviation of the east arm towards the north-east, as at Lichfield. One can see today that Priory Row east of Hill Top turns two to three degrees east-north-east, as apparently did the former bishop's palace,[11] and both the churches of St Michael and Holy Trinity incline even more in this direction. There also appears to be a slight north-east inclination in the south wall of the chapter house, as excavated in 1965-66 (fig. 5),[12] suggesting that the bend began east of the nave. This is a critical point for any reconstruction of the plan of St Mary's.

The first person to try to capture the tangible reality of the lost church through detailed plans and drawings was Thomas F. Tickner F.R.I.B.A. Tickner was an architect practising at 14 Little Park Street, Coventry, in the early years of this century. Following up information from the nineteenth-century Coventry schoolmaster and antiquary, W. G. Fretton F.S.A., and others such as Alderman William Andrews, in 1916 Tickner undertook detailed research into the surviving remains of the medieval cathedral priory. He published his main findings in 1919 in the *British Archaeological Association Journal*,[13] but other unpublished drawings and a notebook are deposited in the Herbert Art Gallery.[14] Three of these plans are reproduced here (figs 1, 2, 3).

[10] E.g. *VCH Warks.*, VIII, 127; Hobley, 86; Thomas, 37.
[11] See J. C. Lancaster, *Historic Towns: Coventry* (London, 1974), map 4.
[12] This deviation disappeared in the published 1967 plan; Hobley, fig. 2. An inclination to the north-east seems also apparent in the length of north choir aisle wall unearthed in 1955 (pl. 6), discussed further below.
[13] Tickner (1919), 24-38.
[14] HAG, notebook and drawings in box-file labelled on spine, 'Tickner's Papers: Coventry Cathedral etc.: Box 10'. The notebook is an address book, with red and gilt bindings, and with the information arranged alphabetically, e.g. 'Arch',

The most significant discoveries brought to prominence by Tickner were two pier bases, about 22 ft. 9 in. (6.93 m.) apart centre to centre, found during work in 1909 on an extension at the back of No. 7 Priory Row (then the Constitutional Club, now the cathedral offices).[15] The general location of the bases suggests that they belonged with the south arcade of the nave, and their distance apart was used by Tickner to reconstruct a nave of nine equal bays, including the west facade block (fig. 2). The presumption should be that their positions relative to No. 7 Priory Row were plotted fairly accurately by Tickner, but evidence from his notebook suggests that they may not be pinpointed exactly;[16] and this becomes a moot point in more recent reconstructions of the plan. Unfortunately no trace of them seems to exist today,[17] though future archaeology needs to bear in mind the possibility that they are still in the ground under the rear of No. 7. Alderman Andrews thought the remains were 'of the Early English period, and ... of the early part of that period ... about 1200-1220',[18] and on this evidence Tickner restored the nave arcades as Early English Gothic (fig. 2).[19] However, Andrews' judgement of style needs to be treated with caution.[20]

Tickner reconstructed an enormous Romanesque east arm over 180 feet (about 55 m.) long,[21] terminating beyond the high altar in a semi-circular

---

'Architect', 'Andrews', etc.

[15] Tickner (1919), 29. In Tickner (1916), 4, he quotes Andrews as saying that the two piers 'were *about* 22' 9" from centre to centre' (my italics).

[16] Tickner (1919), 29, says that he saw these two piers, but he states in his notebook that 'the Builder' (of the Constitutional Club extension) marked them on Tickner's plan 'C.C.' (apparently now lost). Tickner (1916), 29: 'The pencil markings and figures were put on [plan C.C.] by the Builder in 1916 but do not appear to be quite correct. ... The position of one pier is about correct but the piers were 22' 9" from centre to centre.' Moreover, Andrews was his main source of information about the piers, and it is not clear how easily they could be seen or measured. Andrews, column two, states that the piers were discovered in 'five small shafts'. The article also mentions a third pier 'a little to the north', which Tickner did not see (notebook, p. 4) but which he suggested quite plausibly was part of a rood screen, in an offprint of his 1919 article, annotated by hand in 1921, in the Tickner box-file in HAG.

[17] Rigby, 2, item IV.

[18] Andrews, column 1.

[19] Tickner (1919), 35.

[20] E.g. Andrews thought that the ground-course mouldings of the west towers 'have a semi-Norman look; they may be rather older than A. D. 1200' (Andrews, columns 1-2). These mouldings still survive, and are typically Early English Gothic of the first half of the thirteenth century.

[21] Measured between the west crossing arch and the chord of the semi-circular apse. This is now a usual way of expressing the length of the eastern arms of Anglo-Norman great churches, and will be used as standard in this paper; see further Fernie (1979).

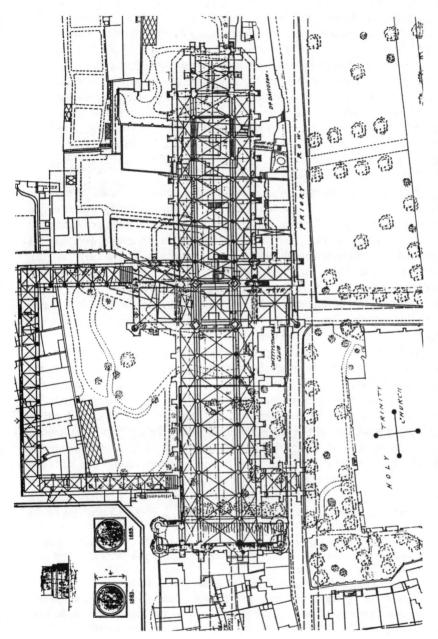

Figure 2. Reconstruction of St Mary's church and cloister, after Tickner (1917).

ambulatory without radiating chapels (fig. 1). The length and number of bays is quite unprecedented in even the largest Norman great churches in this country,[22] and this reconstruction should not be taken seriously either in its general form or its detail.[23] However, his hypothesis that the Romanesque church terminated in an apse and ambulatory remains a possibility, given the popularity of this feature in other Norman great churches in the midlands. If it had no radiating chapels, it would resemble the first design for the east end at Lichfield Cathedral, as Warwick Rodwell's recent excavations have shown.[24] Alternatively, with the more usual addition of radiating chapels, it would recall the original Romanesque east ends of St Peter's, Gloucester, (now the cathedral) and Worcester Cathedral, both Benedictine monastic churches of comparable size to Coventry.

Tickner evidently envisaged at an earlier stage of his research that the east arm was actually Early English Gothic in plan, typically square-ended and with an eastern axial chapel, on the general model of Salisbury Cathedral (fig. 2). Possibly he saw this as replacing the Romanesque east end, as happened at Lichfield around 1200;[25] and certainly it is this Early English Gothic skeleton which underlies the unconvincing size and proportions of his Romanesque plans of 1918 and 1919 (fig. 1). The stylistic evidence which survives today is completely inadequate to substantiate the idea of a major rebuilding of the eastern arm in the thirteenth century, though some remodelling might be expected (see further below).

Tickner's most entertaining reconstruction has been saved for last: the two-storey chapel east of the south transept, which he repeated on the north arm for symmetry (fig. 1). The position of such chapels, obstructing the entrance to the choir aisles, is unprecedented. His interpretation was founded on Fretton's assumption that the standing walls of such a chapel partly survived encapsulated in the Georgian house, No. 9 Priory Row, then owned by Dr Lynes, now the English Studies Centre (pl. 16). Starting from the premise that the stone wall at the rear of this property facing into Hill Top was the lower part of the east wall of the south transept (fig. 2, shown in more detail in fig. 3), Tickner observed a series of features which he thought were medieval. These he listed in his 1919 article.[26] A re-examination of the

22   Maximum of four arcade bays, and usually 100-110 ft. (30.5-33.5 m.) length; exceptionally nearer 140 ft. (42.7 m.) at Peterborough and St Albans, and over 150 ft. (45.7 m.) at Durham.

23   Tickner admitted that it was unproven; Tickner (1919), 34.

24   Rodwell (1989), figs 2 and 3.1; updated in W. Rodwell, 'Lichfield Cathedral: Interim Report on Archaeological Investigations in the South Quire Aisle, May and August 1992', unpublished report for the Dean and Chapter (10 Sept. 1992), 4.

25   Rodwell (1989), 284-5.

26   Tickner (1919), 28-9.

property today casts grave doubt on his interpretation of all these features. In particular, the vital piece of evidence on which he had reconstructed the crypt of the chapel – 'a carved boss in the ceiling which I believe to be *in situ*'[27] – is clearly inserted into the Georgian brick vaults of the house's rear cellar (pl. 14). It is virtually certain that the wall to Hill Top is post-medieval, at best made up of re-used medieval ashlars from the cathedral site.[28]

Nevertheless, the existence of several stone walls in the cellars of Nos 9 and 10 Priory Row, at about medieval floor level, still gives the modern visitor the feeling that one or more of these walls may relate to the layout of the cathedral church in this area. For example, it appears that Brian Hobley considered the front cellar of No. 9 to reflect the existence of a long rectangular chapel off the south transept, as indicated in his final published plan of 1967.[29] More recently, in 1987, part of a medieval skeleton in a stone coffin was uncovered in the cellars between Nos 9 and 10, on an east/west axis,[30] in a position which suggests that it lay just south of the alignment of the south choir aisle wall, but quite conceivably within a chapel adjoining the aisle or transept. All of which suggests that a proper measured survey of these two properties could be beneficial.

There are two other reasons for speculating that the south transept may have been important, and may have incorporated a major chapel off it; neither of which was considered in this context by Tickner. First, the position of the south entrance into the church; and second, the location of the Anglo-Saxon priory church of Leofric and Godiva. We know from the Leet Book that the cathedral possessed a major public and ceremonial entrance somewhere on its south side in the fifteenth century.[31] One account describes it as opening into Holy Trinity churchyard,[32] which led Tickner to reconstruct a large porch on the south side of the nave, facing the north porch of Holy Trinity (fig. 2); and Hobley to look for archaeological corroboration for such an idea in 1967. However, his excavations found no convincing evidence for such a feature,[33] and the possibility should be entertained that it was actually elsewhere in the church. The most feasible

27 *Ibid.*, 29.
28 Rigby, 1-2, item II; Hobley, 86. Rigby could not identify the vesica-shaped 'aumbry', but it is still there, blocked on the former scullery side, but still visible in the west wall of the ground-floor passage at the back of the property. It is *ex situ*, not an aumbry, but a small oval-shaped aperture with a glazing-slot (though the latter may be secondary). There is no sign of the carved 'vesica piscis'.
29 Hobley, fig. 2.
30 Information, Margaret Rylatt and Rafael Salguero.
31 Cited in Fretton, 30; Hobley, 71, 92.
32 Fretton, 30.
33 Hobley, 93. His argument that the presence of a piscina could indicate the proximity of a door is unconvincing: a chapel in the aisle is more likely.

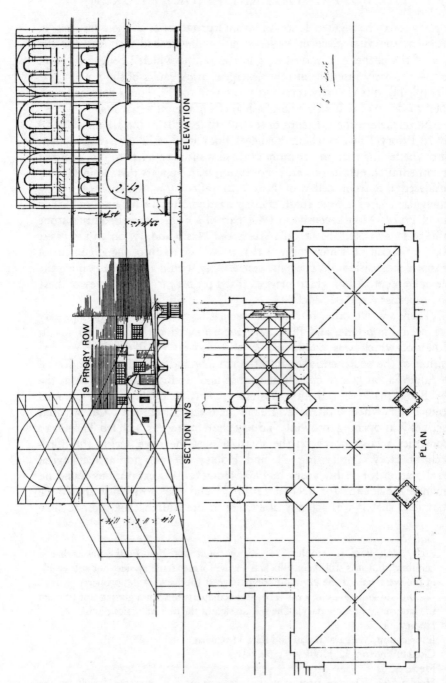

Figure 3. Section/elevation of the Romanesque choir and south chapel (Tickner).

alternative is the south transept, either taking the form of an ornate door in the centre of the south wall, as may still be seen in both transept arms at Lichfield, and the north transept at Westminster Abbey; or just possibly a porch on the west side of the transept, on the general model of the galilee off the south-east transept at Lincoln. Reconstructing a door in any position on the south side needs to take account of the rising land level to the south of over 13 feet (over 4 m.) above the medieval cathedral floor.[34] The example of the transept doors at Lichfield, another church on a sloping site, proves that such a problem is not insuperable; although it could be argued that a west-facing door on the south transept at St Mary's would have allowed the differential in levels to be negotiated more gradually.

If the south transept housed the great south door, one possible explanation for this slightly unusual arrangement could be that the transept incorporated the site of the eastern parts of Leofric's church, including St Osburga's tomb. It must be stated at the outset that no standing fabric has ever been located from any of the Anglo-Saxon churches – St Mary's consecrated in 1043, the contemporary chapel of the Holy Cross, and the nunnery church supposedly destroyed in 1016 (if it ever existed).[35] The topography of the hillside site implies that the Anglo-Saxon St Mary's lay either uphill from the medieval cathedral, perhaps where Holy Trinity church now stands;[36] or it actually occupied part of the medieval cathedral site, which is a more attractive interpretation. Hobley found no trace of it in his limited excavations of the nave site, though terracing for the twelfth-century cathedral church could have destroyed any evidence.[37] Over the rest of the cathedral site, there has been no consistent archaeological investigation, so what follows is entirely speculative.

In suggesting that part of Leofric's church may lie under the south transept, I have in mind the example of Peterborough Cathedral, where the remains of a church of the later tenth century still exist in a similar position beneath the great Romanesque abbey church (fig. 9). We do not know whether Anglo-Saxon St Mary's was cruciform in shape like Peterborough, or Stow in Lincolnshire,[38] but there are strong historical links between both

34 Hobley, fig. 3.
35 See further Hunt, this volume.
36 There are alternative ideas for this site in the 11th century; see Lilley, this volume.
37 Hobley, 89-90. On one copy of his 1966 plan in HAG 'Coventry Benedictine Priory' archive [hereafter HAG CBP], he notes in pencil 'old foundations' in the west bays of both nave aisles; but the source and interpretation of this information is unstated.
38 For dating Stow to c.1034-49, see E. C. Fernie, *The Architecture of the Anglo-Saxons* (London, 1983), 127. Richard Gem (pers. comm.) prefers 1053-55 for the crossing piers.

these churches and St Mary's during Earl Leofric's lifetime.[39] The full dedication of the 1043 church was 'St Mary, St Osburga and All Saints' and it contained a shrine to St Osburga;[40] probably located in the chancel, or possibly in a major chapel like a transept arm, rather similar to Fernie's interpretation of tenth-century Peterborough.[41] We also know that Leofric and Godiva were buried in St Mary's in a pair of *porticus*,[42] perhaps chapels north and south of the chancel and in close proximity to St Osburga's shrine. The veneration of St Osburga and an annual obit mass for the Lady Godiva were continued, or revived, in the cathedral in the later middle ages.[43]

With this information in mind, and superimposing the general model of Peterborough on to a reconstruction plan of St Mary's cathedral church (e.g. fig. 5), one can imagine how the south transept might come to incorporate a chapel of St Osburga, more or less on the same site as her shrine in the 1043 church. One might even speculate that Godiva's burial was also commemorated somewhere in the south transept of the cathedral. The main difference between the twelfth-century churches at Peterborough and Coventry is that the latter is unlikely to have had a south transept of such projection (cf. figs 5, 9). All commentators have reconstructed it as a mirror-image of the north transept, but it need not have been so. The only piece of evidence for the southerly extent of the transept is the account by Poole of the wall with plinth mouldings discovered in 1825 whilst major repairs were being effected to the foundations of No. 9 Priory Row.[44] There must be some doubt anyway about whether a wall only 'about three feet in thickness' could be part of the south terminal wall of the transept; indeed its size suggests more the wall of an Anglo-Saxon church.[45] But even if it was part of the cathedral transept, it need not be reconstructed as underlying the front wall of No. 9, or in line with that wall, as in Hobley's published plan.[46] Given the size of the hole excavated in 1825, the wall could be several feet further south.

[39] Earl Leofric's nephew, Leofric, was abbot of Peterborough, 1052-66, and of Coventry, *c.*1053-66; Earl Leofric and the Lady Godiva made major donations to Stow, 1053-55. See further J. C. Lancaster, *Godiva of Coventry* (Coventry, 1967), 18, 39; and Hunt, this volume.

[40] Lancaster, *Godiva, op. cit.*, 36.

[41] E. C. Fernie, *Anglo-Saxons, op. cit.*, 107-8. Fernie interprets Peterborough as not being truly cruciform like Stow, but having a large side-chapel on each side of the chancel, on the model of some tenth-century German churches. Richard Gem (pers. comm.) reminds me that this interpretation is controversial.

[42] Lancaster, *Godiva, op. cit.*, 31.

[43] See further Sadgrove, this volume.

[44] Poole, 13.

[45] *Ibid.*, 13. For comparison, the Romanesque transept wall at Peterborough is about five to six feet (1.5-1.8 m.) thick.

[46] Hobley, fig. 2.

The possibility of the location of the major door in the south transept may therefore be explained historically as an entrance for visitors to a chapel of St Osburga, on an Anglo-Saxon site. The door may also have come to provide an entrance for the bishop (as at Lincoln), because the palace at Coventry was to the east of the cathedral on the south side from at least the early thirteenth century.[47] A major public entrance in this position would have the advantage for the monks that it would lie away from their entrance to the church, from the cloister to the north. A very comparable parallel for this model of development is the site associated with another midland Anglo-Saxon female saint, St Frideswide's, Oxford (now Christ Church Cathedral). Recent research there has demonstrated that the disproportionate size of the north transept (the arm away from the cloister) results from the continuing veneration of St Frideswide on this, the site of the Anglo-Saxon church.[48] The position of the cloister on the opposite (south) side of the medieval church relates to the refoundation of the house as an Augustinian priory in c.1120,[49] and probably a wish to remove the community away from the public access in the north transept; circumstances which may reflect what also happened at Coventry in the same century.

Let us now return to the main theme of the plan of St Mary's, and more recent discoveries relating to it. In 1955 the remains of the late Gothic eastern termination of the cathedral were located by chance whilst excavating for the foundations of Sir Basil Spence's new cathedral. The lowest courses of two adjoining polygonal chapels were uncovered (pls 2, 3, 4), part of a series of chapels radiating around the east end in the form of a French chevet (figs 4, 5). Part of this masonry is still visible just below the present cathedral car-park (pl. 17). In November 1955, the contractors came across a section of the wall of the north choir aisle, with a window sill and elaborately moulded bases (pls 5-9). Correspondence between Margaret Tomlinson (Victoria County Histories) and the Warwickshire antiquary, Philip Chatwin, reveals the difficult conditions for studying these discoveries at the time:[50]

... Miss Telford's description of the attitude of the contractor who is removing pieces of the sill and will not allow her into the trench is rather disturbing ...

... It is fortunate that the sill was removed. It is just the spot where workmen have to scramble up and down and they would soon have damaged it... (pl. 5)

---

[47] *Ibid.*, 87 and fig. 2.

[48] J. Blair, 'St Frideswide's Monastery: Problems and Possibilities', in *St Frideswide's Monastery at Oxford*, ed. J. Blair (Gloucester, 1990), 228-40, 255, fig. 95.

[49] *Ibid.*, 236-40.

[50] Rigby, annexed copies of 'Extracts from Correspondence concerning discoveries on the Cathedral Site, Coventry, November 1955'.

These finds constituted completely new evidence, yet unfortunately almost all these features were destroyed and none of the loose stones visible in the photographs seems to have survived; nor have the survey drawings made by Spence been located.[51] A brief contemporary report of the finds by Dr G. R. Rigby is filed in the Herbert Art Gallery, but without any measured drawings.[52]

The discovery of the foundations of the chevet substantially modified previous knowledge of the cathedral, and new reconstruction plans were drawn up, first by Paul Woodfield and then by Brian Hobley (figs 4, 5), re-using information from Tickner's measured plan of 1917 (fig. 2). The maximum eastern extent of the medieval church was established, and the floor level of the chevet chapels was shown to be approximately the same as that at the west end, thus dispelling any lingering thoughts that the cellars under Priory Row represented the survival of an extensive medieval crypt.[53]

In 1961, Woodfield published a reconstructed chevet plan of five radiating chapels,[54] subsequently modified to three by Hobley on archaeological grounds (fig. 5).[55] The latter interpretation is more likely to be correct, even though chevets with five or more chapels are the norm, such as Hailes Abbey, Gloucestershire (1270-77).[56] Today the foundations relating to the north-east chapel are still visible,[57] but all traces of the eastern axial chapel have disappeared under the edge of the new cathedral and its car-park. Apparently the only record now surviving of the north foundations of the axial chapel is a photograph by the late Philip Chatwin (pl. 4),[58] providing general corroboration for Woodfield's reconstruction of this chapel (fig. 4) but of no help in taking exact measurements. One point not brought out

---

51   Rigby, 2, item V, notes that the two polygonal apses 'have been drawn out by Basil Spence ... (drawing 259 July 55)'. In the annexed correspondence in the Rigby file is an extract from a letter of 10 Nov. 1955 from P. Chatwin to M. Tomlinson, stating that the Secretary (presumably of the Reconstruction Committee) has 'arranged for the survey [of the north choir aisle wall] to be made, it will be done by the architect' [sic].

52   Rigby (2 pp.), HAG CBP.

53   E.g. Poole, 13, 'one of the finest vaults in England is formed of the underground remains of the monastery cathedral'. Houses with cellars originally extended further east, on the site of the present cathedral car-park, and George Demidowicz pointed out that marks for the barrel racks in the cellars may still be seen on the exterior stonework of the east wall of No. 11 Priory Row.

54   P. Woodfield, 'Warwickshire: Coventry Priory Church', Medieval Archaeology, 5 (1961), 313-4 and fig. 80. The same chevet plan is shown in fig. 4.

55   Hobley, 91; Rigby, 2, item V, also proposed only three chapels.

56   See Thompson, fig. 4, for some comparative chevet plans.

57   Pls 2 and 3 show the foundations in a similar state in 1955.

58   The negative is in the Warwick County Record Office, Warwick, as are those for his other photographs of the chevet and north choir aisle.

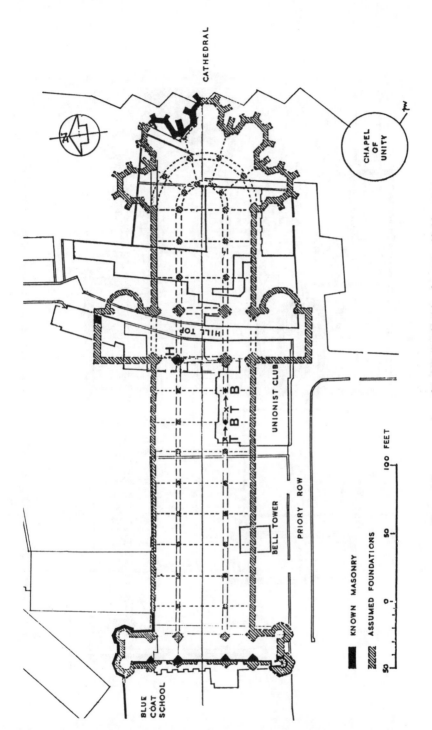

Figure 4. Reconstruction of St Mary's church, after Woodfield, c.1962.

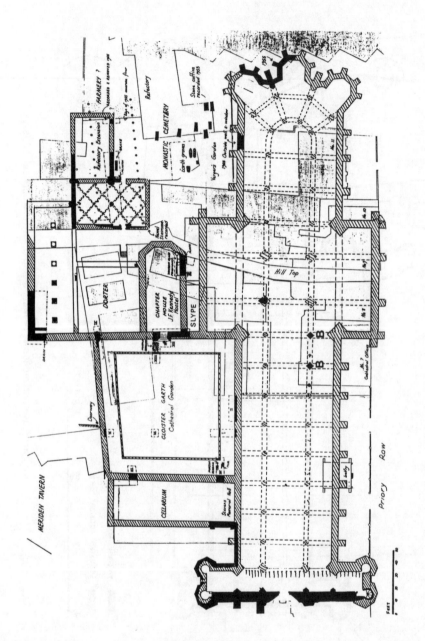

Figure 5. Reconstruction of St Mary's church and conventual buildings, after Hobley (1966).

before is that the pad for the buttress between the chapels (fig. 8A, 'Z') is noticeably larger than the others which are still visible, and must have provided the footing for a major flying buttress rising over the chevet roofs and abutting the north-east corner of the clerestory of the presbytery (fig. 8A, 'Y'). The angle of the footing relative to the main east-west axis shows that the east clerestory wall was narrower than the full width of the main vessel, and the presbytery's eastern termination must have been three-sided by this date (fig. 8A), and not the more conventional English square east end.

Some commentators have suggested that the termination was the survival of an earlier Romanesque apse, and have drawn a parallel with the east end of Tewkesbury Abbey.[59] There, a Romanesque apse and ambulatory plan with three radiating chapels (c.1100) was demolished about 1320 to provide a larger ambulatory and more chapels, but leaving standing the Romanesque presbytery with its three-sided apse (pl. 18).[60] It is possible that the twelfth-century east end at Coventry was of similar plan, which could explain why the chevet form was retained in the later Gothic extension. Tewkesbury was a smaller church than Coventry, so its presbytery of two bays plus an apse probably does not provide the best model for the likely length of the eastern arm. Rather, one should consider three bays plus an apse, like Gloucester (1089), or four bays, like Norwich (1096) or St Bartholomew-the-Great, Smithfield (1123).[61] However, even if Coventry had a Romanesque eastern arm as long as that at Norwich, the apse would still fall short of the position shown on Hobley's 1966 plan (fig. 5), and thus would not come close enough to be linked up later with the Gothic chevet, in the manner of Tewkesbury.[62] Indeed, there is no certainty that a Gothic chevet indicates the former existence of a Romanesque apse and ambulatory plan: Tewkesbury is the only proven example.[63] In fact, if one wishes to argue at Coventry that a Romanesque east end was connected directly to the Gothic chevet without any extension to its arcades, then the very longest eastern arms found in Anglo-Norman churches are actually of the 'three-apse'

[59] *VCH Warks.*, VIII, 127; Hobley, 92.

[60] R. K. Morris, 'Tewkesbury Abbey, the Despenser Mausoleum', *Bristol and Gloucestershire Archaeological Society Transactions*, 93 (1974), 144-5; for a plan of Tewkesbury, see D. Verey, *Gloucestershire: the Vale and the Forest of Dean*, Buildings of England (Harmondsworth, 1970), 358-9.

[61] For comparative plans, see A. Clapham, *English Romanesque Architecture after the Conquest* (Oxford, 1934), chap. 2.

[62] Woodfield and Hobley (figs. 4, 5) show only three complete bays because their arcades, derived from Tickner (fig. 2), are too wide. Also the positions of their apse piers are unconvincing when compared with surviving examples like Tewkesbury.

[63] Westminster Abbey is another possible example: see R. Gem *et al*, *Westminster Abbey, New Bell's Cathedral Guides* (London, 1986), 21.

type, without ambulatory, like Durham (1093) and Peterborough (1118, fig.9).[64] In terms of Anglo-Norman precedent, only an eastern arm of this design could have reached a point far enough east (i.e. fig. 8A, 'X') to enable the 'Tewkesbury conversion model' to work.[65]

The archaeological evidence suggested that the new chevet should be assigned to the later fourteenth or fifteenth centuries, the latter being the more usual choice.[66] Worked stones incorporated into the chapel foundations included a length of stringcourse decorated with oak leaves carved in an undulating style, which Rigby judged could not be earlier than c.1350.[67] The rather late date for the Gothic chevet seems to have worried most subsequent commentators, who would have expected it to be associated more usually with thirteenth-century churches in England, such as Westminster Abbey (1245-69).[68] However, some of the parallels cited were given dates which are no longer acceptable, especially the rebuilt chevet at Tewkesbury which is now placed at c.1320 and not 'late thirteenth century'.[69] Moreover, apsidal chapels and other polygonal features could appear at any date in English late Gothic architecture, as evidenced by Tudor examples at St George's Chapel, Windsor, and Henry VII's Chapel, Westminster; or more pertinently in the midlands around 1400 as, for example, at St Michael's, Coventry (the chancel), and Kenilworth Castle (the oriels).[70] There is no need then to question the idea that the chevet at St Mary's is late Gothic, and the most feasible date appears to be the second half of the fourteenth century because its inspiration may well have come from a site which has not been discussed in this context before: the new chevet at Vale Royal Abbey, Cheshire.[71]

The basis of the formal architectural comparison between Vale Royal and St Mary's lies in the fact that in both chevets, unusually, the polygonal chapels do not directly adjoin each other (figs 4, 5).[72] The contract of 1359 for

[64] For terminology, see Clapham, *English Romanesque, op. cit.*, 20 sqq.; the plan of Durham is fig. 6.

[65] These calculations are based on a position for the crossing as shown in figs 5 and 8A: 'crossing plan A' (see further below).

[66] E.g. Rigby, 2, item V; *VCH Warks.*, VIII, 127; Hobley, 73.

[67] Rigby, 2, item V; illustrated in Hobley, pl. 6. Its position was not directly under the chevet foundations, but in an exterior thickening of the foundations, as shown in other photographs in HAG CBP.

[68] E.g. *VCH Warks.*, VIII, 127; Hobley, 92; Thomas, 34.

[69] Woodfield, *Medieval Archaeology* (1961), *op. cit.*, 314; Hobley, 92; and Thomas, 32, all give 'late thirteenth century'. For the dating of Tewkesbury, see Morris, 'Tewkesbury Abbey', *op. cit.*, 143 sqq.

[70] See further Rigby, 2, item V; and R. K. Morris, 'St Mary's Hall and the Medieval Architecture of Coventry', *Ancient Monuments Society Transactions*, 32 (1988), 17-18.

[71] Noted, but not discussed, in Hobley, 92, note 2.

[72] Thompson, pl. XXIV.

Vale Royal makes it clear that the intermediate spaces there also served as chapels; an arrangement which may also have been followed at St Mary's, though the position of the flying buttress footings makes such a reconstruction less easy (fig. 4).[73] An undercurrent of historical connexions also flows between Vale Royal and Coventry. First, the patron of the new work at Vale Royal in 1359 was Edward, the Black Prince, who resided frequently at Cheylesmore Manor in Coventry and who gave the abbey lands in the city in 1376. Second, the Tichmarsh family of master masons, from Northamptonshire, may provide evidence of a professional architectural link between both sites. In 1312, St Mary's Priory granted a corrody to the royal master mason, Hugh de 'Titemersshe'.[74] Between 1356 and 1361, John de 'Tichmarsh', perhaps Hugh's son or nephew, was the Black Prince's mason for Chester, Flint and North Wales,[75] at the very time that Master William de Helpeston, from another Northamptonshire family, was commencing the new work at nearby Vale Royal.[76] Helpeston succeeded to the position of the Black Prince's mason in Chester on John de Tichmarsh's death in 1361, as well as continuing as the master at Vale Royal until at least 1374.[77] Thus professional and patronage connexions between Coventry, Chester and Vale Royal are quite suggestive.

If one accepts the link, the likelihood is that the St Mary's chevet is derived from Vale Royal, rather than *vice versa*. John Harvey has argued that the direct inspiration for the Vale Royal design, including the interspaces between the chapels, is the east end of Toledo Cathedral, through the intermediary of the Black Prince, Vale Royal's patron, engaged in diplomatic activities in Spain in 1357-8;[78] whereas St Mary's chevet is related to Vale Royal, not Toledo. The Black Death created a shortage of masons and carpenters in the diocese in the 1350s and 1360s, which only the most influential patrons could overcome,[79] so the work at Coventry might well be later.[80] This would place it in the same period as the enlarged chancel at

73 The two chevets differ in other details, e.g. each large chapel at Vale Royal has an axial buttress, and there are also seven smaller polygonal chapels.

74 Lambert in Hobley, 65, citing the Close Rolls. Hugh is obviously the same person as Hugh de 'Tichemers', a master mason in royal service at that period in London and the north of England; for whom see Harvey, 299.

75 Harvey, 299 (also called 'Tychemerssh').

76 *Ibid.*, 134.

77 *Ibid.*

78 *Ibid.*; Thompson, 195-6.

79 See J. M. Maddison, 'Master masons of the diocese of Lichfield: a Study in 14th-century Architecture at the Time of the Black Death', *Lancashire and Cheshire Antiquarian Society Transactions*, 85 (1988), 124-5.

80 We can only speculate as to who designed St Mary's chevet. It might have been Helpeston himself, but differences in the plan imply the relationship with his

Holy Trinity, funded by the priory in 1391, admittedly a more modest commission but with an east window related to the chancel of Nantwich church, Cheshire, another work in the general ambit of Chester and Vale Royal.[81] The chevet could also have acted as the spur to rebuilding the east end of St Michael's in the early fifteenth century on a greatly enlarged scale, and with a polygonal apse.[82] And thus the chevet is very likely to be 'our new work' mentioned in 1409, as suggested by Lambert and Hobley.[83]

However, the story of the cathedral's east end is most unlikely to have been a tidy development of just two phases. Rigby's notes indicate that in November 1955, the contractors came upon several stone features under the chevet, 'much below' the level of the radiating chapels.[84] These included three sections of wall and part of a floor to their east; but measurements and other details are singularly vague.[85] A number of possible interpretations suggest themselves. Possibly foundations for the chevet works? Or perhaps an Anglo-Saxon building of some sort? Or an axial chapel ('lady chapel') extending beyond the Romanesque cathedral?[86] Or the floor of a small crypt under such a chapel? Without more evidence, one can go no further at present.

The discovery of the east chevet was followed in 1959-1960 by Mrs Rosemary Hemsley's excavation of what is usually interpreted as the north-west crossing pier of the church, in the backyard of No. 8 Priory Row. Information about its detail is scanty, with no clues as to dating, but evidently it was a large mass of masonry, free-standing on its north and west

---

work at Vale Royal may be less direct. The only mason documented in Coventry in this period is John Wendulburgh, in 1380, and in 1413 linked to the priory; see Harvey, 329-30.

[81] For the Nantwich east window of c.1390, see Maddison, 'Master Masons', op. cit., 141 and pl. 13. The east window of Holy Trinity, Coventry, was destroyed in World War II, but is shown in Troughton, VIII, 22, and in old photos in Coventry Record Library, e.g. Access No. C and W (M) 5116.

[82] See Rigby, 2, item V; and Morris, 'St Mary's Hall', op. cit., 17-18.

[83] Hobley 73; also VCH Warks., VIII, 125. The chevet may have been partly remodelled after c.1410.

[84] Rigby, extracts from correspondence, 2-3, letter from Rigby to Tomlinson, 20 Nov. 1955.

[85] Ibid., 'A ditch has been dug a little to the west of the east end ... I think the plan below [p. 3] shows what is happening. The ditch has gone through two walls: A is about 3' 6" wide, B about 6' 0". More wall has been exposed very low down at C ... A, B and C are much below this level [of the ground-course of the chevet chapels] but there is a floor at C, which makes Chatwin think it is an earlier building. The distance between A and B is 40 ft. ... The whole position is extremely confusing.'

[86] As happened at Lichfield in the twelfth century; Rodwell (1989), 284-5.

faces (fig. 7).[87] Its size, and its approximate alignment with the axis of the nave north arcade, strongly suggests that it was one of the northern piers of the central tower.

Paul Woodfield reconstructed it as the north-west pier (fig. 4, 'H'),[88] thus placing the crossing 14-15 feet (4.5 m.) further east than Tickner had anticipated, with a nave now over 220 feet (67 m.) long, including the west bay. As a result, Woodfield made several adjustments to Tickner's scheme (cf. figs 2, 4). He lengthened the nave to ten bays, all of 22 ft. 9 in. (6.93 m.) spans except the west bay.[89] More controversially, this entailed moving further to the east the positions of the two nave pier bases located in 1909 and plotted on Tickner's 1917 plan (fig. 4, 'T'-'B'). Third, the proposed new location for the crossing meant abandoning the identification of the west wall of No. 9 Priory Row as the east wall of the south transept.

Hobley's draft reconstruction plan of 1966 accepted all Woodfield's modifications of Tickner, but by then another important discovery needed to be taken on board: namely the firm identification of the chapter house site (fig. 5). In 1965 the excavations located the west door of the chapter house, with fine fourteenth-century bases and a section of the west wall still *in situ*.[90] These features lay about 27 feet (8.25 m.) west of the north-south axis

87 Briefly mentioned in R. and J. Hemsley, 'The Cathedral Church of St Mary, Coventry', *TBWAS*, 78 (1962), 11.

88 A carbon-copy of an anonymous typescript headed 'THE MEDIEVAL CATHEDRAL OF COVENTRY (ST MARY'S PRIORY CHURCH)' (Nov. 1957, 5 pp.), amongst Mr Shelton's papers in HAG, refers to another possible identification for a north-west crossing pier: 'During some excavations made for the foundations of the bakery a little way down Hill Top, medieval work was uncovered. Mr Shelton reports that there was the base of a large column, about 6 ft across, and also five empty coffins were found at a spot 30 feet away in a north-easterly direction ... These coffins were probably burials in the north transept ... the column was in line with the northern respond at the west end of the cathedral and not far from the south to north line of the medieval masonry under No. 9 Priory Row. This leaves little doubt that it is part of the north-western pier of the central tower and that No. 9 Priory Row stands on the site of the south transept ... ' (p. 4). The five coffins seem to be the same ones mentioned in Tickner (1919), 33, and Hobley marked these in the north-east corner of the north transept in one annotated copy of his 1966 plan (similar to fig. 5) in HAG CBP. This suggests that the pier was north of the crossing, and it is unlikely to have been a crossing pier: its shape is wrong, and it was definitely too far east to be the north-west pier. Perhaps it was an arcade pier for an east aisle in the north transept.

89 The surviving remains of the north-west tower show that the west bay was considerably narrower if defined by the tower entrance arches, only 15 ft. 2 in. (4.62 m.) centre to centre. Tickner failed to address this discrepancy in his 1917 plan (fig. 2), but did so in 1918 (fig. 1).

90 Hobley, 95, fig. 5, pl. 17.

of the crossing pier. In the planning of great monastic churches, the west wall of the transept arm almost invariably follows the general alignment of the west wall of the chapter house; though rare exceptions occur (see further below). The application of this planning norm to the circumstances at Coventry would suggest that the transept had a western aisle, as shown by Hobley (fig. 5).

Moreover, the historical precedents for transepts with western aisles demonstrate that they virtually always had eastern aisles as well. Thus Woodfield's speculation about small Norman-style transept arms was shown to be no longer easily tenable (cf. figs 4, 5). We shall call this reconstruction 'crossing plan A', with aisled transept arms and Mrs Hemsley's masonry identified as the north-west crossing pier (e.g. figs 5; 8A, 'H'). Such a reconstruction would place St Mary's in an elite group of major Anglo-Norman cathedrals with aisled transepts, namely Winchester and Ely. However, if this form was employed at Coventry, the reason may be less to do with matters of prestige, and more with contingency. For example, it could have provided more space in transept arms which were restricted in length to the north (and south?) by the topography of the site. The maximum northern extent of the transept was determined by a short length of wall, which Woodfield took to be the north wall of the transept (fig. 4),[91] and which Hobley positively identified as the south wall of the chapter house (fig. 5). Hobley judged that the south face of the wall had originally been external at this end,[92] and therefore postulated that the transept must have been separated from it by a narrow space such as a slype (fig. 5).

We cannot be certain that the south transept mirrored the north arm. For example, it might have projected further south, especially if the remains of the Anglo-Saxon church lay in this area. Indeed the presence of the latter could be an alternative explanation for a west aisle, on the model of Peterborough, where the superimposition of the Norman plan on the Anglo-Saxon one created a space which became a vestry, between the cloister and the south transept (fig. 9). Any arrangement at Coventry could not have followed this exactly, because the cloister is on the north, but it may be that some of the ideas were incorporated: namely that the cloister east wall might have aligned with the west wall of an Anglo-Saxon transept, and perhaps that the western 'aisle' adjoining the cloister might actually have been a room like a vestry.[93]

[91] Drawing by Paul Woodfield on a loose page from a notebook; drawing headed, 'Jan. 1962, Transept Wall', in papers with Rigby, HAG CBP.

[92] Hobley, 92, 96.

[93] Another factor in any reconstruction of the processional entrance from the cloister into the church is the change of about two metres in levels; as shown in Hobley, 95, fig. 3.

The discovery of the chapter house alignment has awkward implications for the articulation of the nave plan. In an aisled transept arrangement, the piers of the first bay of the nave should align with the west wall of the transept. This is how Hobley reconstructed them in 1966, thus manoeuvring the 1909 pier bases about five feet (1.5 m.) further west than their positions in the Woodfield plan (cf. figs 4 and 5, 'B'). However, all this was to change within a year, when the 1967 excavations located the foundations of a third pier base in the nave south arcade.[94] Hobley interpreted this as lying exactly three bays west of the 1909 bases, and therefore that the original positions plotted by Tickner for the 1909 bases were actually correct (i.e. fig. 2).[95] But unfortunately he provided no corroborative evidence, and measurements taken from his final 1967 plan are inconclusive, though this may be a cartographic error.[96] In this and several other aspects, the 1967 plan is less satisfactory for understanding the specific problems of reconstructing the church than earlier plans reproduced here (e.g. figs 4, 5). Without explanation, it returns to a transept with its east wall aligned on the Hill Top side of No. 9 Priory Row, the position advocated by Tickner; and with a long rectangular chapel running east off the south transept, apparently based on the dimensions of the front basement in Nos 9-10 Priory Row.[97] Moreover the problem of interpreting the interior layout of the church is avoided by omitting any bay articulation in the transept, crossing and eastern arm.[98] The two east bays of the nave arcade are absent, and it is unclear how they could relate to the alignment of the west wall of the transept as shown on the 1967 plan.

A difficulty with every previous reconstruction of the nave is the tacit acceptance that all the bays were the same size, and belonged to the same period. The evidence assembled above proves that neither of these premises should be assumed any longer. If we integrate Tickner's locations for the 1909 pier bases with the information from the excavations of Hemsley and Hobley, then only about 40 feet (12.2 m.) would be available for the two east bays of the nave, between the crossing and the first of the 1909 piers: not the

94   Ibid., figs 2, 4.
95   Ibid., 93.
96   Ibid., fig. 2. In this figure, the distance centre to centre between the 1967 base and the more westerly 1909 base is about 65 ft. (19.82 m.), whereas three bays of 22 ft. 9 in. should produce 68 ft. 3 in. (20. 82 m.). To confuse matters further, Hobley's Figure 2 also shows the 1909 bases moved about 3-4 feet west of the positions in Tickner's 1917 plan (fig. 2). Is this a cartographic error? For if one restores the 1909 bases to their 1917 position (fig. 2), the distance from the 1967 base is approximately correct for Hobley's assertion.
97   Hobley, fig. 2. This interpretation is not explained on p. 92, and on p. 86 he rejects Tickner's ideas about No. 9.
98   Ibid., fig. 2.

45 ft. 6 in. (13.86 m.) necessary for two bays of 22 ft. 9 in. each. Less acceptable is the unequal division of the 40 ft. space into a massive first bay west of the crossing (around 27 ft. centre to centre, over 8 m.) and a second bay of only half that span (fig. 8A, 'J', 'K'). The problem is the enormous width produced for the transept west aisle, with which the first bay of the nave arcade should align. This raises the issue of whether the raft of masonry found by Mrs Hemsley has been plotted accurately, and especially whether its interpretation as the north-west crossing pier is really correct.[99]

One way out of some of these difficulties is to identify the pier as the north-east support for the central tower, and thus move the crossing further west. This reconstruction will be termed 'crossing plan B', and would result in a transept with a west wall which could not align with the west wall of the chapter house (fig. 8B): an unusual monastic layout, but not without precedent. At St Frideswide's, Oxford, Richard Halsey has recently proved that the church was entered from the east cloister walk through a door in the end wall of the south transept, before this arrangement was swept away in the rebuilding of the cloister in 1489.[100] Thus originally the transept arm extended further west for the width of the east cloister walk; and a plan based on this idea has been reconstructed for Coventry in Figure 8B.

Such an arrangement would have the advantage of removing the wide west aisle, though its implementation would require the more easterly of the 1909 pier bases to support a south-west crossing pier (fig. 8B, 'G').[101] It would also create an eccentric plan in which the west wall of the chapter house would be out of alignment with both the transept west wall and the west piers of the crossing (fig. 8B); whereas the chapter house wall and crossing piers were on axis at St Frideswide's.[102] If 'crossing plan B' proves to have any validity, then explanations for this discrepancy would need to be sought, almost certainly in the transept and cloister east range being designed at different periods, and perhaps relating to the pre-existing position of the Anglo-Saxon abbey church. Twelfth-century St Frideswide's also included a cloister without a fourth walk running east/west against the nave aisle wall,[103] which is another possible implication for the layout at Coventry. Hobley's excavations in the cloister produced architectural evidence for construction in progress on the north walk in the later middle ages, probably

---

[99] It should also be noted that no fabric from the transept west wall has ever been located to establish its exact position.

[100] R. Halsey, 'The 12th-century Church', in *St Frideswide's Monastery at Oxford*, ed. J. Blair (Gloucester, 1990), 149-52 and fig. 60.

[101] Nothing in contemporary descriptions of the 1909 bases militates against such an interpretation: see further note 16.

[102] Halsey, '12th-century Church', *op. cit.*, fig. 60.

[103] *Ibid.*, 152. As the cloister is on the south side of the church at Oxford, the missing walk is the north one, whereas at Coventry it would be the south walk.

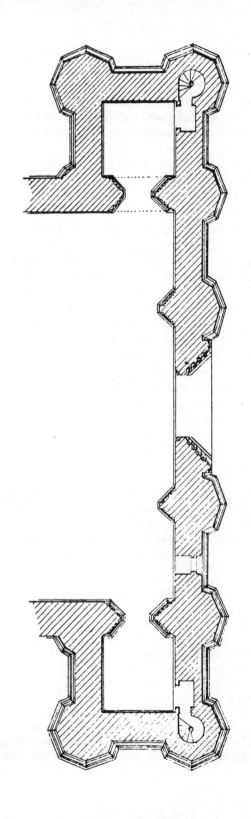

Plan of West Wall

✠ The Cathedral ✠ Coventry ✠

✠

Scale [feet]

Figure 6. Plan of the west front of St Mary's, after Troughton, c.1856.

c.1400,[104] but no certain evidence for an earlier walk in this position.[105] Another implication of this plan would be that the eastern arm of any Romanesque church could not have reached far enough east to link to the later medieval chevet, and therefore a major extension would be likely in the thirteenth or fourteenth centuries.

Evidence for changes in the design of the nave plan comes from a scrutiny of the finds in Trenches XVI and XVII of Hobley's 1967 excavations. In each trench Hobley located the stub of a shallow strip buttress on the exterior of the nave south aisle wall.[106] Measurements taken on his 1967 plan indicate that the buttresses were about 23 feet (7 m.) apart between their east faces, thus tending to confirm that the aisle wall in this middle area of the nave was being laid out for arcade bays of about 22 feet and 9 inches.[107] However, Hobley's plan of Trench XVI also shows quite clearly that the foundation of the south arcade pier base uncovered in this trench is out of alignment by several feet with the reciprocal buttress in the south aisle wall (fig. 8A, 'P', 'Q').[108] Shallow pilaster buttresses of this style suggest a twelfth-century date, and therefore the wall at this level is likely to be the original south aisle wall of the Romanesque or early Gothic church; not a later rebuild. In which case, the most likely explanation for the discrepancy is a break in the building when the aisle wall had been constructed; after which the siting of the pier bases was adjusted when this part of the nave arcade came to be erected. In the west bay of the nave, further adjustments would have been necessary to the bay spacing, just as we know of considerable rethinking in this area at Peterborough in the later twelfth century (fig. 9).[109]

---

[104] Not mentioned in Hobley's text, but illustrated *passim* in Hobley, fig. 4 (Trench XVII, section). HAG CBP has photographs of a large piece of blind arcading found in Trench I in 1965, identified as cloister wall (with the same profile as pieces of Perpendicular style tracery in Troughton, IX, 17); and of a piece of panelled vault or transverse arch from the same trench.

[105] See Hobley, 95. The only possible evidence, not mentioned by Hobley, is a piece of painted plaster seemingly decorated with a Romanesque acanthus pattern, of which there is a poor photo in HAG CBP. The plaster was discovered in Trench II, in the nave north aisle wall on the cloister side. It had presumably been re-used as fill *c*.1400, but whether from an earlier cloister walk cannot be certain.

[106] Hobley, 94, fig. 4, pl. 6a (Trench XVI); and an unpublished photograph of the buttress in Trench XVII in HAG CBP.

[107] No other buttress positions are known for either wall: the one shown in Hobley's 1966 plan (fig. 5) on the north aisle wall just east of the north-west tower is speculative.

[108] Hobley, 94, fig. 4; but he does not comment on this discrepancy.

[109] One possibility at Coventry is that there was a larger pier in the last bay, perhaps because the towers were originally planned to be over the west bays of the aisles, and not projecting beyond them. Tickner adopted the idea of the larger piers in

The western block requires practically no discussion with regard to its plan. Most of the lower parts of the west wall and the north-west tower are still visible today (pl. 13), yet the doors and the buttresses are depicted inaccurately on the most commonly reproduced plan, namely Hobley's of 1967.[110] The buttresses of the towers on the west front were all of semi-octagonal plan, with one of the angles facing forward, as can still be seen for the buttress at the south-west corner of the north-west tower. Dr Troughton, who was present at the time of the clearance of the west front in 1856,[111] was aware of this (fig. 6) and so was Tickner (pl. 10), but the Hobley plans show them as rectangular (e.g. fig. 5). However, the buttresses flanking the central west door are not visible today, and only in the Troughton drawings are they given the same semi-octagonal form (e.g. pl. 10).[112] It is unclear whether his record is based on observation or reconstruction,[113] but investigation of the site in 1989-90 by Coventry Museums Archaeological Unit found traces of the buttress to the left of the door which suggested it was 'wedge-shaped'.[114]

The west facade had a major central door, but an unusual feature was the presence of a small door from the north aisle and the absence of a reciprocal south door. Troughton correctly records this anomaly in most of his drawings (e.g. fig. 6),[115] but all subsequent commentators were uncertain about this asymmetry (e.g. fig. 5),[116] until the existence of the north door was re-affirmed in 1989-90.[117] The decoration of the door included a single order of detached red sandstone nook shafts, of which the weathered stub of the right-hand shaft was still in existence (but in a very friable state) at the time of writing this paper. The purpose of this small door is unclear, but it may have served as an everyday door of convenience towards the west gatehouse and the market square, with the centre west door reserved for ceremonial occasions only. A few Cistercian churches have a similar arrangement of doors, but their purpose is uncertain (e.g. Fountains Abbey and, more

---

[110] 1918 (fig. 1), and Woodfield and Hobley/1966 followed him (figs. 4, 5). Hobley, fig. 2; also in *VCH Warks.* VIII, 126, and Thomas, 30 (the latter with the wrong metric scale).

[111] Soden, 1, implies a date of 1859-60, but 1856 is given in Poole, 14; Tickner, 35; and *VCH Warks.* VIII, 125, n. 8.

[112] See also Troughton, IX, 4.

[113] Tickner (1919), 36, thought the semi-octagonal buttresses continued across the west front.

[114] Soden, 4.

[115] Shown also in Troughton, IX, 5; but omitted in IX, 4.

[116] Fretton, 35, states that there were no side doors. Tickner shows a blocked north door in his plans (e.g. fig. 1), but believed that a south door must have existed for symmetry (e.g. pl. 10); see Tickner (1919), 36.

[117] Soden, 4.

relevant to St Mary's, the contemporary west front at Croxden, Staffordshire).

Turning now to the stylistic evidence for dating the various phases of St Mary's from the building fabric, any assessment must commence with the Norman cathedral.[118] Some doubts might still be entertained as to whether St Mary's was actually rebuilt in the Norman period, because no Romanesque material has yet come to light with a definite provenance from the church. However, the main reason for thinking it was rebuilt is the incontrovertible evidence that some of the conventual buildings were laid out and erected in this period, and presumably the cloister as well. Most English examples of the regular claustral arrangement associated with high medieval monasticism date from after the Norman conquest.[119] It is thus virtually certain that the church would have been rebuilt as well, because few Anglo-Saxon churches except the very grandest would have been able to accommodate the new arrangements.[120]

The conventual buildings of the east range can be shown to be Romanesque in origin, on the basis of their plan and remnants of their fabric. For this we are particularly indebted to Hobley's excavations of 1965-66, which provided for the first time an informed picture of the layout of many of the monastic buildings around the cloister.[121] His investigations in the south-east corner of the chapter house site located what appears to be the foundations for part of a semi-circular apse at a level below the early Gothic structure.[122] Rounded apsidal terminations were common for Norman

[118] The only Anglo-Saxon stone artefact discovered in Coventry to date is the decorated 'cross shaft' found *ex situ* in Palmer Lane on 17 August 1934; now in HAG, and identified more credibly as a length of pilaster or jamb. For the discovery, see P. B. Chatwin, 'Recent Finds in Coventry', *TBWAS*, 58 (1934), 62; and J. B. Shelton, 'Excavations', *Austin's Monthly Magazine*, 27, No. 327 (Sept. 1934), copy in a blue ring binder labelled 'Shelton Extracts, "Austin's Monthly Magazine"', in HAG. I am most grateful to Margaret Rylatt for drawing my attention to the latter. The stone is illustrated in Hobley, pl. 37; and in this volume pl. 20. For a list of other unstratified Anglo-Saxon finds in Coventry, see Hobley, 81; the most relevant are some pre-Conquest glazed tiles from the Benedictine site of St Mary.

[119] See C. Malone in W. Horn and E. Born, *The Plan of St Gall*, 3 vols. (Berkeley and Los Angeles, 1979), II, 343 sqq.. However, Richard Gem (pers. comm.) notes evidence for claustral arrangements at several pre-Conquest sites (e.g. St Augustine's, Canterbury), in addition to Edward the Confessor's Norman-influenced Westminster Abbey.

[120] See also the similar case of St Frideswide's, Oxford, with a similar sized cloister: J. Blair in *St Frideswide's Monastery at Oxford*, ed. J. Blair (Gloucester, 1990), 239.

[121] Hobley, 95-100, fig. 5.

[122] *Ibid.*, 95-6, fig. 6, pl. 19; but he does not discuss dating. There are additional photographs in HAG CBP.

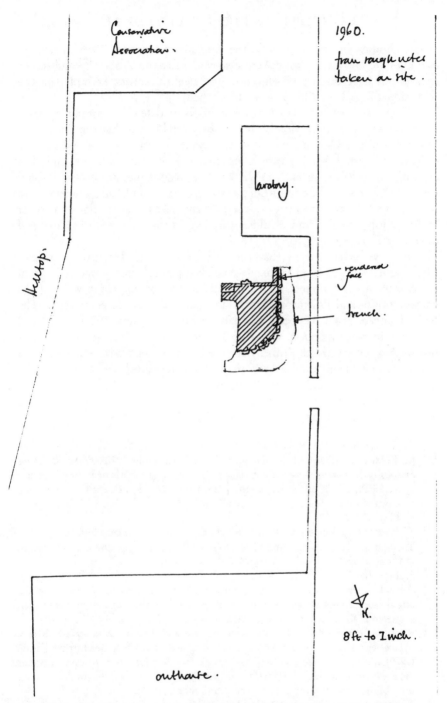

Figure 7. Sketch plan of excavations at the rear of No. 8 Priory Row (1960).

chapter houses and occur only in the Romanesque period. Twelfth-century examples are known at Castle Acre Priory and Reading Abbey,[123] and recent excavations have discovered eleventh- and twelfth-century examples on the same site at St Albans Abbey (now the Cathedral).[124]

There was no associated evidence to help date the Norman chapter house foundations more closely, but Hobley established that the undercroft of the dormitory block to the north was twelfth-century with the discovery of part of a multi-scallop capital on this site.[125] This style of capital is typically late Romanesque, c.1120-70. The reconstruction of the capital showed that it would fit the Romanesque pier stubs and bases uncovered in this area in 1858 and 1883 (fig. 2, inset),[126] and that it was similar to another multi-scallop capital found on the priory site in the nineteenth century and drawn by Troughton.[127]

It is virtually certain that the cloister was also Norman in origin. Measurements taken from Hobley's published plans[128] imply that the size of the cloister may be linked mathematically to key points in the walls of the chapter house and dormitory block, and perhaps the church nave.[129] The cloister appears to have been a square of approximately 105 feet (32 m.) measured between its outer walls (fig. 8A, 'L-M'). The dimension of about 74 feet (22.5 m.) derived from this by the medieval architect's favourite formula of 'one to the square root of two' may have determined the position of the shared wall between the chapter house and the dormitory undercroft (fig. 8A, 'M-N').[130] The same dimension may also have been employed to determine the interior width of the nave with aisles (fig. 8A, 'C-D').[131]

[123] R. Gilyard-Beer, *Abbeys*, HMSO 2nd ed. (London, 1976), 32.

[124] M. Biddle, 'St Albans Abbey Chapter House Excavations 1978', *Fraternity of the Friends of St Albans Abbey, Occasional Paper, No. 1* (a Supplement to *The Alban Link*, 1979), 10-12; an apsidal chapter house of 1077-88, extended at some date between 1093 and 1151.

[125] Hobley, 124, fig. 20.

[126] Tickner (1919), 30; he mistakenly thought they were part of the cloister.

[127] Troughton, IX, 16B, reproduced in Hobley, pl. 27a; perhaps the one referred to in Fretton, 34.

[128] Hobley, figs 2, 5.

[129] What follows is based on measurements taken on Hobley, fig. 2, not from the actual fabric, most of which is inaccessible; therefore these can be no more than suggestions about possible mathematical relationships.

[130] Root-two is the relationship between the side and diagonal of a square: here a square with sides of 74 feet would have a diagonal of 105 feet. See further Fernie (1979) and Fernie (1983); and the basic work on this subject is P. Kidson, 'Systems of Measurement and Proportion in Early Medieval Architecture', 2 vols., unpublished doctoral thesis (University of London, 1956).

[131] The measurement between the inside faces of the west front responds is about 72 ft. (22 m.), but a proper survey is still needed. Unfortunately the most recent plan

In the present state of knowledge it is difficult to attempt to apply these mathematical relationships further. One problem is that the cloister is relatively small compared with the length of the church (on the basis of 'crossing plan A', fig. 5), and makes comparison difficult with other Anglo-Norman great churches. For example, a side of the cloister might typically relate to the length of the nave (including the western block) in the proportion of one to two, as at Ely Cathedral;[132] or to the length of the nave (without the western block) in the proportion of one to root-two, as is likely at Winchester.[133] Neither of these relationships is found at St Mary's, though it is interesting to note that the cloister (105 ft.) seems close to being in the proportion of one to root-two to a cloister side plus the width of the west *cellarium* (fig. 8A, 'L-M': 'B-M'). Also, in 'crossing plan A', the length of the nave as far as the western block (but excluding it) would be close to twice the length of one side of the cloister (fig. 8A, 'E-F': 'L-M'); a variation on the formula at Ely. This could imply that the nave was originally designed to be one bay shorter, an observation which gains some validity from the fact that the western block is clearly a Gothic addition. It was built in a separate campaign from the nave, judging by the difference between its ground-course mouldings and those of the nave south aisle.[134]

One way in which root-two proportional theory could be helpful is in predicting the length of the Romanesque eastern arm. A common formula found in Anglo-Norman great churches is that the length of the nave multiplied by root-two equals the total length of the church to the chord of the east apse.[135] If this were to be applied to 'crossing plan A' at St Mary's, based on approximately 210 feet (64 m.) as the length of the nave excluding the west bay, then the total length of the church to the chord of the east apse would be about 297 feet (90.5 m.).[136] Or a nave of 222 feet (67.6 m.), including the west bay, would give a total length of 314 feet (95.7 m.).[137] These formulae would produce lengths for the eastern arm (including the crossing) of 87 feet (26.5 m.) or 92 feet (28 m.) respectively to the chord of the apse (fig. 8A, 'U', 'V'). In other words, an eastern arm considerably shorter than that of about 130 feet (39.6 m.) which would be the sort of length required to link to the later Gothic chevet, as discussed earlier in this paper. Moreover, similar calculations based on 'crossing plan B' would result in eastern terminations about 51 feet (15.5 m.), shorter still. Without any firm

---

of the west front (in Soden, 8-9) is unreliable.

[132] Fernie (1979), 2-3, fig. 1.

[133] Fernie (1983), 17, fig. 4.

[134] Hobley, pls 6a (nave) and 25 (north-west tower, from Troughton, IX, 13).

[135] See Fernie (1983), 17, fig. 4; and most recently, E. C. Fernie, *An Architectural History of Norwich Cathedral* (Oxford, 1993), 136-40 and Table I.

[136] The more common formula, e.g. Winchester; Fernie (1983), 17, fig. 4.

[137] Less common, e.g. Ely; Fernie (1979), 2.

archaeological information, it is impossible to say which of these formulae for predicting the length of the eastern arm may prove the most accurate. One can say, however, that if the eastern arm was as long as 130 feet, then St Mary's was an exception to the proportions employed in many Anglo-Norman great churches.

With regard to Romanesque decoration, the closest we come to a feature which might be identified with the church is the fragment of a large capital which Tickner saw at the former Coventry School of Art on 8 August 1917.[138] Unfortunately neither the capital nor any visual record of it is known today, so we are entirely reliant on Tickner's description. It was found in Coventry, though the exact provenance was unknown. However, given the fact that he reconstructs it as belonging to a pier almost six feet (1.83 m.) in diameter, it is highly likely that it belonged in a main arcade of the cathedral church. He judged the style of its carving, which was presumably more distinctive than multi-scallop, to be closest to work in St Peter's Church, Northampton, of c.1150-60.[139] The description implies that the capital crowned a cylindrical pier, of the kind common in Anglo-Norman great churches in the west and midlands in the twelfth century (e.g., Malmesbury Abbey, Hereford Cathedral). Or the fragment may have formed part of a capital for a cylindrical pier with some attached shafts, another common twelfth-century type, many variations of which may be seen at Peterborough (fig. 9; pl. 19).[140] The employment of colossal cylindrical piers of the kind found in the earlier naves of Tewkesbury and Gloucester is less likely by this date, but one cannot preclude entirely the possibility of some sort of 'giant order' with cylindrical-type piers, like St Frideswide's, Oxford.[141]

It is impossible to be sure whether this capital derives from the choir, transept aisles or nave, but two possible locations are known which could fit. One is the large cylindrical column base noted earlier this century in the vicinity of the north transept, and the other is the pier foundation in the nave south arcade unearthed by Hobley in 1967 in Trench XVI.[142] The latter might be the more probable location for a Romanesque pier with a capital of such relatively late date, if construction was progressing from east to west in

[138] Tickner (1919), 34-5, and Tickner (1916), 28, 43, 116.

[139] No more specific description of the motifs is given in Tickner (1916).

[140] See further B. Cherry, 'Romanesque architecture in Eastern England', *BAAJ*, 131 (1978), 8 sqq.

[141] For the giant order in the midlands in the twelfth century, see R. Halsey, 'Tewkesbury Abbey: Some Recent Observations', *Medieval Art and Architecture at Gloucester and Tewkesbury* (*BAACT* for 1981, published 1985), 27-9.

[142] For the base in the area of the north transept, see note 88. For the nave base, approximately 9 ft. 6 in. (2.9 m.) in diameter, see Hobley, fig. 4. The diameter of the 1909 bases is not known.

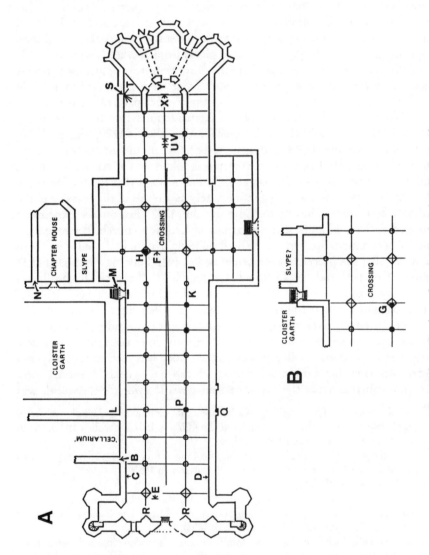

Figure 8. Schematic plans of St Mary's church (Morris, 1993).

a building begun about 1140 or earlier. A date in the mid-twelfth century for work in the central to western parts of the nave would accommodate two other Romanesque stones not previously noted, which could well have come from this area. The stones are carved with lozenge pattern, typical of this period and generally similar to loose pieces of stringcourse at Lichfield Cathedral, which probably belong with the extensive works there of Bishop Roger de Clinton (1130-48).[143] The two pieces from St Mary's were stored in the grilled area under Blue Coat School,[144] and thus may be assumed to have been found when the remains of the west front were uncovered in 1856; in which case, their provenance may well be the western parts of the nave.

Taken as a whole, the few bits of Romanesque fabric from the priory site indicate work unlikely to be much earlier than c.1120, and probably continuing into the 1150s and later, especially in the nave. Setting this information against historical circumstances likely to be conducive to the building of a new Anglo-Norman church, it is evident that there is no proof that anything positive happened immediately as a result of the transfer of the bishop's seat from Chester to Coventry by 1102. Bishop de Limesey is reported to have plundered the treasures of Leofric's church, destroyed the monks' accommodation, and carried off building materials;[145] and it has been suggested that the proceeds were being used to help build new churches at St John's, Chester, and at Lichfield Cathedral.[146] Warwick Rodwell has tentatively proposed a late eleventh-century date for Romanesque Lichfield, on the basis of a similar transept chapel design to Gloucester (begun 1089).[147]

At Coventry, given the apparent depredations of the fabric by Bishop de Limesey, it seems inevitable that some start must have been made on a new church and conventual buildings before the priory was used temporarily as a fortress in 1143; but how much earlier we can only guess.[148] Shortly after 1143 it is obvious from the historical and stylistic evidence that work was

---

[143] R. K. Morris, 'The Lapidary Collections of Lichfield Cathedral', *Medieval Archaeology and Architecture at Lichfield* (*BAACT* for 1987, published 1993), 101-2; these pieces are catalogued as 'LC 19'.

[144] Seen there by the author in 1989, but no longer there in 1993. Rigby, 1, also noted a stone with chevron decoration in this area in 1955.

[145] *VCH Warks.*, VIII, 125.

[146] Dr Richard Gem in a lecture to the British Archaeological Association conference, Chester, July 1992; see also A. B. Clifton, *The Cathedral Church of Lichfield*, Bell's Cathedral Series (London, 1898), 5.

[147] W. Rodwell, 'Lichfield Cathedral: Interim Report on archaeological investigations in the south quire aisle, May and August 1992', unpublished report for the Dean and Chapter (10 Sept. 1992), 4-6; also Rodwell (1989), 283-5, dating it 'c.1085-1100'.

[148] Tickner (1919), 26, saw Bishop de Clinton as the main builder, but he seems to have favoured Lichfield until 1139 or so; which leaves very little time before the troubles of 1143.

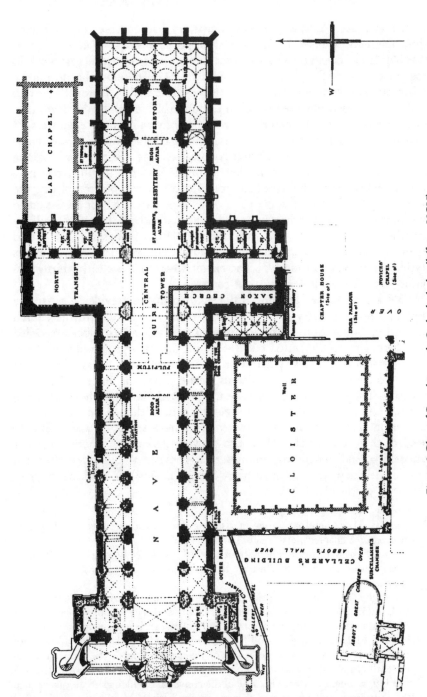

Figure 9. Plan of Peterborough Cathedral, detail (from VCH).

proceeding apace. At this time the monastery had an able and long-lived prior, Laurence (1144-79), and a well-disposed bishop, Walter Durdent (1149-59). It has been argued above that there is evidence to suggest work in progress on the main phase of the nave in c.1150-60, and the dormitory undercroft with its multi-scallop capitals would fit well in Durdent's period. Parallels have been observed between the unusual breadth of the dormitory blocks at Coventry and Canterbury, and the position of their reredorters,[149] and Durdent had previously been the prior of Christ Church, Canterbury. The dormitory undercroft obviously survived the 'destruction' of the conventual buildings by Bishop Nonant in 1189.[150] By his time, one may surmise that work on the nave had ground to a halt without completing the western bays and perhaps some parts of its superstructure; for he is said to have continued the church, which he found 'unfinished'. It is thus unlikely that the slightly earlier seal, attributed to Prior Moyses (1183-9) and apparently showing a complete church with twin west towers, represents anything more than an ideal.[151] The extant west front is clearly thirteenth-century Gothic from its lowest stone-courses.

We are on firmer ground with regard to material evidence when we come to assess the Early English Gothic works associated with the church and priory. In addition to the lower parts of the western block, recorded fabric belonging to the period c.1170-1275 includes a large carved vault boss; some broad-leaf capitals possibly from the cloister; a base from the chapter-house interior; and numerous details from the undercroft of the infirmary. These features substantiate the received view that the west facade with towers was erected in the thirteenth century, though rather earlier in this period than most recent commentators have stated,[152] and definitely ahead of that at Lichfield. They also provide striking testimony to major remodelling and rebuilding amongst the conventual buildings after the anti-monastic depredations of Bishop Nonant (1188-98).[153] And they suggest

[149] Hobley, 46.
[150] Thomas, 31, is therefore wrong in asserting that no earlier conventual buildings survived; the chapter house is another example.
[151] For a summary of information about the seal, see *VCH Warks.*, VIII, 125, n. 8. None of the sources listed illustrate the seal, and I have been unable to locate a drawing of it.
[152] E.g. Rigby, 1, 'second half of the 13th century', 'late 13th-century'; *VCH Warks.*, VIII, 125, 'after the middle of the 13th century'; Hobley, 86, 'a late thirteenth-century date'; and Thomas, 31-2, follows their judgements.
[153] Hobley, 61-2, 88, though not all these buildings are 'after the middle of the 13th century', and the evidence for many of them dating 'from the fourteenth and fifteenth centuries' appears less extensive than he suggests. *VCH Warks.*, VIII, 125 and 129, wrongly ascribes virtually all the conventual buildings to no earlier than the fourteenth and fifteenth centuries, on the basis of Hobley's excavations of

that one or more of the high vaults in the cathedral church was erected in the thirteenth century, a phase of work not noticed before.

The remains of the western block are by far the most informative of these features, because they relate not only to the facade but also to the interior of the nave at its west end. There is no space here to undertake a full analysis of the moulding profiles and other architectural detail, but only some general observations.[154] Along the interior face of the west wall, the four responds survive for up to 7 ft. 6 in. (2.3 m.) above the medieval floor level (pl. 13).[155] The two outer responds carried the entrance arches into the west towers, set outside the aisles (fig. 6), and the two inner ones received the last bay of the nave arcades (fig. 8A, 'R'). All four sit on double-roll bases (pl. 11), which were coming into fashion in the midlands from the 1220s, as in the south transept of Lichfield Cathedral. This feature alone argues that the west wall should be placed more probably in this period rather than in the second half of the thirteenth century, as proposed by Rigby,[156] which has misled virtually all subsequent commentators. In fact, early twentieth-century writers were more correct in their assessment of the date of these western parts,[157] and the terminal date of c.1220 given for the church by Tickner and Burbidge – immortalized on the bronze plaque on No. 8 Priory Row – will do nicely for the approximate commencement of the west front.[158]

The main type of moulding for all the responds is the keel moulding,[159] which is quite compatible with a date in the 1220s. The large keel moulding, found on each of the tower arch responds (pl. 11),[160] had been introduced from France into the Cistercian environment of northern England in the 1160s, and by the early thirteenth century it was commonly employed for

---

1965.

[154] The author hopes to publish a fuller assessment in due course, both for the thirteenth-century and the later Gothic stones. More fieldwork is required at sites such as Lichfield Cathedral, Croxden, Hulton, Kenilworth Priory, Repton and St Mary's Stafford to establish a clearer midland context for the thirteenth-century work.

[155] Soden, 2, 10.

[156] Rigby, 1, item I.

[157] E.g. F. W. Woodhouse, *The Churches of Coventry*, Bell's Cathedral Series (London, 1909), 18, 'first half of the thirteenth century': though applied to the whole of the nave.

[158] Tickner (1919), 34; Burbidge, 117.

[159] R. K. Morris, 'An English Glossary of Medieval Mouldings: with an Introduction to Mouldings *c*.1040-1240', *Architectural History*, 35 (1992), 3, 5, 15, for terminology and dating.

[160] At the time of writing, there are also three other loose stones with large keels in the grilled area under the former Blue Coat School; and another loose at the garden door of the Cathedral's J. F. Kennedy House.

piers in the north and the midlands: in secular and monastic churches of all kinds, e.g. Hulton Abbey (Cistercian), Repton Priory (Augustinian canons) and Wenlock Priory, south transept (Cluniac). Smaller ogee keels are also typical of this period in the west midlands and the south-west, but uncommon deployed in rows, as found along the sides of all four responds at St Mary's (pl. 11); and this usage requires more research. Certainly Tickner's suggestion that the nave responds resembled those at Exeter Cathedral, which are fourteenth-century, is wholly without substance, and misled Burbidge into looking for other similarities with Exeter.[161]

An unexpected feature of the nave arcade responds is that the profile of the large axial shaft (14 in. diameter) is not keeled but semi-circular, more typical of Romanesque design. The form may have been chosen to reciprocate Romanesque piers with axial shafts further to the east, thus providing a possible clue to the form of some of the nave piers. Comparable developments in pier forms may be seen in the western parts of Peterborough nave (pl. 19). However, this interpretation must remain inconclusive at present, because examples of piers with large demi-shafts exist in the midlands in early thirteenth-century works with no obvious Romanesque antecedents on site, such as Repton Priory (founded c.1172).[162] Indeed the fragmentary remains of this church bear several other similarities to the style of the west end at Coventry. For example, detached shafts are placed in front of flat diagonal surfaces on the piers, and filleted shafts are used,[163] both of which recur on the aisle faces of the nave arcade responds at Coventry.[164] A workshop connexion between the two sites looks probable, but the thirteenth-century church at Repton is very poorly dated, and further research is needed.

The lowest stage of the west facade and towers fits comfortably into the second quarter of the thirteenth century, on the basis of the stylistic evidence available. It was entered through a splendid centre door, the design of which is more clearly visible today than is generally realised. The lowest courses of the right jamb show that the door had four orders of detached shafts each separated by a delicate triple roll moulding group, a design not dissimilar in effect to the surviving nave west door of Ely Cathedral, but less sumptuous. The north door of the west facade at Dunstable Priory also looks related.[165]

---

[161] Tickner (1919), 35; Burbidge, 115-17.

[162] Also found in the nave of St Mary's, Stafford; illustrated in N. Pevsner, *Staffordshire*, Buildings of England (Harmondsworth, 1974), pl. 13.

[163] See W. H. St J. Hope, 'Repton Priory, Derbyshire', *Derbyshire Archaeological and Natural History Society Journal* (1885), plans of bases between 152-3.

[164] Seven other pieces of large filleted shaft, *ex situ*, are rebuilt into the wall inside the basement of the north-west tower (see this volume, Fig. 1 opposite page 1, letter 'n' on plan); they are slightly larger than the respond shafts.

[165] Illustrated in N. Pevsner, *Bedfordshire, Huntingdon and Peterborough*, Buildings of

At Coventry, the detached shafts were apparently coloured freestones,[166] rather than the Purbeck-type marble used at Ely, and Iain Soden has pointed out that a similar sort of effect may still be seen in the west door of the former Augustinian priory church at Canons Ashby, Northamptonshire.[167] All these parallels are generally dated in the 1230s or 1240s. It should be noted too that a simpler version of St Mary's door, with detached sandstone shafts, still exists within a stone's throw of the cathedral site, in the inner north porch of Holy Trinity parish church. The porch looks to be about contemporary, judging by the style of its foliage capitals and other architectural details, and is therefore likely to predate the fire which is said to have 'destroyed' Holy Trinity church in 1257.[168]

The tradition for likening the west facade to that of Lichfield Cathedral goes back to Browne Willis,[169] but a comparison with Tickner's speculative reconstruction (pl. 10) brings out how relatively different it would have appeared. This is mainly because the twin towers were set outside the aisles at Coventry (fig. 6, pl. 10), in exactly the same fashion as the contemporary west front at Wells Cathedral. However, the style of architectural detail of the Coventry facade seems to derive from the east midlands, and as wide 'screen' facades are more of a tradition in that area (e.g. Lincoln and Peterborough Cathedrals), the master mason apparently drew his main inspiration from there. The lowest stage of the north-west tower provides the best evidence for stylistic assessment, especially the details shown on it in pre-1856 views (pl. 12), before it was incorporated into the new school buildings, as Fretton laments:[170]

> much to the detriment of the older fragment, for what was left of its characteristic ornamentation has been mercilessly sheared off, and in parts made as clean as a new pin, the turrets being capped with a nondescript species of pyramid, resembling extinguishers rather than anything else.

The use of blind trefoil-headed arcading and extensive vertical shafting for decoration recalls similar features in the west front at Peterborough

England (Harmondsworth, 1968), pl. 27.

166 Burbidge, 116, citing Mr Odell's nineteenth-century diary. `

167 Soden, 4.

168 *VCH Warks.*, VIII, 326.

169 B. Willis, *An History of the Mitred Parliamentary Abbies and Conventual Cathedral Churches*, 2 vols. (London, 1718), I, 69-70; a passage frequently quoted by later authors, e.g. Burbidge, 114. This is the source of the idea for St Mary's having three spires, presumably also in stone. The idea cannot be proven, but is plausible given the fine surviving spires of St Michael's and Holy Trinity, probably intended to outdo those already existing on the cathedral church.

170 Fretton, 35. For other old views predating this restoration, see *VCH Warks.*, VIII, opposite 128; Hobley, pl. 25; Thomas, 35.

(c.1210-20), a source also noted by Tickner,[171] and especially in the nave and Early English parts of the west front at Lincoln (c.1220-50). The unusual buttresses of part-octagonal plan (fig. 6, pl. 10) are more or less replicated in the north transept at Lichfield (c.1240),[172] where the masons' lodge was coming under strong influence from Lincoln from this time on. It is possible that the facade was decorated with statuary, but the only surviving embellishment that may have belonged is a large weathered headstop of a seated figure, two feet (61 cm.) high, which formerly linked two arches of blind arcading, and is now reset in the west wall of the south-west tower.[173]

The only other evidence for work in the cathedral at this period is a large carved vault boss, refixed in the cellar of No. 9, Priory Row (pl. 14).[174] Given the elaboration of the carving and the size of the boss, it is virtually certain to have been part of one of the high vaults of the cathedral church. Stylistically its date looks to be between the 1240s and the 1270s. Perhaps a new vault was being inserted at this date in the choir; the presence of this boss in a property on the eastern part of the cathedral site implies such a provenance. Tickner's notebook records the discovery of another boss in this area about 1901, 'of conventional foliage, very deeply undercut, Early English'.[175] The royal grant of timber towards the fabric of the church between 1247 and 1251[176] may possibly relate to such work, though it could also concern the upper stages of the west front. It should be noted that if 'crossing plan B' were accepted for the Romanesque church, a more comprehensive rebuilding of the eastern arm in the thirteenth century becomes more likely.

Meanwhile work was also under way in the conventual buildings. Hobley's excavations revealed part of the monks' bench against the south wall of the chapter house, and on it a moulded base which would have supported a shaft of the blind arcading of the sedilia.[177] Hobley does not venture an interpretation, but the style of the base suggests a thirteenth-century date, probably c.1220-50, when presumably the whole interior of the chapter house was remodelled and the eastern termination

171 Tickner (1919), 37. His reconstruction of the upper parts of the west towers is indebted to Peterborough (pl. 10).
172 The only difference is that an angle projects forward in each Coventry buttress, as against a side of the octagon in those at Lichfield.
173 This is apparently the same figure as in Troughton, IX, 20; reproduced in Hobley, pl. 29a.
174 The visible part of the boss suggests a diameter of about two feet. It was drawn by Troughton, IX, 24c (apparently already inserted in the basement vault); reproduced in Hobley, pl. 30, but without noting the context.
175 Tickner (1916), 13.
176 Lambert in Hobley, 63.
177 Hobley, 95-6, 118, fig. 6; and other unpublished photographs in HAG CBP.

rebuilt as a polygonal apse.[178] Around the middle of the century, a rectangular undercroft was constructed to the east of the dormitory block, which Hobley identified as the infirmary (farmery);[179] and with this he associated the wall with lancet arches which stood on the east side of Hill Top until the later nineteenth century, and which is remarked on as one of the main survivals from the priory by early commentators.[180] All the moulding details found by Hobley on this site suggest that it was a new build entirely of Early English Gothic style, characterized by the use of the chamfered mitre moulding on the ribs.[181] Two carved roof bosses with similar rib mouldings appear in Dr Troughton's drawings, with their provenance unstated but quite possibly from the same undercroft, which was more or less in his back garden.[182] Hobley also found part of a 'small' capital in the south cloister walk, carved with a simple broad-leaf type of foliage dateable to around 1200.[183] The capital was in a post-Dissolution destruction layer, but it may have belonged to work in this area, such as a new cloister walk or a processional door into the church erected in the later twelfth or early thirteenth centuries. One is left to speculate whether this might be amongst the works which occupied Master Reginald (Reynold), the priory's mason recorded in 1188 and again, perhaps posthumously, in 1224.[184]

Stylistic evidence for work on the church in the Decorated period is meagre, though there must have been considerable renovation, including the provision of larger and more fashionable traceried windows. Indulgences were being granted around 1325 for contributions to the fabric, and amongst

[178] Or, just possibly, the apsidal modification is late medieval, as in the chapter house at Gloucester Cathedral.

[179] Hobley, 98-100, fig. 2 (in which the vaulting is wrongly drawn) and fig. 5.

[180] Ibid., 100, fig. 22. Amongst early commentators, see e.g. Fretton, 35. The feature was drawn by John Carter in 1800 and published in his *The Ancient Architecture of Britain*, part I (London, 1801), pl. XLIII A, B, C.

[181] See Hobley, pl. 20, for the vault springing with this rib profile; and unpublished photographs of fallen sections of rib and other details in HAG CBP. For mouldings terminology, see Morris, 'An English Glossary of Medieval Mouldings...', *Architectural History* (1992), *op. cit.*, 12.

[182] Troughton, IX, 24D; reproduced in Hobley, pl. 29b. Dr Troughton lived at No. 11 Priory Row; see Tickner (1916), 158-9, and Tickner's annotated plans of Priory Row in HAG.

[183] Hobley, 124, fig. 18.4. The dating is mine; Hobley ventures no interpretation. Troughton also illustrates several late Romanesque or Early English foliage capitals of unknown provenance (Troughton, IX, 15 and 16A), one of which recalls the capitals of the north transept door at Lichfield. Also, there is a large squarish stone carved with broad-leaf foliage in the grilled area under the former Blue Coat School.

[184] *VCH Warks.*, VIII, 125 ('Reynold'); Harvey, 249 ('Reginald').

the few chantries recorded are foundations of 1291 and 1328.[185] One of the surviving loose stones of the early Decorated period is a piece of window tracery incorporating a delicate ogee foil.[186] It may well have been found when the west front remains were cleared in the 1850s, in which case its provenance could be an aisle or clerestory window in the western part of the nave; or even the great west window. Without knowing the rate of progress of work on the west front in the thirteenth century, we cannot be sure whether its centre bay held an arrangement of lancets, as proposed by Tickner (pl. 10), or an early bar tracery window. Whatever was there, it is quite likely to have been updated with new tracery in the fourteenth or fifteenth centuries, as happened to the west windows at Lincoln about 1380. In this respect, it is important that an assessment should be made of the 'quantities of high quality painted glass' found during the re-investigation of the west end of St Mary's in 1989-90, to see if they provide a clue to date.[187] Stained glass fragments found during Hobley's excavations on the chapter house site were usefully compared by the late Peter Newton to the existing windows at Stanford on Avon, Northamptonshire, c.1315-26, and thus shown to date probably from c.1310-30.[188] Independent corroboration that renovation work was under way then in the chapter house is derived from the bases of its west door, which look most likely to belong to the first half of the fourteenth century,[189] and from a fragment of ballflower moulding found in the same area.[190]

Another group of stones from the later thirteenth or early fourteenth centuries consists of a series of leering human heads, each set on a large hollow moulding. Two were drawn by Troughton,[191] and one is reset into the upper-level cellar in No. 9 Priory Row, rather out of sight on the far (west) wall (pl. 15).[192] Their size and shape suggest they derive from an exterior stringcourse at the eaves level of a roof, of the sort that may still be seen at Astley just north of Coventry (c.1343). They may have come from an aisle or clerestory, or from one of the towers; Lichfield Cathedral has comparable carved busts used as corbels inside its fourteenth-century crossing tower. Andrews recorded finding at the back of No. 7 Priory Row a block

185 Sir W. Dugdale, *The Antiquities of Warwickshire*, rev. ed., 2 vols. (Coventry, 1730), I, 164-5.
186 Seen by the author in 1989 in the grilled area under the former Blue Coat School, but not there in 1993. This seems to be the stone drawn in Troughton, IX, 19.
187 Soden, 4.
188 Newton in Hobley, 107-11.
189 Hobley, pl. 17b.
190 *Ibid.*, fig. 19.15.
191 Troughton, IX, 27, 30d; reproduced in Hobley, pl. 31.
192 Not mentioned by either Tickner or Rigby.

decorated with ball ornament, like uncarved ballflowers,[193] and this is a form of decoration also associated with towers and high parapets around 1325 (e.g. Salisbury Cathedral spire, Pershore Abbey tower). So, taken together, there are enough clues to suggest that in this period the priory was undertaking work to the church parapets, or possibly a new crossing tower, as was the fashion.[194]

Material signs of construction in the church in the Perpendicular period are restricted to the eastern arm. We have already seen that the new chevet probably belongs to the later fourteenth century, and what we now need to consider are two other late Gothic features revealed by the contractor's clearances in 1955: the mouldings of the north choir aisle wall, and the worked stones from a large vault. The photographs reproduced here are the only record located so far of these features, and more information is still needed about them, and about their local and national context. So what follows is necessarily a preliminary assessment.

There are several loose carved stones in the photograph of the north-east chevet chapel reproduced by Hobley,[195] none of which has ever received any published critical discussion. In the foreground is a stone sculpted with foliage, evidently a vault boss because the stubs for ribs are visible; and directly to its right, a very large piece of cusped blind tracery. Other photographs taken at the same time provide evidence that the two stones belong together. In Plate 3, looking over Mr Shelton's right shoulder, the tracery piece is directly beyond the boss, and this angle makes it possible to see that they both have the same rib profile, mutilated on the tracery piece.[196] The latter is therefore also part of a vault, and one which employed jointed masonry construction,[197] a technique associated with English vaults after the late fourteenth century; notably (but not exclusively) with fan vaulting. Given their size, style and location, the two stones bear testimony to a major new vault in the east end of the church in the fifteenth or early sixteenth centuries, probably the high vault over the presbytery and choir, or possibly in the ambulatory and eastern chapels (like the 'New Building' of c.1500 at Peterborough).

---

[193] Andrews, *Coventry Standard* (1909). For the record, there is also (1993) a stone carved with smaller ballflowers in the grilled area under the former Blue Coat School.

[194] E.g. the new Decorated crossing towers at Salisbury, Lincoln, Hereford, Wells and Lichfield. The suggestion that these features may relate to the crossing tower is based on the assumption that the west towers would have been finished in the thirteenth century, before ballflower (and ball) ornament came into fashion.

[195] Hobley, pl. 5a.

[196] The axial roll moulding is broken off on the tracery piece.

[197] I.e. where the ribs and the panel in between are cut from the same piece of stone; see further W. Leedy, *Fan Vaulting* (London, 1980), chap. 2.

It is tempting to try to relate it to the great fan vaults associated with the early Tudor monarchy, for King Henry VII's interest in the city is well attested, as when he celebrated St George's Day at the cathedral in 1487.[198] However, comparison with the royal group of fan vaults, such as King's College Chapel and Henry VII's Chapel, Westminster, indicates that the Coventry boss is not of a type found in them,[199] and that the geometry of the traceried stone is apparently not that of the classic fan vault immortalized in the Tudor period.[200] So it seems more likely that the design combined aspects of a fan vault and of a more conventional lierne vault[201] with a considerable use of carved bosses, such as may still be seen in the high vaults of Sherborne Abbey, Dorset,[202] and St George's Chapel, Windsor; but examples of which were almost certainly more common in late medieval England before the destruction of many great monastic churches like Coventry. The style of the panelling on the traceried stone indicates the late fourteenth century at the earliest, and overall a date for the vault in the fifteenth century seems most acceptable.

The foundations and worked stones from the north choir aisle have similar diagnostic potential. They focus on two large stones carved with base mouldings (pls 7, 8), which presumably fitted on top of each other to form a respond, from which sprang a group of shafts dividing two bays in the north aisle. The lower of these stones was still attached to the inner surface of the wall (pl. 6), and it appears that the wall in the bay to the west was a bit narrower and adjusting to a slightly different alignment. It is unfortunate (a word which keeps recurring about the 'sorry tale' of 1955)[203] that no record has come down of the exact position of this wall and the window sill which was found with it (pl. 9). From inferences in extracts of correspondence

[198] VCH Warks., II, 57.

[199] The positions of the rib stubs suggest that the Coventry boss comes from an intermediate position on a transverse ridge rib in a lunette over a window; whereas the royal group of vaults tend to use bosses only in the centre of the vaults, or as pendants.

[200] In the Coventry example, the ribs appear to be diverging away from the cusped heads of the panels, rather than converging towards them.

[201] Liernes are the short ribs which create the surface pattern in English later Gothic vaults, except fan vaults: F. Bond, Gothic Architecture in England (London, 1906), chap. XXII, illustrates numerous examples.

[202] Sherborne choir vault was designed before the fire of 1437, and incorporates the feature (observed above at Coventry) of ribs diverging away from cusped heads. See Leedy, Fan Vaulting, op. cit., pl. 27; and J. Gibb, 'The Fire of 1437 and the Rebuilding of Sherborne Abbey', BAAJ, 138 (1985), 101-16.

[203] Margaret Tomlinson of Victoria County Histories called it a 'sorry tale' as long ago as 1965, in a letter to Brian Hobley; copies of correspondence in Rigby file, HAG CBP.

THE LOST CATHEDRAL PRIORY CHURCH

passed by Margaret Tomlinson to Brian Hobley in 1965,[204] it would appear that he has placed the window correctly on his 1966 plan (fig. 5, the area shaded black),[205] in which case the shaft bases were directly to the east of this, one bay before the north-east chevet chapel (fig. 8A, 'S'). The asymmetrical arrangement of the respond suggests that it stood at a point where a regular quadrangular bay of the choir aisle met an irregular bay of the ambulatory, probably triangular in plan (fig. 8A). If a transverse rib dividing the two bays sprang from the mutilated base in the front of the stone in Plate 8, the group of three shafts immediately to its left would be for the various diagonal ribs in the aisle bay; and the base to its right for the single rib (or lesser number of ribs) required in the ambulatory bay (fig. 8A, 'T').

The dating of the moulded bases of the respond and window sill, which are identical (pls 8, 9), is clearly in the Perpendicular period. Dr Rigby, an eye-witness, thought that they suggested 'a late date – between 1450 and 1500',[206] and his judgement has been repeated by most subsequent commentators.[207] At first sight, the bases do have a rather florid appearance which inclines one to think of the so-called 'fantastic' late Perpendicular of Edward IV's reign and the early Tudors. However, no obvious parallel has yet emerged from this group of royal works for the particular combination of bell mouldings displayed on the Coventry bases. Even more ornate bases can be found earlier in the fifteenth century, for example, in the work of Master Richard Winchcombe in the 1430s in the Divinity School, Oxford. Moreover, combinations of bell mouldings for bases and sub-bases, together with tall socles, were common in early Perpendicular works in the second half of the fourteenth century;[208] and these seem to provide parallels at least

[204] *Ibid.*, Margaret Tomlinson to Philip Chatwin, 8 Nov. 1955.
[205] The window moved a bay further east in his 1967 plan, which is less likely to be the correct position; see Hobley, fig. 2.
[206] Extract from a letter from Rigby to Margaret Tomlinson, 20 Nov. 1955; HAG CBP, Rigby file.
[207] E.g. Hobley, 92; Thomas, 32-3 (but contradicted by his summary on 34). *VCH Warks.*, VIII, 127, is more circumspect – 'mouldings of Perpendicular character'. Rigby seems to have misled others in reporting that the bases were of hexagonal form. Photographs appear to show quite clearly that the main bases of the respond and sill were octagonal, though possibly the cluster of minor bases on the respond incorporated hexagonal forms (pls 7-9). In any case, hexagonal bases would not automatically equate with late Perpendicular: the form is especially characteristic of midland architecture in the second half of the fourteenth century (e.g. St Mary's Warwick, Kenilworth Castle).
[208] See J. H. Harvey, *The Perpendicular Style* (London, 1978), fig. 31, e.g. Westminster Abbey porch (pl. 87). For bell bases, see R. K. Morris, 'The Development of Later Gothic Mouldings in England c.1250-1400: Part II', *Architectural History*, 22 (1979), 28-9.

as close in design as any later examples. So the matter remains unresolved from this approach, but an investigation of the exterior plinth moulding of the north wall provides a more promising lead.

The plinth is of an unusual design, with a roll moulding clearly delineated at the bottom of the sloping chamfer course (pl. 5), and comparisons have not been easy to come by.[209] A small version of this idea is incorporated into the very elaborate ground-course mouldings of the Beauchamp Chapel at St Mary's, Warwick (c.1443); and a large chamfered plinth moulding of relatively similar design has been exposed in recent excavations around the east end of the chapel undercroft in Warwick Castle, provisionally dated to the fifteenth century, but the later fourteenth is also possible.[210] However, it is the archaeological evidence still visible in the 1955 photographs which locates this work most precisely in the sequence of rebuilding the east end.

It has already been noted that parts of the foundations of the chevet were made up of re-used worked stones, some of recent Gothic date and apparently in mint condition.[211] What has not been remarked on before is that a stone apparently identical in profile to the north aisle plinth is visible incorporated into the great buttress pad between the north-east and east chapels (pl. 2, by the handle of the shovel; and just visible in centre foreground of pl. 3).[212] It is thus evident that the final form of the chevet, as defined by the plain chamfer plinth moulding on top of these stones (pls 2 and 3), post-dates the choir aisle work. This deduction helps to explain two other observations. The length of foliage stringcourse noted by Rigby and Hobley shares the same unusual delineated roll moulding as the aisle-type plinth, because both are from the same phase of work, re-used. Also, the curious patch of plain chamfer in the choir aisle plinth (pl. 5) must denote a repair or addition effected at the same time as the chamfer plinth of the new chevet. Rigby judged the plinths of the chevet and choir aisle to be at the same level.[213]

---

[209] The most common plinth mouldings are plain chamfer, or bell.

[210] I am most grateful to Nicholas Palmer (Warwickshire County Archaeology Unit) for information about the excavation: see further N. Palmer, 'Warwick Castle: Domestic Range Undercroft: Archaeological Recording (Phase I)', unpublished report, Warwickshire Museum (Warwick, May 1993), 7-8, fig. 6. The suggestion of a fourteenth-century date is mine, based on the profiles of the mullion stubs in the east window of the chapel.

[211] Rigby, 2, item V.

[212] Possibly what Rigby notes as other re-used stones carrying 'a broad fillet' may be more examples of this type, which he saw *in situ*; *ibid*.

[213] Extract from a letter from Rigby to Margaret Tomlinson, 20 Nov. 1955; HAG CBP, Rigby file.

Thus four elements need to be considered in conjunction at the east end. These are – the exterior plinth of the choir aisle; the respond and window sill bases of the interior of the choir aisle; the chevet as built with a plain chamfered plinth; and the ornate panelled vault with bosses. The most likely chronology and reconstruction of events would seem to be as follows.

Construction began on a new eastern extension in the later fourteenth century, in the style of the worked stones associated with the north aisle plinth. The elaborate bases of the respond and window sill are probably also part of this phase, but the evidence available from 1955 is insufficient to prove beyond doubt that the treatments of the inner and outer faces of the choir aisle wall belong together.[214] A hint that this work may have been completed to, or prepared for, a considerable height derives from a large chunk of openwork tracery visible loose on top of the chevet remnants (e.g. pl. 2, centre).[215] Its style is reminiscent of the aisle plinth, with its chamfered surface clearly delineated by incised grooves, and its form suggests that it is part of an exterior pierced parapet at eaves level.

At some stage during this phase, or shortly after its completion, something happened which apparently involved its partial demolition and the re-use of its materials in the new chevet. The mint condition of some of the stones re-used suggests that the two phases followed directly one on the other, or at only a small interval. One possible cause is structural failure, given the potential problems of the sloping site and the massive lower foundations of the new chevet. But an alternative reason is a change of plan, and this might relate to a resurgence of interest in the cult of St Osburga during the work. If one accepts that the chevet design is linked to Vale Royal, and also that either phase one or phase two is the 'new work' mentioned in 1409, then both phases must be relatively close in date to the decade c.1400-10 at the latest. In 1410 it was agreed that the birthday of St Osburga should be celebrated as a local festival and this could supply the explanation for enlarging the 'new work' currently under construction, to provide space for a new setting for her shrine close to the high altar. Burbidge is alone among the commentators in noting a translation of St Osburga in 1462,[216] and I have been unable to find any independent confirmation for this date and event.

214 The responds, etc., might belong with the second phase of the chevet works. Hobley, 92, is misleading in stating that the moulded bases were 'incorporated into the plinth'; they were incorporated into the sill, and contemporary observers considered the piece (pl. 9) to be from the interior.

215 Most clearly illustrated in Hobley, pl. 5a.

216 Burbidge, 118 and 221, from the *City Annals* for 1462: 'Then was St Osborne (St Osburga) translated'. Burbidge's source was a manuscript copy of the Annals known to W. G. Fretton and since lost, probably the Hales Manuscript lost with the Sharp papers in the Birmingham City Reference Library fire of 1879; *ibid.*, 209-10.

However, if it took place and was to the east end, then it would corroborate this argument and supply an absolute terminal date for the new work. The scenario would thus be that phase one, nearing completion at aisle level in 1409, and possibly already incorporating an east end plan influenced by Vale Royal, was partly demolished after 1410. Phase two involved slightly lengthening and re-arranging the plan to make space for the revived cult. Work on this phase, and especially the superstructure and the vaults, may have dragged on intermittently for several decades afterwards, if the 1462 date is a reliable indicator for its completion.

If we could have visited St Mary's in its final medieval state, what would it have felt like architecturally, compared with medieval great churches which still survive for us to admire? In terms of general layout, building periods and size, Gloucester Cathedral[217] is probably the best overall parallel to keep in mind for the church and conventual buildings. It shares with Coventry such features as a cloister to the north, and a substantial Romanesque church with its east end remodelled and extended in the fourteenth and fifteenth centuries. The interior of St Mary's choir and presbytery might have appeared like a longer and taller version of the east arm of Tewkesbury Abbey, in the way that the vista terminates in a three-sided apse with arcades and clerestory (pl. 18).[218] However, there would probably have been more of a feel of late Gothic rebuilding, like Great Malvern Priory; and with the high vault perhaps more like that in the chancel of Sherborne Abbey. For the Romanesque architecture of the nave, which probably survived intact in its main forms until the Dissolution, the twelfth-century nave of Peterborough may provide some ideas (pl. 19). Early English Gothic appeared at the west end of the nave, as in the west bays of Worcester, and at Peterborough, where the change from late Romanesque to Gothic detail may still be observed. Externally, the model of the three spires of Lichfield cannot easily be set aside, but to recreate the truly impressive image of the west front one needs also to look at contemporary Gothic screen facades like Lincoln (pl. 10).

The reconstruction of the main building phases of St Mary's facilitates comparison with the architectural history of Lichfield, the other cathedral church of the diocese, and where the chapter often saw itself in competition with the monks of Coventry.[219] The erection of new Romanesque churches at both sites may be more or less contemporary, and it has even been suggested that Bishop de Limesey (1087-1117) initiated both projects.[220] One

217 Formerly the Benedictine abbey of St Peter.
218 The interior height of St Mary's is likely to have been around 70 feet (21 m.), on the basis of churches of comparable size, e.g. Gloucester (nave), Worcester.
219 Especially in the matter of the election of bishops; see *VCH Warks.*, II, 54; and VIII, 316; also Franklin, this volume.
220 Along with St John's, Chester; Dr Richard Gem at the British Archaeological

gains the impression that Lichfield advanced to completion more rapidly, thanks to the favour shown it by Bishop de Clinton (1130-48), so that by c.1170 a major extension to its east end could be undertaken.[221]

In the meantime, after the disruption of the civil war in the 1140s, the Romanesque cathedral at Coventry was carried forward towards completion through the encouragement of bishops like Durdent and Nonant,[222] changing to Gothic style as it did so. One would estimate that the west facade was finished during the second half of the thirteenth century, at a high point of the priors' wealth and influence. Thus the high medieval great church at Coventry could have been complete well before the existing cathedral church at Lichfield. At the latter, the replacement of the Anglo-Norman church started in earnest about 1200[223] and carried on from east to west for the rest of the thirteenth century. When work was still under way on the north transept, the west front was already rising at Coventry[224] so that the west facade at Lichfield, at least in a general sense, followed Coventry and was inspired by it; and not *vice versa*. However, no sooner was the scaffolding off the facade at Lichfield than work recommenced at the other end of the church in the first half of the fourteenth century. Bishop Langton extended the eastern arm with a new polygonal-apsed Lady Chapel, and the chapter initiated a virtually new choir and presbytery in late Decorated Gothic.

It is therefore no surprise to find that in the later fourteenth century, at the latest, the priory apparently sought to update the eastern parts of St Mary's church, which may still have been essentially Romanesque.[225] In this respect, it would have been no different from a number of other old Benedictine abbeys, like Gloucester and Great Malvern, which had been left behind by the Gothic rebuilding of the secular cathedrals like Lichfield and Salisbury in the previous century. The priory was now to all intents and purposes independent of the bishops, whose interests were almost entirely focused on Lichfield as their cathedral church. Thus the new chevet and the remodelling of the eastern arm at St Mary's were undertaken to bring it back into fashion, with priors like Richard Crosby (1398-1437) assuming a major role. And just as interest was revived in St Chad at Lichfield in the fourteenth century, so it appears that the cult of St Osburga was rekindled in the fifteenth at Coventry.

Association conference, Chester, 1992.
[221] Rodwell (1989), 283-5.
[222] Nonant encouraged the completion of the cathedral, but not monastic life.
[223] Rodwell (1989), 283-5.
[224] The architectural detail of the two works is so close that they must be about contemporary, probably by the same workshop.
[225] In that there is no evidence as yet for any major earlier Gothic rebuilding of the eastern arm; though 'crossing plan B' would very likely entail this.

This paper had originally been offered with the primary intention of discussing the stonework still visible today at the east and west ends of the medieval cathedral site, and the worked stones from the excavations which Brian Hobley directed in 1965-67. However, in the course of research large quantities of previously unpublished materials emerged, and this process is by no means exhausted. As a result, the paper has also taken on the form of a critical review of past discoveries, to explain how certain features of the church plan have been ascertained and, often, why they have been re-interpreted since. In mitigation of the resultant length of the paper, I must plead that it deals with a whole church comparable in size to Gloucester or Worcester cathedrals, and for which Tickner's article in 1919 has been the only previous attempt at an extended architectural history.[226] Yet the amount of evidence has increased enormously since Tickner's time.

This account should be regarded as a starting point, and certainly not a definitive exposition. It will have succeeded if it has drawn attention to the potential significance of even the smallest details, and therefore the necessity of preserving them if at all possible, or recording them professionally and ensuring the long-term survival of those records. All loose worked stones in the area should be reported and properly protected. The sorry saga of what happened in 1955 is obvious with hindsight, but carved stones still continue to go astray. With regard to the conservation of standing fabric, the lower parts of the north-west tower are in urgent need of remedy from destruction through rising damp, as pointed out in Iain Soden's report in 1990, but about which nothing has been done.[227] We are in danger of losing the only well-preserved length of the ground-course mouldings of the tower because of this delay.

A priority for the future is the production of a new measured survey map for the priory area, locating exactly the modern topography and buildings, the medieval standing fabric and, as far as possible, every feature known through previous discoveries. This is essential for any attempt at detailed reconstruction of medieval St Mary's, and as a master plan to provide context for any future archaeological investigations, which would undoubtedly prove beneficial. I am painfully conscious that in concluding with these pleas, I am reiterating the published sentiments of Thomas Tickner in 1919[228] and Rosemary and John Hemsley in 1962.[229] Of course,

---

[226] Those in *VCH Warks*. VIII, Hobley and Thomas, are all brief accounts, of necessity.

[227] Soden, 2, 3, 5.

[228] Tickner (1919), 37: 'If the work I have attempted will only serve as an incentive to the carrying out of excavations ...'

[229] R. and J. Hemsley, 'The Cathedral Church of St Mary, Coventry', *TBWAS*, 78 (1962), 11: 'Mr. Chatwin has for some considerable time tried to effect such an excavation ...'

in the meantime the excavations supervised by Brian Hobley have taken place. Nevertheless there still exist a number of sites of considerable promise for our increased knowledge of the cathedral church – the properties in Priory Row and their back-yards; Hill Top and Priory Row itself; and the area between the Provost's House and the new cathedral. However, the outstanding opportunity for a research excavation lies on the site of the west bays of the nave and the west range of the cloister, beneath the path which runs from Priory Lane to the former Blue Coat School and the derelict nineteenth-century building in the yard to the north. Apart from the archaeological advantages, the opening up of this area would greatly enhance the setting of the west front of the most forgotten medieval cathedral in England.

Acknowledgements
I am most grateful to the following for facilitating access to various properties on the former priory site – the Very Reverend John Petty; Jim Helliwell; Paul Melia; Rafael Salguero and the staff of the English Studies Centre; Duncan Elliott; Barbara Olds; and the Reverend David Urquhart. For answering enquiries about archive materials, I should like to thank Margaret Rylatt; Ed Dickinson; David Hardhill; Iain Soden; David Rimmer; Paul Woodfield; John Rathbone; the Venerable Jessie Proctor; and Jonathan Hemsley. I am indebted to many of the participants at the symposium for helpful discussion and ideas, but particularly to Margaret Rylatt; George Demidowicz; Michael Franklin; and the Reverend Canon Michael Sadgrove, to whom go special thanks for originating the idea of the symposium. Richard Gem kindly commented on a draft at short notice and put me right about a number of Anglo-Saxon and Romanesque matters, though time has prevented me from incorporating all his points in the final article. I am grateful to Warwick University for sabbatical leave, during part of which the research for, and writing of, this paper was undertaken. Finally, I have benefited more than they realise from the keen-eyed students from Warwick University who have accompanied me on course visits to the priory site.

ABBREVIATIONS

BAACT: *British Archaeological Association Conference Transactions*
BAAJ: *British Archaeological Association Journal.*
TBWAS: *Birmingham (and Warwickshire) Archaeological Society Transactions.*
CBP: 'Coventry Benedictine Priory' archive at HAG.
HAG: Herbert Art Gallery and Museum, Coventry.

Andrews: Alderman W. Andrews, 'The Ancient Coventry Cathedral, Discoveries at the Constitutional Club', *Coventry Standard* (Feb. or March 1909), two-and-a-half columns, copy pasted into the front of Tickner (1916).

Burbidge: F. B. Burbidge, *Old Coventry and Lady Godiva* (Birmingham, n.d., c.1950).

Fernie (1979): E. C. Fernie, 'Observations on the Norman Plan of Ely Cathedral', *Medieval Art and Architecture at Ely Cathedral* (BAACT for 1976, published 1979), 1-7.

Fernie (1983): E. C. Fernie, 'The Grid System and the Design of the Norman Cathedral', *Medieval Art and Architecture at Winchester Cathedral* (BAACT for 1980, published 1983), 13-19.

Fretton: W. G. Fretton, 'The Benedictine Monastery and Cathedral of Coventry', *TBWAS* 7 (1876), 19-38.

Harvey: J. H. Harvey, *English Mediaeval Architects: a Biographical Dictionary down to 1550*, rev. ed. (Gloucester, 1984).

Hobley: B. Hobley *et al.*, 'The Cathedral and Priory Church of St Mary, Coventry', *TBWAS* 84 (1967-70, published 1971), 46-139.

Poole: B. Poole, *Coventry: its History and Antiquities* (Coventry, 1870).

Rigby: G. R. Rigby, 'Report on Remains of Cathedral Church, St. Mary's Priory, October 1955', unpublished typescript (2 pp.) and copies of correspondence attached, HAG CBP.

Rodwell (1989): W. Rodwell, 'Archaeology and the Standing Fabric: Recent Studies at Lichfield Cathedral', *Antiquity* 63 (June 1989), 281-94.

Soden: I. Soden, 'Excavations at St. Mary's Benedictine Priory, Coventry, 1989-90', unpublished report, HAG Archaeological Unit (n.d., c.1990), 11 pp.

Thomas: J. Thomas, *Coventry Cathedral*, New Bell's Cathedral Guides (London, 1987).

Thompson: F. H. Thompson, 'Excavations at the Cistercian Abbey of Vale Royal, Cheshire, 1958', *Antiquaries Journal* 42 (1962), 184-207.

Tickner (1916): T. F. Tickner, unpublished notebook, begun on 28th October 1916, in HAG (see further reference 14).

Tickner (1919): T. F. Tickner, 'The Cathedral and Priory of St. Mary of Coventry and an approximate restoration of the plan of the church', *BAAJ*, n.s. 25 (1919), 24-38.

Troughton: Dr. N. Troughton, Sketches c.1850-68, 10 vols., unpublished (Coventry Record Office).

VCH Warks., II: *The Victoria County History of Warwickshire* (London, 1908).

VCH Warks., VIII: *The Victoria County History of Warwickshire* (London, 1969).

Revisiting the Archaeological Evidence for the Priory
MARGARET RYLATT

Archaeologists and historians alike have long sought evidence, through their own particular disciplines, for the origins of religious life on Coventry's hill top; evidence which, if found and assembled, would contribute greatly to our knowledge and understanding of the very origin of Coventry itself. The symposium at last brought together researchers from many disciplines to pool their knowledge in an attempt to draw some firm conclusions on the history of the Benedictine Priory of St Mary before 1581 when a survey of Coventry records '... there is also upon the same ground stone which is left of the steeple and church there....'[1] In archaeological terms, there is no stratified evidence for any settlement in Coventry before the twelfth century. Therefore, evidence for earlier periods must be sought from documentary sources, the reporting of the few objects found in the city and, last but not least, tradition.

Objects from the pre-Conquest period are rare from Coventry, and those that have been found are generally unprovenanced and of the type that, one could argue, are easily lost by travellers passing through the area, such as a coin or a brooch. However, there are two objects that certainly do not fall into such a category: a fragment of Saxon stonework, found in Palmer Lane in the 1930s and a wooden vat, dated c.1000, found at the bottom of Bishop Street. For many years the fragment of worked sandstone was thought to be part of a Saxon cross, but Richard Morris has recently suggested that it is in fact part of a tenth-century door jamb (Plate 20). Both of these objects are, of course, important, but being unstratified can only be used as evidence in a much wider picture.

Research into traditions is also important for the historian, and Coventry has a strong tradition that in the tenth century St Osburga founded a nunnery here, which in 1016 was destroyed by marauding Danes. The tradition continues that Leofric and Godiva founded a church on, or near, the site of the nunnery in 1043, but this date is now considered to be more likely that of dedication rather than foundation.

The earliest recording of remains certainly belonging to the medieval Cathedral of St Mary was carried out in 1856-57 when the old Blue Coat School was being rebuilt, fortunately avoiding the west end but incorporating the north-west tower. The artist, Dr Nathaniel Troughton, made many sketches of the masonry uncovered at the time, which are most useful, but it is evident that much demolition had accompanied the process and the original plan to preserve the tower at its original height was not carried out.[2]

---

[1] Coventry Record Office, BA/A/A/2/3, 1581 survey.

No records were made of the archaeological levels and only a brief sentence in a description of the work tells of some human bones found together with medieval encaustic tiles.

In 1909 T. F. Tickner recorded the existence of two pier bases in the south nave and aisle and in 1919 he published a plan of the cathedral which has greatly assisted archaeologists and historians in more recent research.[3] (See Morris Fig. 1, p. 16)

Some recording was also done in 1955 when the new cathedral was under construction, including the notable discovery of the foundations of two polygonal apses with projecting buttresses (Plates 2-4). These clearly pin-pointed the eastern end of the medieval cathedral, establishing its total length as about 130m (425 ft).

This then was the knowledge, sometimes uncertain and often fragmentary, that the archaeologists possessed when a programme of major archaeological work was undertaken by Coventry Museum in 1965-7 under the direction of Brian Hobley. The excavations, nearly nine hundred years after the death of Lady Godiva, were the first, and possibly will be the only, opportunity archaeologists will have to excavate such a large part of this monastic site. The project was intended to recover as much evidence as possible about the Benedictine house and its great cathedral church, but the prime objective was to locate remains of the pre-Conquest church built by Leofric and Godiva, in which they are both reputed to have been buried, and with a little luck, uncover evidence of St Osburga's nunnery.

In 1967 work towards this prime objective was undertaken on the site of a disused graveyard belonging to Holy Trinity in Priory Row.[4] Documentary sources pointed to this site as being an important one to investigate but its recent use as a graveyard posed many problems for the archaeologists. Eighteenth-century tombs had to be avoided, and also the mature trees. Consequently there was only room for trenches to be excavated. Unfortunately, no evidence was found of pre-Conquest structures, but what did become evident was the fact that the medieval builders had levelled the site down to bed-rock, effectively removing any earlier archaeological strata.

Somewhat out of sequence, but relevant to this point, it is worth mentioning the fact that in 1989-90 Coventry Museum's Archaeology Unit returned to the site of the west end to examine and record fully the state of

2   Coventry Record Office, 1/9/1-15, c.1856-1860 collection of sketches of St Mary's Priory; Coventry Record Office, 1490/1, Specification for works to Blue Coat School.

3   T. F. Tickner, 'Cathedral and Priory of St Mary, Coventry', *Journal of the British Archaeological Association*, n.s. XXV (1919), 24-38.

4   B. Hobley, 'Excavations at the Cathedral and Benedictine Priory of St Mary, Coventry', *Transactions of the Birmingham and Warwickshire Archaeological Society*, 84 (1971), 45-139.

preservation of the thirteenth-century wall and, through excavation, to establish whether or not it shared a common foundation with an earlier structure.[5] It was found that the west end did not stand on earlier foundations and, arriving at the same conclusion as the 1967 work, it is suggested that evidence for earlier structures be sought elsewhere, most likely under the eighteenth-century buildings in Priory Row.

Before the 1965 excavations very little was known of the layout or extent of the conventual buildings except that they lay to the north of the church towards the River Sherbourne. A number of small trenches were then excavated in the garden of J. F. Kennedy House, which produced evidence of the cloister, cloister garth, chapter house, cellarium and what was later identified as the south wall of the frater. Of the cloister walls virtually nothing was found *in situ*, as extensive stone robbing had taken place. Of the floor, only a few tiles had survived in position and below the floor level a number of disturbed graves were found.

Located centrally along the east cloister walk a two-metre-wide doorway into the chapter house was discovered with its south jamb still in position. A trench excavated below the floor of the dining room of J. F. Kennedy House exposed part of the south wall of the chapter house, which on the inside face incorporated stone seats. Also found *in situ* was a single shaft base. The quality of the masonry found, as with the west end a hundred years earlier, was of a very high standard.

The main area of excavation during 1965-7 was undertaken in an area just west of Hill Top alley. Here the dorter, frater and kitchen were the main buildings uncovered (Plate 21). As in other areas, there had been extensive wall robbing, but the actual level and quality of the remains were quite remarkable considering the destructive activity on these sites since the Dissolution in 1539. A twenty-metre section of the north wall of the frater, which contained two window openings and a doorway, was found (Plate 22). A very short length of the west wall was also located and, as previously mentioned, a short section of the south wall during the excavations in the garden of J. F. Kennedy House. Thus three sides of the building were established.

Just north of the frater, and linked by a pentice, lay the kitchen. This was the only building to be completely excavated. It measured 9.1m x 6m and had one doorway, located in the south wall. It is suggested that there may possibly have been another doorway in the north wall giving access to the kitchen court, but this wall had been robbed down to foundation levels, thus obliterating any evidence of an opening. The inner north-west corner of the kitchen had a massive foundation which was interpreted as the base of an

5   M. Rylatt and I. Soden, 'Coventry, St Mary's Benedictine Priory', *West Midlands Archaeology* 33 (1990), 94-95.

oven or chimney. East of the kitchen a heavily cobbled area with two stone drains running through it was identified as the kitchen court. The drains capped with large sandstone slabs, were in such a good state they could have been used today (Plate 23). Both appeared to flow northwards towards the River Sherbourne, as one might expect. East of the kitchen court, walls two metres wide and in some places two metres high established the north wall of the dorter and the west end of the reredorter.

Both the dorter and reredorter were built on the soft silt of the Sherbourne river terrace, creating subsidence problems for the medieval builders. In an attempt to counteract this, the north wall was constructed on massive sandstone foundations, but it was evident that the north-west corner of the reredorter had collapsed in the medieval period.

Considering the extent of the excavations of 1965-7 and 1989-90 relatively few objects were found. Building materials were, of course, plentiful. Carved, decorated stonework, fragments of roof tile and slate, floor tiles (Fig. 1) and window glass (Fig. 2) all contribute to our knowledge of the aesthetic nature of this great house and can only make us wonder at the tremendous effect it had on those who visited it.

Archaeological excavations can never answer all the questions asked of them; more often than not the findings pose even more questions. In cities such as Coventry, historical phases pass quickly and sites of once great buildings are eventually built over, and what once stood there is forgotten. Consider what has happened to the centre of Coventry since the Second World War; only those who were alive before the Blitz can remember. This is why it is essential that historians and archaeologists work together to document and publish the results of their research.

Prior to the 1965-7 excavations archaeological work that had taken place on this site was, in today's view, poorly documented, if at all. Therefore the publication by Brian Hobley of the 1960s excavations is an invaluable piece of work bringing together, as it does, all known evidence of previous discoveries, as well as the report on work done at the time. But even this has now become open to reinterpretation, as the papers at this symposium exemplify. New research, new archaeological techniques, new dating methods bring us nearer to a true understanding of this once great monastic house which dominated the life and skyline of Coventry for several hundred years. Those interested and working on the history of the site are forever hopeful that one small archaeological trench which will turn up the evidence of an earlier foundation: the remains of the church built by Leofric and Godiva would be a major breakthrough.

I am sure that the outcome of this symposium has provided archaeologists with new ideas and let us hope that some of the site remains available for future excavations.

Figure 1. Medieval floor tile from Priory site.

Figure 2. Two fragments of painted window glass from the chapter house.

Coventry's Topographical Development: The Impact of the Priory

KEITH D. LILLEY

Introduction

The origins of medieval Coventry remain largely enigmatic despite a plethora of studies on the subject during the past two decades. Opportunities were offered by the radical redevelopment of the city centre after 1945, but work by archaeologists has concentrated mainly on the surrounding medieval defences of Coventry.[1] The elusive castle and associated ditch-system has also attracted recent attention,[2] leaving domestic sites relatively untouched by comparison.[3] The historians' approach has been more wide-ranging, but their treatment of medieval Coventry has tended to concentrate on particular questions concerning the 'unity' or 'division' of the medieval town and the forged charters.[4]

Valuable though these detailed studies are, they do not attend to the topography of medieval Coventry, which remains relatively neglected, both as a source, and as an object of study. The exception is the *Historic Towns Atlas* fascicule on Coventry,[5] but this has been subject to criticism by local scholars[6] and does not compare favourably with historic town atlases

[1] E. Gooder, C. Woodfield & R. E. Chaplin, 'The Walls of Coventry', *Transactions of the Birmingham Archaeological Society* 81 (1966), 99-138. J. Bateman & M. Redknap, *Coventry: Excavations on the Town Wall 1976-78*, Coventry Museums Monograph Series 2 (Coventry, 1986).

[2] M. Rylatt, *Coventry Archaeology and Redevelopment*, Coventry Museums Monograph Series 1 (Coventry, 1977). See also the annual reports in *West Midland Archaeology*.

[3] Except for excavations at Much Park Street, although these were restricted to three limited excavation-sites; see S. M. Wright, 'The Medieval Development of Much Park Street, Coventry: the Evidence of the 1970-74 Excavations', *Transactions of the Birmingham and Warwickshire Archaeological Society* 92 (1982), 1-133.

[4] The differing views on these subjects are more recently covered by: R. H. C. Davis, *The Early History of Coventry*, Dugdale Society Occasional Papers 24, (Oxford, 1976); A. & E. Gooder, 'Coventry before 1355: Unity or Division?', *Midland History* 6 (1981), 1-38; T. John (ed), *Medieval Coventry – A City Divided?* (Coventry & Warwickshire Pamphlets 11, 1981); P. R. Coss (ed), *The Early Records of Medieval Coventry* (London, 1986).

[5] M. D. Lobel (ed), *The Atlas of Historic Towns II: Coventry* (London, 1975).

[6] A. & E. Gooder, 'Review of Historic Towns II: Coventry', *Transactions of the Birmingham and Warwickshire Archaeological Society* 88 (1976). P. R. Coss, 'Review of Historic Towns: Coventry', *Midland History* 4 (1977).

published elsewhere in Europe.[7] The medieval and post-medieval topography of particular Coventry streets has been examined[8] but the town as a whole has not been systematically studied, and yet a suitable methodology for topographical analysis has been known to historical geographers for over a quarter of a century.[9] Furthermore, a substantial amount of medieval documentary material has been published for Coventry and, together with recent archaeological excavations, such material can be used to provide historical detail for analysis. In this paper, by using a combination of geographical methods and historical information, the impact of the priory on the topographical development of medieval Coventry will be assessed.

The priory has been the subject of a number of past studies examining both historical and archaeological aspects of its development.[10] However, the topography of the priory precinct has not been reconstructed satisfactorily and the impact of the priory on the surrounding urban topography even less so. Yet the priory, as the earliest feature documented in Coventry's history, may itself yield clues to the origins of the town. The priory, after its foundation, certainly influenced the tenurial development of the medieval town as it accumulated properties and rights which were eventually to lead to the prior's claims over his, so-called, half of Coventry and its market rights.[11] The subject of the date of the forged charters relating to the prior's claims over his half of Coventry, the prior's fee, has been examined recently,[12] and

7   T. R. Slater & K. D. Lilley, 'The British Historic Towns Atlas: a Critique', *Urban History* (forthcoming, 1994).

8   N. W. Alcock, 'Coventry Streets: West Orchard and the Sherbourne, Development and Topography, 1600 to 1940', *Transactions of the Birmingham and Warwickshire Archaeological Society* 91 (1981), 83-116. N. W. Alcock, 'The Catesbys in Coventry: a Medieval Estate and its Archives', *Midland History* 15 (1990), 1-36.

9   The development of this work can be followed through: M. R. G. Conzen, *Alnwick, Northumberland, a Study in Town-plan Analysis*, Institute of British Geographers Publication 27 (London, 1960); T. R. Slater (ed), *The Built Form of Western Cities* (Leicester, 1990); N. J. Baker & T. R. Slater, 'Morphological Regions in English Medieval Towns', in *Urban Landscapes, International Perspectives*, ed. J. W. R. Whitehand & P. J. Larkham (London, 1992).

10 W. G. Fretton, 'The Benedictine Monastery and Cathedral of Coventry', *Transactions of the Birmingham and Midland Institute Archaeology Section* 8 (1880), 19-38. T. F. Tickner, 'The Cathedral and Priory of St. Mary and an Approximate Restoration of the Plan of the Church', *Journal of the British Archaeological Association* New Series 25 (1919), 24-40. B. Hobley with M. W. Lambert, 'Excavations at the Cathedral and Benedictine Priory of St. Mary, Coventry', *Transactions of the Birmingham and Warwickshire Archaeological Society* 84 (1971) 45-139.

11 John, *Medieval Coventry*.

12 Coss, *Early Records*.

the extent of the town's unity discussed.[13] In seeking to address the topographical impact of the priory on the development of medieval Coventry, two main themes will be explored. One concerns the form of the precinct, that is the religious topography of the priory. The second theme examines the shaping of the secular landscape by the priory outside the precinct.

Reconstructing Coventry's Medieval Urban Topography
A suitable methodology for using town plans as research tools in urban history has been used by geographers in Britain following the introduction of analytical techniques from Europe by Professor M. R. G. Conzen.[14] Recently the methodology of town-plan analysis has been applied to a number of English medieval towns[15] and gradually improved upon to provide a rigorous tool for revealing urban topographical development.[16] In particular, doctoral research at the University of Birmingham by the present author has sought to utilise town-plan analysis in order to reconstruct the origins and development of medieval Coventry and so further contribute to a firmer methodological basis.[17] It is part of this research which forms the essence of this paper.

Any analysis of Coventry's medieval topography will be hampered by the loss of visible remains, sustained in particular during the twentieth century. However, there are abundant cartographic and documentary sources available for analysis, together with a growing archive of archaeological information from recent excavations. A combination of these sources provides the plan-analytic procedure with chronological information to help reconstruct the topographical development of the medieval town. The cartographic base of the analysis is the first edition 1/2500 scale Ordnance Survey (OS) plan of Coventry, published in 1889; a source used in other plan-analyses of English medieval towns.[18] This reliable and accurate

---

13 Gooder, *Unity or Division.*
14 Conzen, *Alnwick.*
15 T. R. Slater, 'Medieval New Town and Port: a Plan Analysis of Hedon, East Yorkshire', *Yorkshire Archaeological Journal* 57 (1985), 23-51; *idem,* 'The Topography and Planning of Medieval Lichfield: a Critique', *Transactions of the South Staffordshire Archaeological and Historical Society* 16 (1986), 11-35; *idem,* 'English Medieval New Towns with Composite Plans', in Slater (ed), *Built Form,* 60-82.
16 Baker & Slater, *Morphological Regions.* K. D. Lilley, 'Coventry's Town Plan: New Perspectives', Urban Morphology Research Group, School of Geography, University of Birmingham (unpublished, 1991).
17 K. D. Lilley, *Medieval Coventry: a Study in Town-plan Analysis* (unpublished University of Birmingham Ph.D. thesis, forthcoming 1994).
18 See Baker & Slater, *Morphological Regions,* for an attempt to set out the methodology of town-plan analysis, and also Lilley, *Medieval Coventry.*

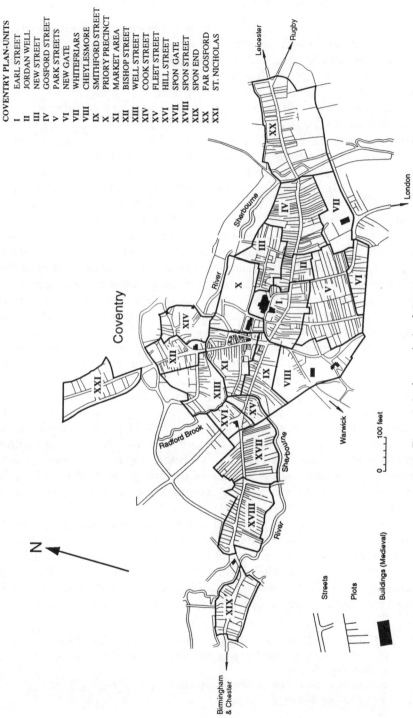

Coventry

COVENTRY PLAN-UNITS

I	EARL STREET
II	JORDAN WELL
III	NEW STREET
IV	GOSFORD STREET
V	PARK STREETS
VI	NEW GATE
VII	WHITEFRIARS
VIII	CHEYLESMORE
IX	SMITHFORD STREET
X	PRIORY PRECINCT
XI	MARKET AREA
XII	BISHOP STREET
XIII	WELL STREET
XIV	COOK STREET
XV	FLEET STREET
XVI	HILL STREET
XVII	SPON GATE
XVIII	SPON STREET
XIX	SPON END
XX	FAR GOSFORD
XXI	ST. NICHOLAS

Streets

Plots

Buildings (Medieval)

0   100 feet

N

Figure 1. A plan analysis of Coventry

cartographic source is simplified into three plan-elements; the street-system, plot pattern and major institutional structures (such as churches and defences), which constitute the town plan. Elsewhere in Britain the stability of these plan-elements from the medieval period into the modern has been proven archaeologically and is now gaining widespread recognition.[19]

On the basis of differences in the form of the three plan-elements, the town plan can be disaggregated into discrete areas, known as plan-units. Each plan-unit is recognisably distinct from its neighbours because of characteristic differences in the street-system and plot pattern. Most English town plans are composite types as they are composed of a number of individual plan-units.[20] Furthermore, plan-units have been taken to represent individual phases in the topographical development of medieval towns, although it is often difficult to determine when each unit first originated.[21] The town plan of Coventry is also composite in form, composed of twenty-one separate plan-units, each unit perhaps representing a stage in the town's topographical development (Fig 1). In particular, two plan-units are relevant for an understanding of the former priory precinct and its topographical influence on the development of the town. A description of the morphology of these two plan-units is useful to show how distinct they are from the surrounding plan-units and also to suggest why they should be so distinctive.

The first plan-unit, the priory precinct, is approximately rectilinear in overall form and located between the River Sherbourne to the north and Earl Street to the south (numbered Plan-unit X on Fig. 1). The plan-unit boundary (plan-seam) encircles an area which had relatively few urban plots, even at the time of the 1/2500 scale survey in 1889. Within the plan-unit area the parish church of Holy Trinity, together with the site of the priory ruins and other ecclesiastical antiquities shown by the Ordnance Survey, form a distinctive ecclesiastical enceinte. The plan-seam probably reflects the former precinct boundary. However, because so little of the priory remained in 1889, it is necessary to test this assumption by reconstructing the religious topography of the precinct.

The second plan-unit (Unit XI) covers the market area and is quite distinctive in comparison to the priory precinct unit (X) to the east, due to three different arrangements of plots within the street-system (termed sub-units) (Fig. 1). The whole plan-unit is centred on a triangular-shaped market place, which has undergone infilling which has obscured its earlier, more open form. Small irregular plots, densely covered with buildings in

19 N. J. Baker, H. Dalwood, R. Holt, C. Mundy & G. Taylor, 'From Roman to Medieval Worcester: Development and Planning in the Anglo-Saxon City', *Antiquity* 66 (1992), 65-74.
20 *Ibid.*; Slater, *English Medieval New Towns.*
21 Lilley, *Medieval Coventry.*

1889, can be identified within the centre of the market place on the 1/2500 scale OS plan. These distinctive plots are indicative of market colonisation and have been recognised in other medieval market places.[22] Not all of the market place in Coventry was built upon; instead narrow interconnecting lanes can be seen which have street names based on the types of marketing functions carried out there (e.g. Little Butcher Row and Potter Row). It seems likely, therefore, that the medieval market place was segregated according to different market functions.

Triangular market places are often associated with ecclesiastical urban growth and frequently lay outside monastic precincts, forming a focus outside their gates (for example, St Albans, Peterborough and Ely).[23] Furthermore, the Benedictine order of monks is known to have been actively engaged in the development of new towns in England during the eleventh and twelfth centuries.[24] At Coventry, therefore, the triangular market place could also be indicative of a phase of urban development initiated by the Benedictine monastery outside its precinct.[25] The plan-seam which separates the two plan-units (X & XI), if it represents the former precinct wall, demonstrates the close connection between the market area and the adjacent monastic precinct. This juxtaposition may be explained by the two plan-unit areas being closely associated in their origin and development. In other words, could the market area represent a contemporary or near-

---

[22] See Conzen, *Alnwick*, and also Slater, *English Medieval New Towns*, for further examples of this phenomenon.

[23] T. R. Slater, 'Urban Genesis and Medieval Town Plans in Warwickshire and Worcestershire', in *Field and Forest*, ed. T. R. Slater & P. J. Jarvis (Norwich, 1982). M. Aston & C. J. Bond, *The Landscape of Towns* (London, 1976).

[24] T. R. Slater, 'Benedictine Town Planning in Medieval England', in *Medieval Towns and the Church II*, ed. G. Rosser & T. R. Slater (Leicester, forthcoming 1994).

[25] Triangular market places have also been said to originate from pre-urban greens that developed into market areas through urban growth, as at Hedon, a medieval 'new town' in Yorkshire (Slater, 'Medieval New Town and Port'). Another explanation uses the idea of the morphological frame (see K. D. Lilley, *Topographical Frameworks and the Concept of the Morphological Frame*, School of Geography working paper 60, University of Birmingham 1992), where three earlier roads intersect and form a triangular open-space at the junction, as at Alnwick (Conzen, *Alnwick*). In the case of Coventry the origins of the market place as a green cannot be ruled out. A 'village green' seems inappropriate but a former open-space in front of the precinct is possible, such as the one still visible outside the former precinct wall at Evesham (another Benedictine foundation; see Slater, *Urban Genesis*). The road-junction hypothesis can be ruled out more firmly because the Coventry market place is situated north of the principal road intersection (Earl Street/Broadgate) (see Lilley, *Medieval Coventry*).

contemporary monastic foundation, or perhaps even form part of the original monastic endowment, as the prior was later to claim?

Using the town plan as a base, the various and disparate documentary references can be brought together with the archaeological record to locate medieval features in each of the two plan-units. However, before the historical information is plotted onto the plan-units it is necessary to redraw the plans at a larger scale using the 1851 Board of Health (hereafter BOH) plan as a base. The BOH plan is recognised as the earliest accurate and detailed plan of Coventry[26] and allows comparison between the two plan-units. Historical cartographical sources, such as John Speed's plan of 1610 and Bradford's 1750 plan, add further information to the topography of the plan-units and go together with the BOH plan to produce a reliable cartographic base.

Archaeological features are located onto the base plan and provide some evidence for their date and function, although not all excavations have been published for the two plan-units under discussion. Documentary information is mainly derived from the thirteenth-century deeds, calendared and transcribed by Coss,[27] as well as the published part of the priory rental of 1410-11, known as the Pittancer's Rental.[28] The Coventry Leet Book[29] also contains a wealth of fifteenth-century topographical detail to add to the plans. Of course, published studies on the topography of the priory area are also considered in the analysis, as is unpublished work, principally by J. B. Shelton and N. W. Alcock.[30]

The method by which all of this historical and topographical information is added to the base plan is a complex one and has been discussed more fully elsewhere.[31] In the following part of this paper the medieval topographies of the two plan-units are considered in turn, to show how their medieval topographies took shape and to show how they continued to exert an influence upon the topography of Coventry. Finally, the possible link between the monastic precinct and the development of the market area is discussed.

[26]   A copy of this plan is housed at Warwick County Record Office under reference Z734(u), although the original is kept at Coventry City Record Office. For the development of the BOH plans in Warwickshire, see J. B. Harley, 'The Ordnance Survey 1:528 Board of Health Town Plans in Warwickshire 1848-1854', in Field and Forest, ed. Slater & Jarvis, 347-84.

[27]   P. R. Coss (ed), The Langley Cartulary, Dugdale Society Publication XXXII (Stratford upon Avon, 1980); idem, Early Records.

[28]   A. & E. A. Gooder (eds), The Pittancer's Rental, 1410-11, Department of Extramural Studies, University of Birmingham (Birmingham, 1973).

[29]   M. Dormer Harris (ed), The Coventry Leet Book, 1420-1555, Early English Text Society Original Series 134 and 135 (London, 1907-13).

[30]   This unpublished work is housed in the Coventry Museum Archaeological Unit (CMAU) archive in the care of M. Rylatt.

[31]   Lilley, Medieval Coventry.

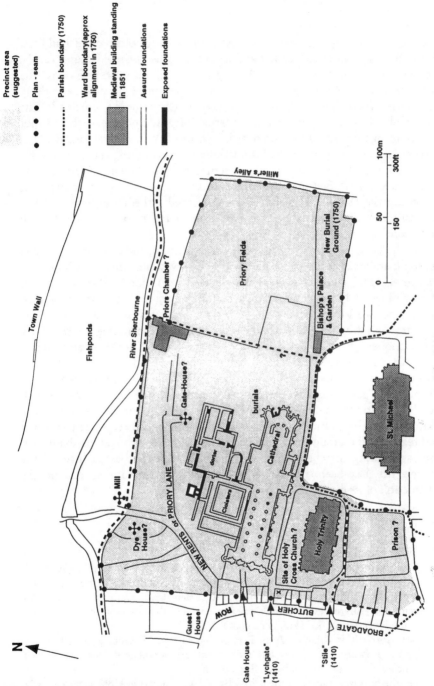

Legend:

Precinct area (suggested)

••• Plan - seam

•••••••• Parish boundary (1750)

—•—•— Ward boundary(approx alignment in 1750)

Medieval building standing in 1851

Assured foundations

Exposed foundations

Town Wall

Fishponds

River Sherbourne

Mill

Dye House?

NEW RENTS

Guest House

Gate House

"Lychgate" (1410)

ROW

BUTCHER

"Stile" (1410)

BROADGATE

Gate-House?

Priors Chamber ?

PRIORY LANE

Cloister

Cellar

burials

Cathedral

Site of Holy Cross Church ?

Holy Trinity

Prison ?

St. Michael

Priory Fields

Bishop's Palace & Garden

New Burial Ground (1750)

Miller's Alley

N

0   50   100m
0   150   300ft

Figure 2. The Priory Precinct plan-unit

The Priory Precinct Topography

The medieval priory precinct contained a whole range of different buildings within its walls, and the location and layout of some of these features can be plotted on the base plan (Fig. 2). Together with Bury St Edmunds, the cathedral church of the priory was one of the few in England to be entirely demolished following the Dissolution, leaving few standing remains.[32] The topography of the priory and its internal organisation are therefore not readily reconstructed, as Fretton noted.[33] Some of the medieval cathedral has been excavated and parts of its foundations exposed during the past century and a new conjectural plan has been attempted[34] (see Richard Morris, Fig. 8, p. 4, this volume). Because the former north-west tower of the cathedral is shown on the 1851 BOH plan, the reconstructed cathedral ground-plan can be positioned onto the large-scale base plan of the plan-unit (Fig. 2) with some confidence.

At its greatest extent, by the fourteenth century, the cathedral extended approximately 425 feet in length on a true east-west alignment. Although no structural remains of the earliest church have been found, clear evidence of an east range of Norman conventual buildings suggests it too was rebuilt in this period (see Morris, this volume). The strict east-west orientation of the cathedral building is also indicative of liturgical replanning in the early post-Conquest period.[35] The earliest structural foundations that can be dated with any confidence (c.1220-1250) belong to the west front and include an impressive central doorway.[36] The lack of the earliest structural remains of the priory in general has been explained in terms of large-scale changes which involved periodic rebuilding, documented during the later thirteenth century.[37] As excavations have shown, this probably necessitated levelling and terracing the ground north of the cathedral for the conventual buildings, thus accounting for the late date of finds.[38] However, as so little of the church site has been excavated, it would be premature to assume the destruction of its earliest phases.

---

[32] Hobley, *Excavations at the Cathedral*, p. 77.

[33] Fretton, *The Benedictine Monastery*, p. 35.

[34] Hobley, *Excavations at the Cathedral*.

[35] The orientation of churches in towns is discussed by R. Morris (*Churches in the Landscape* (London, 1989), pp. 208-9), who suggests that 'a desire for greater strictness in orientation arose out of the Benedictine reforms of the tenth century'. Differences in church orientation have also been noted in Worcester and Gloucester (N. J. Baker, pers. comm.).

[36] See Morris (this volume). Also, Fretton, *op. cit.*, p. 35; Hobley, *op. cit.*, p. 86, pp.90-94 (where the door and west front are reproduced from an original nineteenth-century sketch by N. Troughton).

[37] See the historical survey of the priory by M. W. Lambert in Hobley, *op. cit.*, p.62.

[38] Hobley, *Excavations at the Cathedral*, p. 90.

The layout of the conventual buildings can be plotted onto the base plan, using Hobley's ground-plan from his excavations.[39] The conventual buildings form a compact group north of the cathedral rather than their more usual position on the south side. This reversal may be explained by the need to provide a water supply from, and drainage to, the river Sherbourne and possibly because it kept the monastic offices more secluded, away from the town to the south. So far the cloisters, chapter house and kitchen have been located, together with some clerical burials east of the cathedral.[40] In this area, too, the few pre-Conquest finds may be taken to indicate the site of the earliest Benedictine foundation before liturgical replanning took place.

Clearly it was the cathedral and conventual buildings which dominated the priory precinct, occupying the western portion of the suggested precinct area, closest to the market area and therefore overlooking it. Within the precinct various other buildings can be identified and, in particular, a group of industrial-type activities along the street that became New Rents. Here the mill was to be found, which the amateur Coventry archaeologist J. B. Shelton recorded when excavations exposed the leat and timbers.[41] Shelton's finds correspond with a curving plot boundary which probably represents the course of the former mill leat, and can be also recognised on Speed's plan of 1610 (Fig. 2).[42] It seems likely that the priory dye-house was located adjacent to the mill,[43] where Shelton recorded 'stone foundations' together with a well and mortared stone-wall.[44] A concentration of industry-related and craft-based activities thus forms a water-side complex within the priory precinct, but away from the prior's private accommodation, to the east, and segregated from the main conventual buildings to the south.

The prior's chamber is mentioned among the conventual offices,[45] and is probably the building, constructed partly of stone, shown on a nineteenth century painting next to the river Sherbourne.[46] It is also shown on Speed's plan as an unnamed building and, later, as an antiquity of the priory on the

39 See Morris (this volume) for a reproduction of this plan.
40 Ibid., p. 95.
41 A plan of Mr J. B. Shelton's finds in the Trinity Street area is reproduced by M. Rylatt & A. F. Adams, A Harvest of History (Coventry, 1982), p. 36.
42 Lilley, Medieval Coventry.
43 Fretton, The Benedictine Monastery, p. 37; Lambert in Hobley, Excavations at the Cathedral, p. 78.
44 This position for the dye-house is different from that suggested by M. D. Lobel in the Historic Towns Atlas (Map 7), which placed the dye-house where K. D. Lilley (Medieval Coventry) located the prior's chamber.
45 Fretton, The Benedictine Monastery, p. 36.
46 See the frontispiece of A History of the County of Warwick Volume III, The City of Coventry and Borough of Warwick, ed. W. B. Stephens (London, 1969).

1851 BOH plan.[47] It would seem most likely that the prior would have had his private accommodation away from the main area of conventual buildings in this more secluded position. Connecting his chamber with the industrial complex, and then with the market place, is a street shown on Hollar's engraving of Speed's plan, which after the Dissolution formed part of New Rents. This street-system probably originated as part of the medieval precinct topography, providing it with internal access, as well as providing private access out of the city through Priory Gate to the north-east.

The eastern side of the precinct plan-unit includes Priory Fields, so-called on the 1849 Tithe Award map of Holy Trinity parish.[48] These fields extend up to the Miller's Alley, a narrow lane which is shown first on Speed's plan and in more detail on the BOH plan, and were probably used by the priory for horticultural purposes, providing food for the brethren. To the south of the fields and occupying the south-eastern corner of the precinct lay the Bishop's Palace, shown by Speed on his plan of 1610 and, in more detail by both Samuel Bradford's plan of 1750 and the 1851 BOH plan. The BOH plan shows that the palace lay only just north of the parish boundary, close to New Street properties,[49] and attached to a long plot which extends up to Miller's Alley. In 1793 this plot, shown also by Bradford (1750), became the New Burial Ground which was supposed to have been 'part of the bishop's garden'.[50] In 1224 the prior granted Bishop de Stavensby a plot of land next to the priory graveyard for a residence, but by 1283 the palace was in need of repair and was thus enlarged and had a garden added.[51] The location and extent of the thirteenth-century palace and garden can, therefore, be placed with some certainty onto the base plan (Fig. 2). Furthermore, its longevity shows again how medieval features within the priory precinct continued to exert an influence upon the post-Dissolution townscape.

South of the priory cathedral site lies the only remaining building of the former medieval precinct, the parish church of Holy Trinity. Documentation for the church has been covered elsewhere in detail.[52] From this it would appear that its origins are to be found as a church for the prior's tenants, built by 1101x13,[53] probably when the abbey became a cathedral priory and the bishop transferred his see to Coventry from Chester. The earliest Norman

47 Sheet 17 of the BOH plan, Warwickshire County Record Office Z734(u).
48 The Tithe Award map of Holy Trinity parish is held at Warwickshire County Record Office (CR569/81).
49 New Street was developed over the prior's orchard which had previously been called the Earl's Orchard (see Lilley, *Medieval Coventry*).
50 Fretton, *The Benedictine Monastery*, p. 33.
51 Stephens, *County History*, p. 316.
52 *Ibid.*, pp. 321-9.
53 This date is suggested by P. R. Coss (*Early Records*, p.xvii), although the origins of Holy Trinity may be as an earlier cemetery chapel.

church was destroyed by a fire in 1257 but it was subsequently rebuilt.[54] In 1851 the small churchyard was encompassed by streets, as it may have been in the medieval period, with access being provided from the market place to the west. A chapel dedicated to the Holy Cross also existed (c.1183-4) and may have lain within Holy Trinity churchyard as both church and chapel were described as *infra cemiterium sitis*.[55] However, it must be stated that contrary to the *Historic Towns Atlas* plan,[56] the exact location of the chapel remains uncertain. During the construction of Trinity Street, in the 1930s, Shelton observed an 'archway crypt facing south'[57] beside Trinity Lane on the west side of the churchyard. Perhaps this is the remains of the lost chapel, which could have originated as a small mortuary chapel serving the priory within its cemetery. The very small size of the Holy Trinity churchyard raises the question of where the later-medieval townspeople of Coventry were laid to rest as, so far, no medieval burial ground has been uncovered: perhaps the Holy Cross chapel was used as a charnel house in the north-west corner of Holy Trinity churchyard.

The parish boundary changes its course markedly to accommodate both the church and churchyard, and also the next street-block to the south. This curious diversion may have encompassed a former burial ground for Holy Trinity parish or, equally plausibly, it could have contained the prior's prison. This particular feature is documented as early as 1186-7 and, so far, remains unlocated with any certainty.[58] It seems likely that the prior's prison was the same as the prison which the burgesses of Coventry had the right to keep in 1345, probably itself being sited in the place occupied by the one of 1675 within 'the area bounded by Pepper Lane, Derby Lane and Trinity Lane'.[59] This prison site, also shown by Bradford on his plan of 1750 on the corner of the street-block south of Holy Trinity church, is contained within the prior's (i.e. Holy Trinity) parish, and thus accounts for the southward deviation in the parish boundary (Fig. 2). The twelfth-century prison may, therefore, partly explain the parish topography, although the recent excavations east of Derby Lane failed to produce any significant medieval material to confirm this hypothesis.[60]

54   Stephens, *County History*, p. 326.
55   *Ibid*, p. 329.
56   Map 7 in Lobel, *Historic Towns*.
57   Site number 26 on the plan in Rylatt & Adams, *op. cit.*
58   See Stephens, *County History*, p. 296. *The Historic Towns Atlas* equates the site of the prior's prison with the Bastille House although there is no evidence for this (see Map 7 in Lobel, *Historic Towns*).
59   Stephens, *County History*, p. 296.
60   Post-medieval disruption on the Derby Lane site meant few medieval structural remains were found (Coventry Museum Archaeology Unit, archive reports).

So far emphasis has been placed on those features within the priory precinct plan-unit that are believed to have been contained within the precinct walls. To complete the reconstruction of the priory topography the alignment of these walls also needs to be determined, reviewing whether the plan-seam reflects their course, and the wall-alignment suggested by the *Historic Towns Atlas*.[61] It may be that the precinct wall did not extend across the river to the north, contrary to the *Historic Towns Atlas*, for this would have been expensive. The fact that the fifteenth-century town wall was being built on a new alignment, and that its presence caused the prior's dispute with the town in 1480,[62] enhances such an argument. If the precinct wall had existed north of the river then it might be expected that the new town wall would have made use of its defensive attributes, but no mention is made of a pre-existing wall. However, the new town wall did enclose some of the prior's ground, including fishponds, 'certain stewes and seint Osburn pole';[63] but these lands of his extended much further north into Harnall and were well away from the precinct area.[64] For these reasons the northern wall of the precinct, if one existed, probably ran along the south side of the river Sherbourne, on the same course as the ward boundary on Bradford's plan of 1750.

The northern precinct wall may have turned southward at the prior's chamber to run along the north side of Priory Fields as far as Miller's Alley (thus excluding the Bastille House). The alley would then represent the eastern section of the wall although, alternatively, the wall could be reflected by the ward boundary that divides the Priory Fields from conventual buildings to the west (see Fig. 2). The former course is preferable, however, as it would enclose the Bishop's Palace and garden, which are known to have been on ground granted by the prior next to his cemetery (see above). The southern section of the wall would then run against the south side of the bishop's garden and along the north side of St Michael's churchyard, pursuing the same course as the parish boundary and thus accommodating Holy Trinity churchyard and, perhaps, the prison. The parish boundary almost certainly reflects the precinct wall as it also represented the boundary with the earl's fee. Again this illustrates the longevity of the priory influence on the topography of medieval Coventry; but what of the western section of the wall abutting the market place? Much of the evidence for this section actually comes from documentation and excavations relating to features within the market place.

---

61 Lobel, *Historic Towns*, Map 7.
62 The dispute is covered in the *Coventry Leet Book* (Dormer Harris, *op. cit.*, pp. 443-473).
63 *Ibid*, p. 463.
64 Lilley, *Medieval Coventry*.

Already it has been suggested that the plan-seam separating the priory and market plan-units represents the former western wall of the precinct. The plot pattern shown by the accurate 1851 BOH plan shows the suggested wall alignment in more detail as a straight, but intermittent, plot boundary, running north-south from Broadgate to the river Sherbourne (Fig. 2). To test whether this boundary does indeed represent the precinct wall, and to locate likely entrances into the monastic enclosure, relies on archaeological information which can be plotted onto the base plan with some confidence. Much of this information is derived from Shelton's observations of the 1930s and his plan of sites, but it can be further supplemented by more recent, systematic excavations in Broadgate.[65]

Of particular interest is the site where Shelton found 'heavy stone foundations, eight feet below ground level'[66] which, when plotted onto the base plan, correspond exactly with the suggested precinct boundary alignment. Furthermore, the foundations are within a plot which pierces the presumed wall alignment at the place where Speed shows the priory gate on his plan of 1610, opposite Little Butcher Row (Fig. 3). Therefore, it seems likely that both the foundations and the plot represent the site of the priory gatehouse and the main entrance into the priory court. This location of the gatehouse is supported by Fretton who states that, following the demolition of the 'stone arch, or entrance gate into the western court of the priory', the site became The Dog public house (Fig. 3).[67] This inn is shown on the 1851 BOH plan and occupies part of the deep plot outlined above. With some confidence, therefore, it is possible to locate the priory gatehouse and the entrance-way from the market into the precinct and so confirm that the plan-seam represents the precinct wall. Moreover, the gateway clearly led from the market into the west door of the priory cathedral to provide access for the prior's tenants into their half of the church. After c.1102x13, however, the prior's tenants attended divine service in their own church of Holy Trinity (see above) and so the cathedral-gatehouse-market alignment is probably earlier in date.[68]

The precinct wall and gatehouse are set back from the street frontage probably as a result of encroachment onto the market by properties abutting the wall, which would account for the gradual loss of the line of the wall and the very small properties shown on the BOH plan (Fig. 3). Other entrances into the precinct are likely to have existed and again Shelton's record

[65] J. B. Shelton's plan in Rylatt & Adams, *op. cit.* The excavations at Broadgate are as yet unpublished but the report is housed in the Coventry Museum Archaeology Unit archive.

[66] Numbered as site 62 on Shelton's plan in Rylatt & Adams, *op. cit.*

[67] Fretton, *The Benedictine Monastery*, p. 37.

[68] This alignment may reflect a ceremonial processional route, linking the town with the church and thus emphasising the bond between them (see note 91).

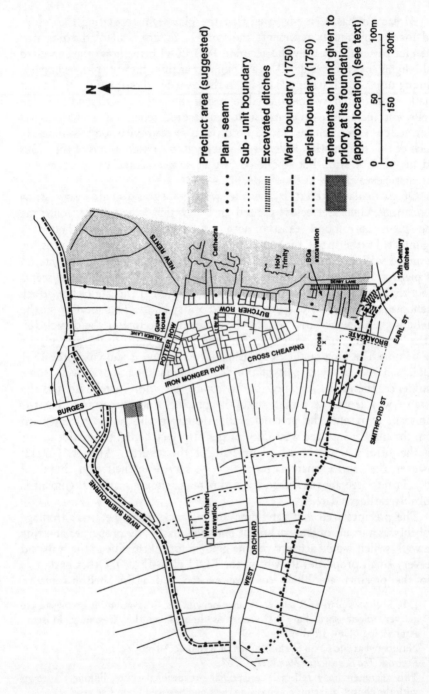

Figure 3. The Market area plan-unit

Legend:

- Precinct area (suggested)
- Plan - seam
- Sub - unit boundary
- Excavated ditches
- Ward boundary (1750)
- Parish boundary (1750)
- Tenements on land given to priory at its foundation (approx location) (see text)

N

100m
300ft
0   50   150

Map labels:

NEW RENTS
Cathedral
Holy Trinity
BGs excavation
DERBY LANE
12th Century ditches
Guest House
PALMER LANE
Lett Lane
POTTER ROW
BUTCHER ROW
IRON MONGER ROW
CROSS CHEAPING
Cross
BROADGATE
EARL ST
SMITHFORD ST
BURGES
RIVER SHERBOURNE
West Orchard excavation
WEST ORCHARD

confirms this. He observed 'two doorways from the cathedral, eight feet deep', to the south of the priory gatehouse, which correspond with the later line of Priory Row and so probably represent access into the precinct for the townspeople to reach Holy Trinity church. Other circumstantial evidence suggests that New Rents was a medieval street providing access into the priory (see above).

Although the western precinct wall alignment and gate position can be proven using the BOH plan and Shelton's archaeological record, no evidence for the southern section of wall was found in the recent excavations of Broadgate.[69] Instead the area between Derby Lane and Broadgate produced evidence for occupation only after the thirteenth century. However, when the excavated structures and property boundaries are plotted onto the base plan of the plan-unit and compared with the suggested precinct wall alignment, some correspondence can be seen. Again encroachments onto the street-space in front of the wall appear to have taken place, and this is supported by Alcock's documentary analysis of medieval properties in this street-block.[70] Furthermore, one of the smaller ditches[71] found in the excavations is on the same east-west alignment as the parish boundary to the west and Pepper Lane to the east. This ditch was also the earliest found, dated to the early twelfth century, and had an 'uncertain relationship' with the larger ditch to the south, which suggests the latter was dug through the earlier ditch.[72] This evidence points to the earliest ditch being representative of the former precinct-wall alignment. However, this still leaves the problem of why thirteenth-century domestic and industrial structures occupy an area within what appears to be the priory precinct.

The problem caused by the conflicting topographical and archaeological evidence could be resolved by further excavation, but on the basis of the present evidence may be explained by changes to the precinct wall during the civil war of Stephen's reign. It is possible that the precinct boundary was damaged or breached during the conflict and therefore re-aligned to the north and east afterwards, thus leaving a large vacant area available for re-occupation once the large ditch to the south had been infilled, by c.1200.[73] The impact of the war on Coventry's early defences may have been responsible for a number of other changes in the topography south of the priory; indeed it is known that the priory itself was fortified during the conflict.[74] It is for this reason that the alignment of the precinct wall south of

[69] Coventry Museum Archaeology Unit archive (report ref. BGe74-5).
[70] *Ibid.* N. W. Alcock's contribution on tenement histories forms a detailed part of the archive report.
[71] This is ditch (F2a), as identified on the plans in the archive report.
[72] This observation is based on the archive excavation report.
[73] *Ibid.*
[74] On the fortification of the priory, see Lilley, *Medieval Coventry*; Lambert in

Holy Trinity church remains largely hypothetical. The western alignment and the priory gate can be identified, however, and it shows the long-standing influence of this feature on Coventry's topography.

On the basis of the priory topography reconstructed so far, the plan-unit area defined in the town-plan analysis can be seen to reflect the former precinct, thus illustrating the continuity of the priory's influence upon the modern townscape. This well-defined and compact ecclesiastical *enceinte* formed one topographical impact of the priory on the development of Coventry's medieval topography, exerting an influence since its foundation by c.1043 (see Hunt, this volume), and perhaps even disclosing the outline of a much earlier monastic site.[75] The second topographical impact of the priory, hypothesised on the basis of the town-plan analysis, is the market area plan-unit.

The Market-Area Topography

The plan-analysis of the market area suggested three episodes of topographical development, the first being the triangular market place itself, perhaps developed by the priory outside and adjacent to its precinct. At some time this market place appears to have undergone infilling, possibly to accommodate more stalls and shops on a permanent basis and therefore adding to the prior's profits. Finally, it seems that properties were developed along West Orchard behind Cross Cheaping properties, again within the prior's parish and fee, perhaps as a response to increased demands for property and, of course, profit. Each of these suggested developments can be explored by reconstructing the medieval topography of the market area plan-unit, using the various historical sources to add to the plan-analysis, and by plotting this information onto an accurate base plan comparable with that of the precinct plan-unit (Fig. 3).

In fixing the position of the gate and precinct wall the market place can be seen to have formed a once wide and open space adjoining the priory precinct (in an area now occupied by Broadgate, Ironmonger Row and the upper part of Trinity Street). Already mention has been made of encroachments onto the market place by small properties adjoining the precinct wall and gate. These encroachments, as well as the more extensive infilling of the market place, can be explained more fully by reconstructing the former medieval property pattern using part of the priory cartulary. In particular, the Pittancer's Rental of 1410-11[76] records a series of entries that allows the schematic reconstruction of priory-held property in the infill

---

Hobley, *Excavations at the Cathedral.*
[75] The details supporting site-continuity are covered in Lilley, *Medieval Coventry*, but were suggested as long ago as 1880 by Fretton, *The Benedictine Monastery.*
[76] Gooder *et al, The Pittancer's Rental.*

block, between Butcher Row and Cross Cheaping (Fig. 4). The details behind the construction of the formal layout of the priory property have been covered elsewhere,[77] and so the main features of interest can be summarised here.

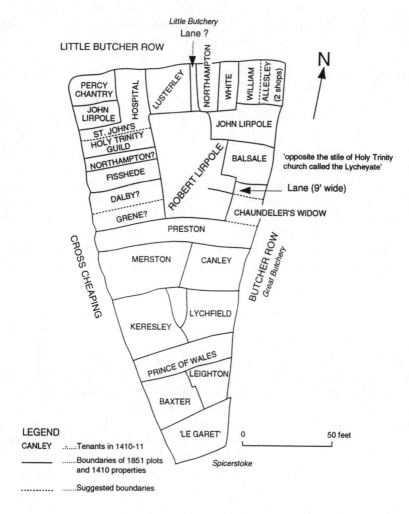

Figure 4. The Market infill in 1410-11

The reconstruction is based on the continuous sequence of abuttals in the Rental for Butcher Row (Great Butchery), starting with a corner tenement called the 'Garet' (in Spicerstoke) and running north to the corner of the Little Butchery, where another sequence continues the abuttals west to Cross

[77] Lilley, *Medieval Coventry.*

89

Cheaping (Fig. 4). Properties fronting Butcher Row between the Garet and the tenement of John Chaundeler's widow all extend back to properties fronting Cross Cheaping, implying that the south end of the infill block was only two plots deep. North of the widow's tenement and along Little Butcher Row, properties extend back to a common property held by a butcher called Robert Lirpole. Thus, the northern end of the infill block appears to be wider than the southern end, as some Cross Cheaping properties also extend back to Lirpole's tenement. The overall shape of the formal tenement layout is therefore triangular, the same as the shape of the infill block shown on the 1851 BOH plan.

The formal tenement layout of c.1400 can be matched with the plot structure of the infill block, based on the BOH plan (Fig. 4). The correlation between the two plot layouts is very marked, especially at the southern end of the block where the mid-nineteenth-century plot structure matches the tenement layout almost exactly. At the north-east corner two shops of William Allesley's chantry can be identified as a corner plot on the BOH plan, divided into two smaller units. Similarly the complicated tenement structure in the north-west corner, where the abuttal sequence is incomplete, can be clarified and Robert Lirpole's large central plot is clearly defined.

Not surprisingly, most of the Little and Great Butcher Row properties recorded in the Rental were held by butchers in 1410-11, reflecting the medieval segregation of the market area according to different functions (note also Potter Row, Corn Market, The Poultry, Ironmonger Row). Some of the property entries also include references to other topographical features which were located nearby. For example, at the north end of the block, the tenements of John Lirpole and William Balsale lay opposite the lychgate of Holy Trinity church. By using the formal plot layout and the BOH plan it can be seen that the lychgate was located at Priory Row, where Shelton had recorded two doorways beneath the street, confirming the longevity of this entrance into the precinct. Furthermore, a second, lesser entry to the church (a stile) is recorded in the Rental and can be located to the south, near Spicerstoke and the Garet. The Garet itself may mean 'watch tower', derived in Middle English from the Old French word *garite* (OED). During the development of Trinity Street in the 1930s this infill block was demolished and Shelton observed cellars thirty feet deep in a quarry where the Garet had stood. This tenement may, therefore, represent the site of a medieval watch-tower, built in the prior's market place.

Essentially, the close correlation of the formal tenement layout of c.1400 with the 1851 plot structure reinforces the hypothesised longevity of medieval plot boundaries in the market area. By 1410 the infill block had clearly been developed for permanent structures which were all held by the priory, and had perhaps been initiated by the prior as part of a development to increase his rents in an organised and well-controlled manner. The date of origin for this infill development is difficult to determine, but the early deeds record stalls in the market by c.1250[78] and Shelton makes reference to timber structures found beneath Butcher Row properties in the 1930s.[79] These he interpreted as farmhouse foundations and cattlesheds, but they are more likely to be the first market place structures, probably wooden structures. Perhaps, therefore, the interior of the market place was being developed with properties by the early thirteenth century to increase the prior's rents. If this is the case, then the priory can again be seen to have had a dramatic impact on the medieval townscape of Coventry.

The evidence so far seems to support the origins of the market place as an initiative by the Benedictines to provide extra revenue for their cathedral and convent. There seems to be a strong topographical link between the market place (and property within it) and the priory precinct, both being separated by the precinct wall but having interconnecting access by way of three different entries. Thus, the market place seems to have been subject to direct control by the priory from an early date, perhaps from the time of the priory's foundation or shortly after. Evidence for the earliest phase of occupation in the market can be found in the two series of plots surrounding the market place on the west and north sides, that is along Cross Cheaping and Potter Row.

The medieval layout of properties fronting the west side of Cross Cheaping along Ironmonger Row, north of West Orchard, has been reconstructed by Alcock.[80] The thirteenth-century property layout to the south can also be reconstructed schematically,[81] and both plot layouts can be related to the 1851 plot structure on the BOH plan (Fig. 3). By the thirteenth century the basic structure of the Cross Cheaping plot series seems to have consisted of large properties each within a deep and broad primary plot, which itself contained the capital messuage mid-way along its length, reached from the street by narrow access lanes. Within these large plots, at the street-front, a number of smaller commercial properties existed, quite densely arranged. This pattern of buildings has also been demonstrated in Shrewsbury, at Pride Hill, in common with other examples elsewhere.[82]

[78] For example; Coss, *Early Records*, deed 680. Also deed 385 of the late 1260s, which records 3s. rent 'from the waste ground in the prior of Coventry's market place against the butcher's stalls on the western side'. Selds are recorded from c.1210 (deed 661) and shops from c.1200 (deed 600).

[79] See Lilley, *Medieval Coventry*.

[80] Alcock, *Catesby Estate*.

[81] Based on deeds from Coss, *Early Records*, and outlined in Lilley, *Medieval Coventry*.

[82] N. J. Baker, J. B. Lawson, R. Maxwell & J. T. Smith, 'Further Work on Pride Hill, Shrewsbury', *Transactions of the Shropshire Archaeological and Historical*

In Coventry, the thirteenth-century deeds provide some indication of the small size of these properties. For example, in 1298 a messuage 'in the market place where corn is sold' measured only eleven feet in width but extended sixty feet in length.[83] The high density of buildings within these plots, at this time, is suggested not only by the small size of properties, but also by a deed of 1301 which granted the water that dripped from the gutters of one tenement to an adjacent tenement.[84] As early as c.1200 the internal structure of properties in the market place is also suggested by a reference to stalls situated in front of a capital burgage.[85] The outlines of these properties are apparent in the plot structure of 1851, so testifying to their survival, even where commercial activity was intense. This evidence, therefore, provides a contrast with the view taken by Scrase in his study of corner plots in Wells.[86]

This urban fabric along the west side of Cross Cheaping was certainly being intensified through the thirteenth century, as the deeds show, but it may have existed for some time before. Excavations in West Orchard,[87] just west of deep plots fronting Cross Cheaping, revealed twelfth- and thirteenth-century pits and evidence of industrial activities. Also, in one of these pits, a fragment of Anglo-Saxon tufa was found and this may be related to the (re)development of Cross Cheaping properties. Together with a fragment of a cross,[88] the tufa represents one of the few pre-Conquest finds to suggest the presence of a settlement contemporary with the earliest monastic foundation. Both finds are located within plot-series next to the market place and may, therefore, reflect earlier properties fronting the market place edge, along Potter Row, Ironmonger Row and Cross Cheaping (Fig. 3). In support of this suggestion is a reference in the Pittancer's Rental to a row of properties along Ironmonger Row just south of the Sherbourne.[89] Three contiguous tenements recorded in the Rental were 'situated on the ground part of the original endowment of the ... Cathedral church' (in solo fundacionis ecclesie

---

Society 68 (1993), 3-64, pp. 54-9.

83 Coss, Early Records, deed 694.

84 Ibid., deed 700.

85 Ibid., deed 524 and see also p. xxxvii.

86 A. J. Scrase, 'Development and Change in Burgage Plots: the Example of Wells', Journal of Historical Geography 15 (1989), 349-65.

87 For this excavation see the unpublished Coventry Museum Archaeology Unit archive report (WO87/90) and also the West Midland Archaeology annual reports for 1987 and 1989.

88 This fragment of cross has been variously dated to the period c.800-c.1000 and is even suggested to be part of the convent sacked by the Danes in AD 1016 (see P. B. Chatwin, 'Recent Finds in Coventry', Transactions of the Birmingham Archaeological Society 58 (1937), 56-62, p. 62; Stephens, County History, p. 7). Could it be a market cross?

89 See Gooder et al., Pittancer's Rental, pp. 31-2.

Cathedralis...). This wording suggests that the property deeds commemorate their origin as part of the land on which the priory was originally founded, by c.1043, by Earl Leofric. It seems likely that other properties within this plot-series along Cross Cheaping also had their origin as part of the market foundation and were perhaps contemporary with it. The deep plots fronting the north side of the market place, along Potter Row, may also be contemporary in date, thus accounting for the presence of the Prior's Guest House in the market area, on the corner of Palmer Lane (Fig. 3).

The medieval market place occupied a large area and left little space for further growth, being bounded on the south side by the Earl's property along Smithford Street and on the east by the priory precinct. Land to the north, near the river, was liable to flooding, which only leaves land to the west available for building. A distinctive series of plots can be seen in 1851 on the BOH plan, arranged along the street called West Orchard as far as the Sherbourne, where the street crosses the river to join Fleet Street. On the basis of this street-system it would appear that West Orchard street originally formed a diversion providing access directly into the prior's market place, thus avoiding the congestion and tolls along Smithford Street with its bar.[90] Furthermore, the line of West Orchard continues across the market place by way of Little Butcher Row and so meets with the priory gate (Fig. 3). This is surely no coincidence, and must have been planned so that the prior did not have to circumnavigate the market infill to gain access to West Orchard or to exit from the town westwards. Again, this suggests that the market was infilled by a controlled process, almost certainly authorised by the prior.[91]

The creation of the new street diversion and bridge suggests that West Orchard was planned to develop properties in the former 'waste garden' (*in Wasto Gardino*) as it was called in the 1250s,[92] perhaps to relieve the market area and to increase revenue. However, properties of the later thirteenth century in West Orchard, near to the bridge, appear quite spacious and rural from their description in the deeds, which suggests their development was actually piecemeal.[93] By the fifteenth century entries in the Pittancer's Rental (1410-11) mention institutions in the western portion of West Orchard, such as the grammar school and St Nicholas's Hall. These are the type of institutional buildings normally associated with urban fringe-belt locations

[90] The site of this bar has been established in Lilley, *Medieval Coventry*.
[91] At Gloucester and Pontefract there may also have been controlled infill of the medieval market places. The alignment of West Orchard and Little Butcher Row also matches with the cathedral doorway and gatehouse and may, therefore, have formed part of the suggested processional way (see note 68). My thanks to Dr N. Baker for these suggestions.
[92] Coss, *Early Records*, deeds 648-9.
[93] *Ibid.*, deeds 649, 657; see also Lilley, *Medieval Coventry*.

and represent a hiatus in property development.[94] Nearer to Cross Cheaping, property development seems to have been more intensive, and excavations revealed evidence of fourteenth-century structures and property boundaries. These developments probably account for the truncated plot tails of Cross Cheaping plots, which is also an indication of intensive demands on property (see Fig. 3). Overall, the relationship between the market place, priory and West Orchard again gives some indication of the prior's involvement in the development of Coventry's medieval topography, by the later thirteenth century.

The Topographical Impact of the Priory
By reconstructing the medieval topography of the priory and market area plan-units a much clearer view of their development emerges. It is now possible to reconsider in more detail the hypotheses which were based on the town-plan analysis. Clearly there existed a strong topographical link between the priory precinct and the market area. Although the precinct wall separated the monastic community from the lay one, the presence of gateways through the wall shows that the two areas were interdependent. Such a close connection suggests that the market was the prior's possession, and his involvement in the development of properties, both in and outside the market place, shows the strength of this connection. Also the location of the priory cathedral at the west end of the precinct shows that the monastic community was involved with the trading and marketing process, being part of the town rather than enjoying monastic isolation.

The Benedictines were not new to the idea of town plantation, indeed the second abbot of Coventry, Leofric, is known to have also administered the abbeys of Burton-upon-Trent and Peterborough in 1053, where towns were subsequently planted.[95] The triangular-shaped market place and its plots could represent such a plantation in front of the priory gate, perhaps developed by Abbot Leofric in the later eleventh century, to facilitate marketing in Coventry. In the earl's fee there is no evidence for any market place in the town plan[96] and the earl's tenants made no claim for a market place of their own during the dispute with the prior in the late thirteenth century.[97] This in itself is evidence that Earl Street represents the pre-Conquest settlement nucleus of Coventry, as market places were largely absent in the topography of pre-Conquest *burhs*.[98] The market place is

[94]   J. W. R. Whitehand, 'Fringe Belts: a Neglected Aspect of Urban Geography', *Transactions of the Institute of British Geographers* 41 (1967), 223-33.
[95]   Fretton, *The Benedictine Monastery*, p. 21; Slater, *Benedictine Town Planning*.
[96]   Lilley, *Medieval Coventry*.
[97]   This argument is presented by Coss, *Early Records*.
[98]   This important point has not been noted in Coventry before. For similar examples see M. Biddle & D. Hill, 'Late Saxon Planned Towns', *Antiquaries*

located not on the east-west Earl's Street but astride the north-south route from Tamworth to Warwick, which also passed through Coventry, outside the prior's gate, so the market could easily have attracted trade passing between these other two Warwickshire *burhs*. Thus, it seems likely that the abbot astutely recognised the need for market provision at an early date and used part of his land for a market. Because the market place (together with the precinct) occupied only part of the land endowed by Leofric, a piece of the land left over to the west became known as the waste garden. This then explains the origins of West Orchard as priory land, which later became used for the diversion street leading into the market place and the priory gate.

These conclusions support Professor R. H. C. Davis's suggestion that Coventry 'as a town... is both older and more important than its historians have hitherto believed';[99] and it seems that the priory foundation represents one of the later developments in Coventry's pre-Conquest topographical history. The impact of the priory on the origins of medieval Coventry, as reflected in its topography, suggest that the claims made by the prior in his forged charters may have been legitimate. The lack of legitimate evidence at the prior's disposal to support his claims for the market meant fabrication of early charters was necessary, although the town-plan itself actually provides enough evidence to substantiate his case.

Overall, on the basis of the town-plan analysis, the priory can be seen to have had three significant impacts on the topography of Coventry. First, there was the enclosure of the priory precinct itself, which contained the cathedral and conventual buildings, as well as industrial and horticultural areas. Here, too, was the bishop's palace and garden, the prior's prison and his chamber, and the parish church serving his tenants. All of this was in place by the later twelfth to thirteenth centuries and was surrounded by a precinct wall (which probably marks the area of the first Benedictine monastery, and is perhaps the site of an even earlier foundation).[100] The second impact of the priory is the market area which lay against the precinct wall, outside the priory gate. The market may, therefore, have been founded contemporaneously, or soon after the priory as part of Leofric's grant of *c.*1043. A series of early properties first surrounded two sides of the triangular market place (the third side being the precinct wall), but additional commercial properties developed on the market place in an ordered manner, leaving a clear entrance into the priory gateway. Soon after, so it seems, the prior developed West Orchard as a street, probably as a diversion to avoid using Earl Street, and properties were being developed along it by the fourteenth century. What is remarkable about this sequence of events is not

99 *Journal* 51 (1971), 70-85.
    Davis, *Early History*, p. 19.
100 Lilley, *Medieval Coventry*.

just that the priory played a key part in Coventry's medieval development, but that these developments are embodied in the mid-late nineteenth-century town-plan. This in itself illustrates the longstanding impact that the priory had on Coventry's topographical development.

Acknowledgements
My thanks are due to Dr T. R. Slater (University of Birmingham) who supervised my doctoral research on which this paper is based, and suggested improvements to earlier drafts. Further comments on this paper were gratefully received from Dr Nigel Baker (University of Birmingham). The kind help received from Coventry Museum Archaeology Unit, particularly M. Rylatt and I. Soden, is also acknowledged. The plans were drawn by Kevin Burkhill but based on draft plans prepared by myself. Any inconsistencies belong with the author.

Piety, Prestige or Politics? The House of Leofric and the Foundation and Patronage of Coventry Priory

JOHN HUNT

On October 30, 1057, Earl Leofric of Mercia died and was buried in the family foundation of Coventry Priory;[1] in recording this event the *Anglo-Saxon Chronicle* described him as 'very wise in all matters, both religious and secular',[2] a characterisation followed slightly later in the *Vita Ædwardi Regis* as 'Earl Leofric, an excellent man, very devoted to God'.[3] Barlow rightly put this into perspective when he pointed out that Leofric's was a 'devotion of a fashionable type',[4] but more recently Fleming has sustained Leofric's reputation for piety when she commented that 'The earl and his wife founded a Benedictine monastery at Coventry, an extravagantly expensive act of piety, and they granted a number of large estates to other ecclesiastical institutions'.[5] It is not the purpose of this paper so much to challenge this reputation, but rather to look at the broader range of concerns that attended upon such acts of piety. This requires that the foundation and patronage of Coventry be examined within the context of the wider pattern of family patronage and the contemporary scene.

There can be little doubt that Coventry was indeed an impressive foundation. Florence of Worcester, for example, was impressed not only by the level of landed endowment from Leofric and his wife Godiva, but also at 'the abundance of gold, silver, jewels, and precious stones' that could not be bettered anywhere in England.[6] Such was the wealth of the house that Robert de Limesey was said by William of Malmesbury[7] to have extracted 500 marks of silver from one of the beams of the shrine. Exaggeration perhaps, but it conveys the impression that the priory church gave to contemporaries and the level of generosity and patronage that they associated with Leofric and his wife.

---

[1]   *Anglo-Saxon Chronicle* [hereafter 'ASC'], s.a. 1057; cf. William of Malmesbury, *De Gestis Pontificum Anglorum*, 311, ed N. E. S. A. Hamilton (London, 1870); Matthew Paris, *Flores Historiarum* I, 576, ed. H. R. Luard (London, 1890).

[2]   ASC, 'D' s.a. 1057.

[3]   F. Barlow, *Vita Ædwardi Regis* (London, 1962), 21.

[4]   F. Barlow, *The English Church 1000-1066: a Constitutional History* (London, 1963), 57.

[5]   R. Fleming, *Kings and Lords in Conquest England* (Cambridge, 1991), 58.

[6]   *Florentii Wigorniensis Monachi, Chronicon ex Chronicis*, ed. B. Thorpe (London, 1848-9), vol 1, 216; cf. *Flores Hist.*, I, *op. cit.*, 576.

[7]   *Gesta Pont., op. cit.*, 309.

The foundation of the priory is generally dated at about 1043;[8] the spurious foundation and confirmation charters refer to Leofric as the founder of Coventry Priory, as does the *Anglo-Saxon Chronicle*.[9] However, there is also a strong tradition associating Godiva with her husband in the foundation and patronage of not only the priory, but also of several other religious houses.[10] Although this tradition is derived principally from post-Conquest sources, those Anglo-Saxon grants which have survived are sufficient to indicate that it is a genuine one,[11] further elaborated in the case of Coventry by the famous legend of Lady Godiva's Ride. Godiva was regarded by some chroniclers as having a particular devotion to the cult of the Virgin Mary[12] and Katherine French has highlighted the point[13] that for Roger of Wendover and Matthew Paris it was at the instigation of Godiva that Leofric undertook his patronage of the church. This however appears to be an instance of post-Conquest elaboration. Godiva may indeed have felt a particular devotion for Mary,[14] but this did not of itself make her especially devout and one might suspect this attribution to be determined by the respectful chroniclers writing at a time when the cult was at its height.[15] The

---

[8] Problems surrounding the date of foundation are discussed further below. The date of 1043 is found in the spurious confirmation charter discussed in F. E. Harmer, *Anglo-Saxon Writs* (Stamford, 1989), 215; however, perhaps more reliably, J. C. Lancaster, *Godiva of Coventry* (Coventry, 1967), 36, cites the now lost Chronicle of Geoffrey, Prior of Coventry; cf. W. Dugdale, *Monasticon Anglicanum*, III (London, 1849), 177. Harmer, *ibid.*, no. 46, is an authentic confirmation writ addressed to Abbot Leofwine of Coventry, dated by the editor as 1043-53, presumably established by the accession of Edward and the elevation of Leofwine to the bishopric of Lichfield. However, it does not necessarily follow that the confirmation charter actually dates the foundation, as it may simply reflect the confirmation at some point after the event by a new king.

[9] ASC, 'E', s.a. 1066.

[10] Cf. *Flor. Wig.*, *op. cit.*, 216, 'the noble countess Godiva, a worshipper of God, and devoted friend of St Mary'; Symeon of Durham, *Historia Regum*, ed. T. Arnold (London, 1882 & 1885), Vol II, 173, s.a. 1057; *Gesta Pont.*, *op. cit.*, 309; William of Malmesbury, *De Gestis Regum Anglorum*, ed. W. Stubbs (London, 1887), 237 associates Godiva with Leofric in the patronage of several houses, as does *Flores Hist.* I, *op. cit.*, 576 and *Rogeri de Wendover, Chronica, sive Flores Historiarum*, ed. H. O. Coxe (London, 1841), vol I, 497-8. Similarly, the endowment of Stow St Mary was undertaken by both Leofric and Godiva: see A. J. Robertson, *Anglo-Saxon Charters* (Cambridge, 1956), no. 115.

[11] Robertson, *op. cit.*, nos. 13, 15.

[12] See K. L. French, 'The Legend of Lady Godiva and the Image of the Female Body', *Journal of Medieval History* XVIII, no. 1 (1992), 4.

[13] *Ibid.*, 10.

[14] According to *Gesta Pont.*, *op. cit.*, 311, as Godiva was dying she hung a circlet of gems worth 100 silver marks, that she had used as a rosary, around a statue of the Blessed Mary.

authentic grants that have survived[16] betray no sense of Godiva leading her husband in matters of church patronage, and Hemming's account of lands at Chaddesley Corbett and Belbroughton shows Godiva making grants to Worcester, but retaining the leases for herself and not arranging for the reversion of these estates to the church, her sons Edwin and Morcar retaining them.[17] There can be no doubt that Godiva was intimately involved with the patronage of Coventry Priory and other religious houses, but this seems to have been a genuine partnership with her husband, with shared ambitions and attitudes. To this extent, it was a family affair.

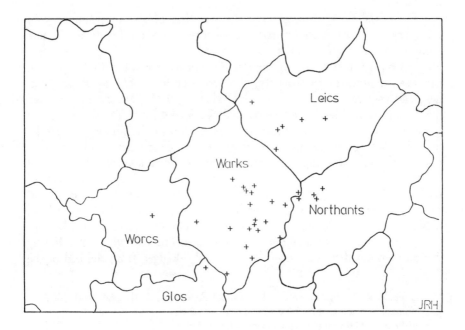

Figure 1. The Lands of Coventry Abbey in 1086

Coventry Priory was endowed with lands in (Fig. 1) Warwickshire, Leicestershire, Northamptonshire, Worcestershire and Gloucestershire; whilst the extant versions of the foundation charter cannot be trusted in its details, it is the case that many of the estates mentioned may be verified in the folios of Domesday Book,[18] where it is also apparent that between *c.*1043

15 Cf. R. & C. Brooke, *Popular Religion in the Middle Ages* (London 1984), 31-3.

16 Robertson, *op. cit.*

17 Hemming, *Hemingi Chartularium Ecclesiae Wigornensis*, ed. T. Hearne (Oxford, 1723) I, 261; cf. Barlow, *The English Church, op. cit.*, 173.

and 1086 the Priory had further supplemented its holdings; in Warwickshire, for instance, Binley was purchased from Osbern son of Richard, and Clifton upon Dunsmore was a gift of Alwin the Sheriff. The level of landed endowment, in Warwickshire particularly, is one indicator of the pre-foundation holdings of the house of Leofric in the shire, but it cannot be assumed that the tenurial pattern that may be reconstructed for 1066 necessarily applied also in c.1040. In addition, the Priory was richly endowed with silver and gold; there was a shrine for the remains of St Osburga, and to these relics was added the arm of St Augustine of Hippo, purchased in Pavia by Archbishop Æthelnoth[19] and given to Coventry, where it was placed in a silver shrine.[20]

The relics of St Osburga raise the tradition of an earlier nunnery in Coventry, and with it the question of whether Coventry Priory was a new foundation, or a refoundation. Unfortunately, there is little scope for real progress on this matter. By the fourteenth century it was believed that there had been a nunnery in Coventry,[21] a tradition reiterated by Rous[22] and Dugdale[23] where it was also maintained that in 1016 a Danish army crossed the Thames into Mercia and devastated Warwickshire.[24] This campaign, it has been assumed, brought about the destruction of the nunnery.[25] Whilst there is nothing inherently improbable in this reconstruction of events, it remains the case that there is no corroborative documentary evidence, and the archaeological evidence cited by Lancaster is unconvincing.[26] The carved sandstone fragment is not necessarily part of a cross shaft[27] and there is no reason to assume it comes from the nunnery. The so-called Viking axe-head may have come into Coventry in any number of circumstances, as it belongs to a type common throughout the eleventh century,[28] whilst the Viking stirrup mentioned by Lancaster[29] was actually dredged from the bed of the

---

18 Dugdale, *Mon. Ang.*, iii, *op. cit.*, 177; *Domes. Book*, 238d, 231b, 222c, 174b,166a.
19 William of Malmesbury, *Gesta Regum*, *op. cit.*, 224.
20 William of Malmesbury, *Gesta Pont.*, *op. cit.*, 309.
21 Discussed in Lancaster, *op. cit.*, 14.
22 Rous, *Historia Regum Angliae*, 104.
23 W. Dugdale, *The Antiquities of Warwickshire* (Coventry, 1765), 91.
24 Cf. M. K. Lawson, *Cnut: the Danes in England in the Early Eleventh Century* (London, 1993), 16; ASC, s.a. 1016.
25 Cf. Lancaster, *op. cit.*, 15.
26 *Ibid.*, 14-15.
27 M. Stokes, *Catalogue of the Later Saxon Artefacts in the Collections of the Herbert Art Gallery and Museum* (Unpublished), No. 2, in J. Hunt and M. Stokes, *Early Medieval Coventry*, in preparation.
28 D. C. Devenish, W. M. Elliott, 'A Decorated Axe-Head of Viking Type from Coventry', *Medieval Archaeology* 11 (1967), 251-52.
29 M. Stokes, *op. cit.*

River Avon near Chippenham in 1934, and subsequently deposited in the collections of the Herbert Art Gallery and Museum.

However, the gift of the relic of St Augustine is not without its problems. If Malmesbury is to be trusted, he states that Aethelnoth transmitted the relic to Coventry on returning home; in 1022 he had visited Rome to receive the pallium and be consecrated as archbishop of Canterbury, returning in the same year. Thus, it is possible that the relic came to Coventry in 1022, and if it was a personal gift of Aethelnoth, it cannot have come later than 1038, the year of his death. This clearly has major implications. It could point to the presence of a religious foundation in Coventry pre-dating the foundation of the priory by Leofric and Godiva, which might be identified with the nunnery of St Osburga that had survived, if indeed it had ever suffered, an attack by the Danes in 1016. Although there is no corroborative evidence, this scenario would fit well with the long received tradition of a earlier foundation. Further, it would point to Leofric and Godiva undertaking a refoundation of a monastic house, representing a late example of a widespread phenomenon.

Alternatively, given that the foundation date of 1043 is derived from an eighteenth-century reference to a lost early thirteenth-century chronicle, there might be scope to question its reliability. There is nothing inherently improbable in the foundation of Leofric and Godiva being dated earlier than 1043, and at or before 1038. It might be supposed that the forged charters citing the foundation date of 1043 are likely to be correct in at least this detail, yet this cannot be simply assumed. That the lost Chronicle of Prior Geoffrey should record the building and dedication of the priory in the same year, which if correct would suggest that the project was completed at great speed, might indicate that the dates of foundation and dedication had become conflated. The process of foundation was generally one spread over several years, and it was usually the case that there was a lapse of time between foundation and dedication; if the precise date and circumstances of the initial foundation became hazy, the most convenient date for the monastic chroniclers to settle upon would be that of the dedication. Thus, it might be argued that whilst 1043 represents the date of dedication, the actual foundation pre-dated this; to place this within the period 1023/32 to 1038 would be consistent with William of Malmesbury's account of the relic of St Augustine; furthermore, this was without doubt an important relic, the gift of which one might have expected to attend upon some important event or reflect a special relationship. Although Malmesbury does not make any specific reference to Leofric and Godiva, the undertaking to establish a 'modern' Benedictine foundation in Coventry would provide a realistic and appropriate context for such a gift. In which case the priory was founded in or before 1038, and there is no reason to retain references to an earlier house.

In addition to their patronage of Coventry, Leofric and his family also supported several other religious houses. William of Malmesbury commented that Leofric and Godiva built many monasteries[30] but in Florence of Worcester may be found a more detailed and precise account.[31] Whilst noting Coventry as the foundation of Leofric and Godiva, the chronicler added that these patrons enriched the houses of Leominster and Wenlock, Chester St John and Chester St Werburgh, and St Mary's, Stow. In addition, they also gave lands to Worcester, and added to the buildings, ornaments and endowments of Evesham Abbey. This list of benefactions is reiterated in Matthew Paris[32] and partially in Roger of Wendover.[33] Leofric also had interests in Burton Abbey.[34] In all, this is not an unimpressive list, nor necessarily a complete one.

The benefactions included some of the leading churches of the region, principally within the dioceses of Lichfield and Worcester but also reaching into those of Hereford and Dorchester. Worcester and Lichfield lay at the heart of the Mercian earldom and so it is perhaps surprising not to see the cathedral church of Lichfield as more prominent. It is however unwise to draw hasty conclusions from this; it is improbable that the earls of Mercia would have ignored such an important local church, and the appointment in 1053 of Leofwine, abbot of Leofric's foundation at Coventry, as bishop of Lichfield is suggestive of the influence of the comital family in episcopal affairs.[35]

Worcester, Evesham and Burton were all houses that had been touched by the Monastic Reform of the tenth and early eleventh centuries. Worcester and Evesham were particularly respected centres, whose stature in the tenth century was further enhanced by the translation of relics.[36] Evesham seems

---

[30] William of Malmesbury, *Gesta Regum*, op. cit., 237.

[31] *Flo. Wig.*, op. cit. 159.

[32] Matthew Paris, *Flores* I, op. cit., 576.

[33] Wendover, *Flores*, op. cit., 497-8. There are differences, however, in that Wendover omits Stow and Leominster and records Stone and Lenton. Whilst there is a possibility of a pre-Conquest foundation in Stone, it is not well established; cf. *Victoria County History, Staffordshire*, III (London, 1970), 240. In the case of Lenton there is no reason to regard it as anything other than a post-Conquest foundation of c.1109-1125; cf. *Victoria County History, Nottinghamshire*, III (London, 1910), 91. It therefore seems probable that Wendover's attribution of Stone and Lenton to the patronage of Leofric and Godiva is mistaken and perhaps based on a misreading of his source.

[34] *Domesday Book*, 239a, Austrey; cf. *Lancaster*, op. cit., 38; J. Hunt, 'Land Tenure and Lordship in Tenth and Eleventh Century Staffordshire', *Staffordshire Studies* 4 (1991-92), 12.

[35] Cf. Barlow, *The English Church*, op. cit., 109, note 3.

[36] D. Rollason, 'The Shrines of Saints in Later Anglo-Saxon England: Distribution and Significance', in *The Anglo-Saxon Church*, ed. L. A. S. Butler and R. K. Morris

to be the earliest demonstrable instance of the patronage of Leofric and Godiva, occurring before 1038,[37] although Worcester might rival this. There is clear evidence of family donations in the 1050s[38] but there is also a charter of c.1023[39] concerned with a dispute over land at Inkberrow, bought from a Leofric of Blackwell, Blackwell being one of the manors granted by the earl and his wife to Worcester in 1052-57. Robertson suggested that Leofric of Blackwell should not be identified with Earl Leofric, but this writer would not discount that possibility. There is obviously a link through the estate, and the chronology does not seem to present significant problems. If so, it may be that there was a relationship between Leofric and Worcester by the 1020s; alternatively, more in keeping with Robertson, it is possible to regard Leofric of Blackwell as a dependent thegn of Leofwine and Leofric, Blackwell reverting to the earl later; in any case, there clearly was a relationship with Worcester by the 1050s.

Thus, the house of Leofric may be seen associated with the most important and prestigious religious centres of the region, whilst their links to the monastery of Burton on Trent, made before 1057 as a result of family affiliations and the prominence of the comital family, and the foundation of Coventry, both Benedictine houses, reflect the position of Leofric and his wife within the main flow of contemporary religious sentiment. However, as Barlow noted,[40] there is nothing here to cast Leofric as a reformer.

Yet, neither can we assume, within the secular norms of the day, that his religious sentiment was not real enough. The endowments were made, and when he and Godiva gave a charter in favour of St Mary's, Stow,[41] providing lands for the food and clothing of the priests, it was explicitly stated that divine service should be celebrated 'as it is at St Paul's in London'. More than a passive interest would seem to be signalled here.

On the western fringes of the earldom Leofric and Godiva may be instanced supporting Leominster, Wenlock and Chester. Leominster had since the seventh century been the principal centre of Christianity in north-west Herefordshire[42] and was the site of both a monastic community

---

(CBA 1986), 32-40; D. Rollason, *Saints and Relics in Anglo-Saxon England* (Oxford, 1989), 178.

37 *Chronicon Abbatiae de Evesham*, ed. W. Macray (London, 1863), 84. Leofric and Godiva are shown granting lands and undertaking building works before the death of Prior Æfic in 1036-38.

38 Robertson, *op. cit.*, no. 113.

39 Robertson, *ibid.*, no. 83.

40 Barlow, *The English Church, op. cit.*, 57.

41 c.1053-55; Robertson, *op. cit.*, no. 115.

42 B. Kemp, 'Some Aspects of the Parochia of Leominster in the 12th Century', in *Minsters and Parish Churches: the Local Church in Transition 950-1200*, ed. J. Blair (Oxford, 1988), 83; 'The Monastic Dean of Leominster', *English Historical*

and of secular clergy serving its *parochia*. Since the house was dissolved in 1046 it may be presumed that Leofric's patronage predates this, but it does not seem clear whether this should be associated with the nuns or with the secular clerks. In the case of both Wenlock and Chester St Werburgh, secular clerks were the recipients of comital patronage. Finberg[43] has shown Wenlock to have survived its traditional destruction at the hands of the Danes and suggested that it transformed itself into a house of secular clerks; whilst the endowment of Wenlock by Leofric and Godiva is not in doubt, the assumption that they refounded the house in *c*.1050[44] cannot be accepted, and the attempts made to identify through excavation structures that might be associated with such refoundations[45] can no longer be substantiated.[46] Apart from the earl's gifts, the grant to Wenlock by Cnut, releasing the canons from tax on 4 hides,[47] may reflect in part the advantages of counting Leofric as a patron.[48] In the case of Chester, the translation here of the relic of St Werburgh from Hanbury in the tenth century reflects the emergence of another religious centre of importance, with which Leofric and Godiva associated themselves.

Only at Evesham and Coventry, however, does general endowment go further, to be reflected in building activities.[49] At Evesham the church of Holy Trinity was built, perhaps a reflection of the affection between Leofric, Godiva and Prior Ælfic, their father confessor;[50] this might also account for the relatively early date at which their patronage of this house can be instanced.

However, only at Coventry do we appear to have Leofric and Godiva actually establishing a religious house, whether or not it was more properly a refoundation. In terms of the family of Leofric, it was clearly intended as something special. Whilst there was no regional translation of relics to confirm its spiritual credentials, the foundation did boast the relics of St Osburga in a richly appointed shrine, reflecting local sentiment, and in addition acquired a relic of St Augustine of Hippo, which must have been regarded as something of a significant and prestigious coup for the

Review, 83 (1968), 505-6.

43 H. P. R. Finberg, *The Early Charters of the West Midlands* (Leicester, 1972), 197-8.

44 Cited by Lancaster, *op. cit.*, 40.

45 D. H. S. Cranage, 'The Monastery of St Milburge at Much Wenlock, Shropshire', *Archaeologia* 72 (1922), 105-32, especially 108.

46 H. Woods, 'Excavations at Wenlock Priory, 1981-6', *Journal of the British Archaeological Association*, 140 (1987), especially 59-63.

47 *Domesday Book*, 252c.

48 Lawson, *op. cit.*, 151.

49 Although this does not deny, as we cannot know, that endowments elsewhere did not facilitate building projects.

50 *Chronicon Abbatiae de Evesham, op. cit.*, 83.

community. Furthermore, Coventry was to be a family mausoleum, both Leofric and Godiva being buried here;[51] it was their *eigenkirche*, just as Burton on Trent had been for Wulfric Spott. The promotion of family mausolea in monastic houses is a well attested phenomenon in France of the eleventh century, reaching its apogee during the late twelfth and early thirteenth centuries with such dynastic burials *ad sanctos* ('among the saints') as at Fontevraud. It was equally commonplace in England, not only after the Conquest, but, as Coventry and Burton suggest, before 1066. By the early eleventh century, seigneurial families were well aware of the political as well as religious benefits of such mausolea, that enhanced further the traditional tenurial advantages of a family monastery.

The patronage of Leofric and Godiva is in keeping with what might be expected of an important regional family. It is striking, however, that, in so far as it may be reconstructed, their patronage was essentially localised, although their son, Ælfgar, did grant the Staffordshire manors of Meaford and Hamstall Ridware to the church of St Rémy, Rheims,[52] and Leofric's father Leofwine is noted as a benefactor of Peterborough,[53] a link that may have been preserved in some form, as earl Leofric's nephew, also named Leofric, became abbot of Peterborough in 1052 and was praised by Hugh Candidus. Nonetheless it is apparent that patronage was generally forthcoming within the context and framework of the Mercian earldom. Just as their tenurial possessions, though extensive, were predominantly regional in nature,[54] so too was their pattern of patronage; and this was no matter of simple coincidence. There was a very real relationship between the tenurial and patronage patterns that reflects the reality of the contemporary scene.

Illustrating in part the religious motivations behind monastic patronage, the grant to Worcester of Wolverley and Blackwell[55] was made to the monks by Leofric and Godiva 'on condition that they intercede for our souls'. It was undoubtedly the view of Hemming that such intercession was more than called for in the case of Leofric. For Hemming Leofric and his kin were despoilers of the church of Worcester, although by no means the only ones.

Hemming, a monk of Worcester, has given his name to an eleventh-century cartulary[56] that describes the fate of lands regarded as *ad victum monachorum* ('for the monks' supplies'), for the support of the brethren of

---

51 William of Malmesbury, *Gesta Pont.*, 311.
52 *Domesday Book*, 247c; the same church also held Lapley in Staffordshire from the king.
53 Hugh Candidus, *The Peterborough Chronicle*, ed. W. Mellows (Peterborough, 1941), 35.
54 F. M. Stenton, *Anglo-Saxon England* (Oxford, 1971), 574; D. Hill, *An Atlas of Anglo-Saxon England* (Oxford, 1981), map 182.
55 Robertson, *op. cit.*, no. 113.
56 Hemming, *op. cit.*

Worcester.[57] More particularly, it is an account of those estates which Worcester had been deprived of 'by force and fraud and secular power',[58] at least in so far as it was viewed by the Church.

The Danes established in the region during the reign of Cnut[59] were viewed by Hemming as great despoilers, in particular referring to the lands seized by Earl Hakon and his *milites*,[60] and to the acquisitions of Earl Ranig and his men in Herefordshire.[61] In some cases, these lands were lost as a result of the manipulation of the taxation system by which those acquiring the land paid the tax due upon it, and thereby claimed it.[62]

However, such charges were not laid solely at the door of the Danes. The English nobility, and particularly the family of Earl Leofwine, figure prominently in the pages of Hemming. Eadwine, the brother of Earl Leofric, acquired estates by paying the tax that was due on them, obtaining Bickmarsh in Warwickshire and Wychbold in Worcestershire, together with lands in Shropshire.[63] Another brother, Godwin, held the manor of Salwarpe[64] which the church tried unsuccessfully to recover, as his son and heir, supported by his uncle, Leofric, frustrated the attempt. By 1086 there were two manors in Salwarpe, one of five hides that had been held by Æthelwine, Leofric's nephew, and another that had been granted to Coventry Abbey. Similarly, Bishop's Itchington appears to have been a Worcester estate that was acquired perhaps by Leofwine and transferred to Coventry by Leofric.[65] It would seem that Leofric or his kin had taken the opportunity to endow their foundation, or at least part of it, with land that they had seized from Worcester church and which that church still sought to recover.

At Hampton Lovett, Erngeat son of Grim successfully resisted Bishop Wulfstan's attempts to recover the manor, as a result of the support Leofric gave him;[66] Leofric likewise supported one of his Danish thegns, Sigmundr,

---

[57] N. R. Ker, 'Hemming's Cartulary', in *Studies in Medieval History Presented to F. M. Powicke*, ed. R. W. Hunt, *et al.* (Oxford, 1948), 63.

[58] A. Williams, 'Cockles Amongst the Wheat: Danes and English in the Western Midlands in the First Half of the Eleventh Century', in *Midland History* 11 (1986), 13.

[59] Williams, *ibid.*

[60] Hemming, *op. cit.*, I, 251. 'Milites' in this context refers to the warrior retainers of Earl Hakon.

[61] *Ibid.*, I, 274.

[62] *Ibid.*, I, 278; discussed in Barlow, *The English Church*, *op. cit.*, 73; Lawson, *op. cit.*, 13.

[63] Hemming, *op. cit.*, I, 278.

[64] *Ibid.*, 259-60.

[65] R. R. Darlington, *The Vita Wulfstani of William of Malmesbury*, Camden Series 40 (London, 1928), xxii-xxiv.

[66] Hemming, *op. cit.*, I, 260.

in his attempts to secure land in Crowle.[67] The same thegn also held Shelsley[68] of Earl Edwin, from which he could not withdraw without permission,[69] a manor which Hemming also regarded as rightfully belonging to Worcester church.[70]

The tenurial tangle that these disputes might create is well illustrated in the Domesday entry for Alveston in Warwickshire.[71] Before 1066 a man named Brictwin had held the manor, but as far as his two sons and four others were concerned, they did not know whether he held the land from the church of Worcester, or 'from Earl Leofric, whom he served'. However, as far as the sons were concerned, they had held the land of Leofric. Such confusion was inevitable after a period of time, and it worked to the benefit of the comital family and their thegns.

Leofric did return some of the lands acquired by his father, the manors of Wolverley and Blackwell for instance,[72] but more generally, it seems to have been a case of either refusal or unfulfilled promises. His promise to revert Chaddesley Corbett, Belbroughton, Bell Hall and Fairfield to the church on his death came to nothing when Godiva subsequently arranged for gifts and payments to Worcester, but did not revert the lands[73] which in turn were passed[74] to her sons, Edwin and Morcar, who continued to deprive the church.

The eloquence of Hemming leaves the impression that the house of Leofwine and his descendants had somehow singled out Worcester for special treatment, but allowing for the fact that the sheer scale of Worcester's landholding rendered it a vulnerable target, this seems not to have been the case. The lands of Burton Abbey appear to have been treated in a similar way[75] and there are hints that other lands in Warwickshire were similarly treated. Myton contained three manors in 1086, all held by members of the comital family. However, two pre-Conquest grants[76] show Cnut endowing Abingdon Abbey with land here, grants which no longer figure in 1086.[77] At

---

[67] Ibid., 264-5.

[68] Domesday Book, 176d.

[69] I.e., this was a dependent tenure.

[70] Hemming, op. cit., I, 251.

[71] Domesday Book, 238c.

[72] Above, p. 103.

[73] Hemming, op. cit., I, 261.

[74] In Hemming, seized.

[75] J. Hunt, op. cit., 12-13; cf. Austrey, Domesday Book, 239a, where Leofric is said to have given this manor to Burton. Since it figured in the will of Wulfric Spott, the reference in Domesday must either be a confirmation of possession by Leofric, or reflect seizure and subsequent restoration of the manor.

[76] P. H. Sawyer, Anglo-Saxon Charters: an Annotated List and Bibliography (London, 1968); S. 987; S. 973.

Salford Priors an uncertain charter of 714[78] grants lands to Evesham Abbey, which in 1066 were held by Godiva. More speculatively, if the fragmentary charter S.1855 of Bishop Lyfing is to be associated with Wootten Wawen, and this manor with Waga or Vagn, then this again might reflect church interest in lands held by a thegn of Leofric. Wormleighton is yet another Warwickshire manor that had been granted to Abingdon Abbey[79] but was no longer in their possession by 1066, being held instead by secular lords. It is arguable therefore that the Warwickshire estates of Abingdon Abbey and perhaps Evesham Abbey were as vulnerable to the needs of Leofric and his kin as were Worcester and Burton on Trent. These acquisitions reflect a process by which the family had over several generations been building up its influence, through its tenurial base, in midland England. It has been rightly pointed out that the tenurial pattern at Domesday should not be regarded as static[80] and that the problem of identifying dependent tenure has tended to obscure the full reality of comital landholdings in 1066;[81] however, it is also the case that the tenurial pattern associated with the house of Leofric in 1066 was one that had only recently been achieved,[82] in which the 'despoiling' of church lands and the patronage of the church were simply two sides of the same coin, both part of a strategy for maintaining the position of the family in the region and enhancing its power (Fig. 2).

Land tenure was fundamental to effective lordship and central to this was the need to be able to promote and maintain dependent tenures.[83] In enhancing family holdings and supporting the aggrandisement of their thegns, this is precisely what Leofric and his kin were doing, in which their treatment of the church and its lands was central. It has been pointed out that prior to the Reform Movement, cathedral lands tended to consist of several individual prebends, which the Reform process sought to 'communalise'.[84] That Oswald of Worcester may be found granting an estate for three lives to prior Wynsige suggests that the Reform did not remove the concept,[85] whilst the flexibility and adaptability of it would have continued to recommend itself to magnates in need, like Leofric. Reinforced by a society that must have often perceived the church as greedy and exploitative,[86] it was natural

77 *Domesday Book*, 239a.
78 Sawyer, *op. cit.*, S. 1250.
79 *Ibid.*, S. 937.
80 P. Stafford, *Unification and Conquest: a Political and Social History of England in the Tenth and Eleventh Centuries* (London, 1989), 111.
81 J. Hunt, *op. cit.*, 11.
82 E.g. the case of Alveston and the confusion that attended upon it.
83 R. P. Abels, *Lordship and Military Obligation in Anglo-Saxon England* (London, 1988), 185; for a regional perspective, J. Hunt, *op. cit.*, especially 9 ff.
84 E. John, *Orbis Britanniae* (Leicester, 1966), 164.
85 *Ibid.*, 165.

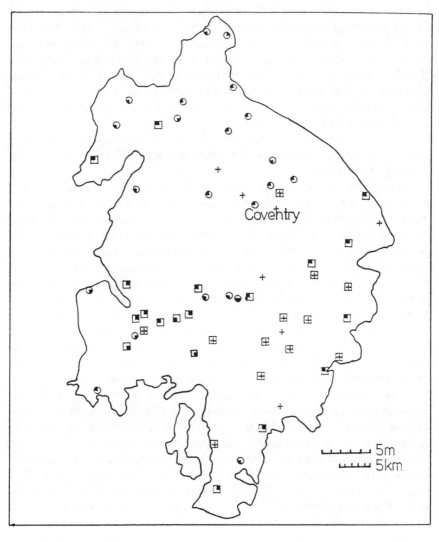

◐	Held by Earl Leofric TRE	
◑	Held by Godiva TRE	
◓	Held by Earl Edwin TRE	
◕	Held by Earl Ælfgar TRE	
+	Held by Coventry Abbey	
⊞	Tenure claimed in 'Foundation Charter'	

Possible Dependent Thegns:
- ◨ Wulfwin
- ◪ Waga
- ◧ Sigmundr
- ▣ Men of Earl Leofric

Figure 2. Warwickshire and the House of Leofric, *tempore Regis Edwardi*

that secular lordship should simply make use of a traditional system that had been geared to the support of the individual. Furthermore, where the family had a link through patronage, and even more so as being, or having taken the place of, the founding kin, it was perceived as their right – as simply an extension of their family estate. In this sense, the granting of estates to a church, especially to one's own foundation, was not to be seen as an alienation, but rather as an investment in lordship. So it was in the case of Coventry, where there was the added bonus that at least some of the lands granted were usurped from Worcester.

There was however a further dimension to the patronage of the house of Leofric that can be related to the contemporary political scene and the standing of the family.

Some studies have argued that the patronage of a church, generally monastic houses, might offer the patron the means of achieving two particular objectives. Firstly, as R. W. Southern illustrated in his discussion of the expansion of Anjou in the tenth and eleventh centuries,[87] the patronage of a church could provide an entrée into an area not properly under the patron's control, or on which he had ambitions, around which he might then extend his influence. Secondly, it was a means by which family interests in an area might be further enhanced and consolidated; not only[88] by virtue of the lands with which the house was endowed and which the patron's family might subsequently exploit for secular purposes, but also as a focus that might foster cohesion and a sense of community between the patron, those men bound to him and his family, and perhaps the wider neighbourhood. To promote such a community of interest and identification with the principal family was clearly an effective means of enhancing seigneurial influence and power. This theme has been developed in relation to post-Conquest studies[89] but it is one that in its essentials seems equally applicable to the pre-Conquest context, particularly the tenth and eleventh centuries, when the needs of developing and maintaining family identities and political patronage were just as vital. In this writer's opinion, both of these themes may be applied to the foundation of Coventry Abbey, all the more so when it is recalled that this house also seems to have been intended as a family mausoleum, and as such yet another means by which the profile

---

[86] Cf. Barlow, *The English Church, op. cit.*, 175.

[87] Here with reference to the church of St Martin at Tours. R. W. Southern, *The Making of the Middle Ages* (London, 1967), 81-7.

[88] Above, p. 108.

[89] Cf. J. C. Ward, 'Fashions in Monastic Endowment: the Foundations of the Clare Family, 1066-1314', *Journal of Ecclesiastical History* 32 (1981), 427-37; R. Mortimer, 'Land and Service: the Tenants of the Honour of Clare', *Anglo-Norman Studies* 8 (1985), 177-97; J. Hunt, *An Archaeological and Documentary Study of the Honor of Dudley c.1060-1325*, in preparation.

of the family might be enhanced within the locality. To this might be added the ability of patrons to influence, to the advantage of their kin, ecclesiastical appointments. The first Abbot of Coventry, Leofwine, may have been a member of the family[90] but whether he was or not there can be little doubt that his elevation to the bishopric of Lichfield in 1053 was of benefit to the Mercian comital house and the influence that it might exert. Similarly, Earl Leofric could after 1052[91] look to his nephew and namesake as Abbot of Peterborough, an appointment which again probably owed much to the influence of the earl,[92] as his extensive interests must surely do. A pluralist, he also held the abbacies of Burton on Trent, Coventry, Crowland and Thorney,[93] putting him in a very powerful position to defend and promote the interests of the family. It might also have been expected by Earl Leofric that with a nephew at Burton and Coventry, family dispositions of their manors might attract less hostility than appears to have been the case at Worcester.[94]

The need for Leofric to regard church patronage in these ways stemmed not only from the normal and conscientious practices of seigneurial families to maintain their position, but also from the particular experience of the west midlands since the reign of Cnut and the implications of this for the house of Leofwine. In this much centres on the history of the individual earldoms, which unfortunately cannot be reconstructed in detail[95] although E. A. Freeman made some attempt in his *History of the Norman Conquest.*[96]

In 1017 Eadric Streona, Ealdorman of Mercia, was murdered, clearing the way for a reorganisation of Mercia by Cnut.[97] He was followed by Leofwine, Ealdorman of the Hwicce, but it is not clear if his authority was as extensive as had been that of Eadric. As might be expected of an ealdorman of the Hwicce, Leofwine already had some landed interests in Warwickshire, having received lands here in 998,[98] including the manor of Southam that was

90 E. A. Freeman, *The Norman Conquest* (Oxford, 1870), ii, 360; Barlow, *The English Church, op. cit.,* 218.

91 Hugh Candidus, *op. cit.,* 33; ASC, 'E', s.a. 1052.

92 Barlow, *The English Church, op. cit.,* 57.

93 ASC 'E', s.a. 1066.

94 The appointment of Leofric as Abbot of Peterborough may also bear some reflection upon the origins of his grandfather, Leofwine, suggesting ongoing interests in the East Anglian region; Williams, *op. cit.,* 8; Earl Leofric's son, Ælfgar, also received in 1051 the earldom of East Anglia during the temporary disgrace of the house of Godwin; F. Barlow, *Edward the Confessor* (London, 1970), 115.

95 F. M. Stenton, *op. cit.,* 415.

96 E. A. Freeman, *op. cit.,* Appendix G.

97 For a more detailed discussion of these events see Williams, *op. cit.,* 6 ff; Lawson, *op. cit.,* 186-7.

98 P. H. Sawyer, *op. cit.,* S. 892.

subsequently given to Coventry Abbey. Leofwine disappears from the charters in the early 1020s[99] to be succeeded as earl by his son, Leofric, at some point between 1023 and 1032.

However, in addition to the establishment of Leofwine as earl of Mercia, Cnut also appointed a number of Danes to earldoms in the west midlands. Hrani was settled in Herefordshire between 1016 and 1019, Hakon Ericson in Worcestershire by 1018, and Eilaf Thorgilson in Gloucestershire at about the same time.[100] What is not clear, however, is the relationship between these new earls and the earls of Mercia. On the one hand they might have all operated independently of each other, but alternatively it is possible that the traditional authority of those holding the earldom of Mercia was maintained, and the Danish earls were therefore regarded formally as subordinates. This latter interpretation has been favoured by both Freeman[101] and Williams.[102] Whichever was the case, there can be little doubt that the freedom for action of the earls of Mercia was now constrained, and that whereas their family might have previously been the obvious focus of attention and service within the locality, there was now the possibility of an alternative focus. In so far as it was ever the case, the earls of Mercia could no longer simply assume their authority and right of political patronage. Now they had to ensure that they defended, maintained and further enhanced it in those areas that were less directly under their control, even if still under their authority. Where they clearly remained unchallenged was within the north-west midlands, particularly Cheshire, Shropshire and Staffordshire, their strength here reflected at the time of Domesday by the number of their holdings in the area;[103] this was the focus and traditional heartland of their authority (Fig. 3).

Williams has argued[104] that the changes made by Cnut were short lived, the new earldoms dying with their earls, but even during the reign of the Confessor there remained an element of 'fragmentation' in the west midlands. Most clearly, Herefordshire was to pass from Hrani via Swegn Godwinson and Ralph of Mantes to Harold Godwinson. The earldom created in 1045 for Beorn Estrithson seems to have included Leicestershire, Derbyshire and Lincolnshire,[105] areas that subsequently were held directly by the earls of Mercia. Freeman supposed that the murder of Beorn in 1049 might indicate the point at which these territories passed to Leofric, and that the earl's patronage of Stow might reflect the incorporation of this area into

---

[99] M. K. Lawson, *op. cit.*, 186-7.
[100] A. Williams, *op. cit.*, 6-7.
[101] E. A. Freeman, *op. cit.*, 564.
[102] A. Williams, *op. cit.*, 8.
[103] Cf. D. Hill, *op. cit.*, map 182.
[104] A. Williams, *op. cit.*, 15.
[105] Cf. F. Barlow, *Edward the Confessor, op. cit.*, 89-90; E. A. Freeman, *op. cit.*, 558, 561.

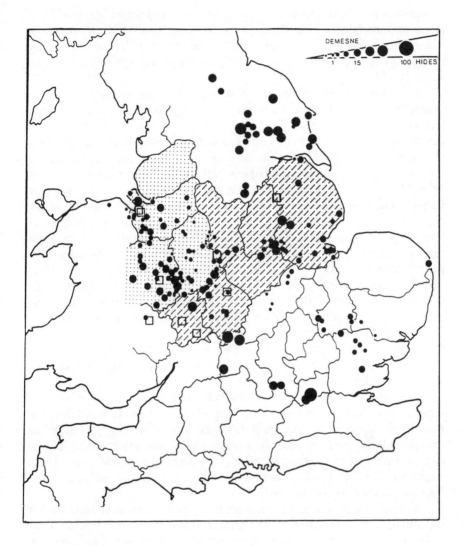

- Demesne lands of the Leofric family in 1066 (after Hill, 1981).
□ Religious houses endowed by Leofric and Godiva.
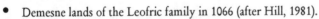 Earldom of Leofric in 1045 (after hill, 1981; Freeman, 1870). The
  tenurial heartland of the Leofric family.
The greater Mercian Earldom held in addition to the heartland by
  Edwin in 1065 (after Hill and Freeman).   JRH

Figure 3. Religious Patronage and the Mercian Earldom
Adapted from Hill, Atlas of Anglo-Saxon England with the permission of Basil Blackwell Ltd.

113

his earldom by *c*.1053; this is not certain, however, and patronage could have preceded incorporation. It should also be noted that by 1066 Coventry Abbey was holding several manors in Leicestershire, reflecting the landed holdings of the house of Leofric, quite probably predating the formation of Beorn's earldom.[106]

It is particularly frustrating, however, that the situation of both Worcestershire and Warwickshire remains ambiguous. Freeman conjectured that these shires were held in 1045 by Ralph of Mantes,[107] presumably supposing that he must have been established in an earldom since 1041, having come to England in the entourage of Edward, and that the territory of the Hwicce was not otherwise attributed. However, it is not known whether or not Ralph came to England in 1041, and Barlow[108] has pointed out that Ralph could have still been a child in 1041; not until 1050 does he clearly appear as an earl,[109] although Barlow is prepared to postulate that Ralph was following Swegn in Herefordshire by 1047.[110] Alternatively, Robertson has suggested that Odda may have been the earl of Worcestershire between 1052 and his death in 1056,[111] and has also placed Ralph in Worcestershire in 1051, to follow Swegn in Herefordshire in the following year;[112] if Ralph did hold Worcestershire before 1052, it is not improbable that this could have extended also into Warwickshire, as the territory of the Hwicce had done.

However, it is against this varied and at times confusing backdrop that the pattern of patronage followed by Leofric and Godiva should, in part, be examined; a pattern that it has already been suggested was closely related to the territorial framework and ambitions of the earldom.

The support given to Chester, Wenlock and Burton occurred within the tenurial heartland of the earldom, acts of piety that also fulfilled the traditional expectations and obligations of secular nobility towards the church, which certainly did nothing to undermine the standing of the comital house in the region. However, the patronage offered beyond this heartland, whilst still clearly within the context of a Mercian earldom, might have had further benefits in mind.

The patronage of Leominster, within Swegn Godwinson's earldom but on the borders with Mercia, may represent an attempt to develop some influence in that locality, countering a loss of territory in the earldom that

---

[106] Wulfric Spott held estates in Leicestershire, and the union of his family with that of Leofric might have supplemented their landed holdings here and elsewhere, including Warwickshire.

[107] E. A. Freeman, *op. cit.*, 563-6 and maps facing 568.

[108] F. Barlow, *Edward the Confessor, op. cit.*, 76.

[109] *Ibid.*, 89.

[110] *Ibid.*, 93.

[111] A. J. Robertson, *op. cit.*, 456.

[112] *Ibid.*, 467.

resulted from Cnut's reorganisation of the region. In Worcestershire, the tenurial aggrandisement of the family at the expense of the church combined with schemes of patronage to bolster comital authority. The early patronage of Evesham might reflect a response to the influence of the recently deceased Earl Hakon, not to mention that of the bishops of Worcester, and the need of the earl to build up a party or following in the locality that was directly bound to him, even if Leofric had by this date recovered direct control of the region. If Ralph of Mantes was established in the shire by 1045 to 1051, the need to be seen as patrons of Evesham and Worcester was all the more convincing.

Within this pattern, the foundation of Coventry remains striking but can also be understood. It represents the establishment of an *Eigenkloster*, a family monastery and mausoleum, in which (as the symposium demonstrated) the acts and reputation of Leofric and Godiva would never be forgotten. Yet, although it is clear that Leofwine had possessed lands in Coventry since the late tenth century, it was not an area at the heart of their earldom. Rather than establish their family foundation at the heart of their possessions and affinity, as one might have expected, they chose instead an area where their tenurial position was comparatively weak, albeit perhaps stronger than in Worcestershire;[113] furthermore, if the traditional foundation date of 1043 is accepted, this took place early in the reign of a new king. This foundation might be seen as something of a spearhead into a region in which the family wanted to develop its standing further, to consolidate its tenurial position and its focus for the political community of the shire. If Ralph of Mantes did exercise any influence in the region in the 1040s, the need for such action was heightened, whilst the extensive earldom of Swegn Godwinson to the south of Worcestershire and Warwickshire may have also prompted the Mercian earls into action in order to forestall any unwanted extension of the influence of the house of Godwin, as had already happened in Herefordshire. If Coventry was indeed a foundation conceived in the 1020s or 1030s, then it may be seen within the context of a response to the reorganisation and political circumstances of Cnut's reign, compensating for and addressing the influence of the Danish earls and their legacy. Furthermore, the absence of any large religious houses in the region between Worcester and Peterborough presented a situation that must have facilitated the foundation of the new house at Coventry.

By 1066 the areas where patronage by the house of Leofric had taken place were undoubtedly parts of the Mercian earldom, and this in itself is some reflection of the effectiveness of family policy. Eric John has

[113] There are inherent dangers in projecting the tenurial picture of 1066 as revealed by *Domesday Book* back to the 1040s; as the case of Alveston reminds us, the earls may have greatly improved their tenurial position between 1043 and 1066.

highlighted the way in which the kings of England took an interest in the reform of monasteries as they became centres of royal influence and cultivated the cult of the royal family.[114] In a more modest way, the patronage generally, and the foundation of Coventry in particular, could do the same for the house of Leofric. They could promote their family's position within the localities of their earldom and provide a framework through which they could respond to the influence of other lords and foster communities of interest closely tied to the comital family.

This paper has concerned itself with an examination of three dimensions to the patronage of the house of Leofric, which has at the same time partially illuminated their relationship with the church. Firstly, there was clearly a dimension of piety, in its own way genuine and commonplace to the nobility of the eleventh century,[115] whose spiritual rewards were prayers for their souls and a place for burial. But it was also a piety of a conventional type, that was not allowed to stand in the way of the wider needs of the family, and indeed was perhaps seen as a potential contributor to the wider political standing of the family. The prayers of those who received their support ensured that the family and its influence were kept to the forefront locally; their memory was assured. It was also a direct enhancement of family prestige, something that was further reinforced by the association of Leofric and Godiva with churches of regional importance, within the context of the earldom; *ipso facto*, Leofric and Godiva shared in the power and prestige of the religious houses that they supported.

In many respects, the tenth-century reformation did little to change the attitudes of patrons to the church[116] and, as Stafford has observed, even the new monasteries did not cease to be seen as family monasteries. Patronage of the church was seen as an extension of family business, and thus it was not inconsistent to look to these family interests when needs dictated. Those who had the power, like Leofric, went further and exploited church lands more widely. Nonetheless their method and attitude was a combination of traditional perceptions of family rights and expectations, together with the equally traditional opportunism of powerful families in taking advantage of their neighbours, and especially of extensive church estates. Thus the second dimension of their patronage was to view the church as an abundant reservoir of landed holdings that was within their right or within their power to utilise as they saw fit.

Thirdly, church patronage generally, but more particularly the foundation of a religious house, might be utilised as an entrée by the family into an area where it felt a need to consolidate its position and influence.

114 E. John, *op. cit.*, 179.
115 P. Stafford, *op. cit.*, 190.
116 *Ibid.*, 189-91.

Such strategy to develop the role of the family as a focal point of influence and interest within the locality was a key contributor to maintaining their prestige and political strength. Monastic patronage was undoubtedly related to the development of lordship, and was indeed an investment in it.[117] As Dominique Barthélémy has observed of eleventh-century France, 'A special relationship with a monastery was an important milestone along the way to acquiring lordship of the ban'.[118] In essentials this is also true of eleventh-century England and is exemplified in the foundation of family mausolea, which provided a focal point for family identity, prestige and political loyalty. This was the context for the foundation of Coventry.

Piety, prestige and politics all had a part to play in the foundation of Coventry Abbey, as they did in the family's wider approach to patronage. Patronage and 'despoliation' were simply two shades of the same strategy for the promotion of the family and the securing of its base of power through projected images and solid tenurial foundations.

Acknowledgements
I would like to thank Professor Chris Dyer and Mr M. Stokes for reading and commenting on an earlier draft of this paper.

[117] E. John, *op. cit.*, 179.
[118] D. Barthélémy, 'Kinship', in *A History of Private Life: Revelations of the Medieval World*, ed. P. Aries and G. Duby (Harvard, 1988), 101.

The Bishops of Coventry and Lichfield, c.1072-1208
M. J. FRANKLIN

The Anglo-Norman bishops of Coventry themselves have attracted little attention in recent historical writing, though there has been plenty of discussion of their changing titles. Two rather amorphous quotations from the *Victoria County History* will confirm this: 'Walter Durdent ... left few traces of his tenure ... Richard Peche ... left little impression on the diocese or on his own times...';[1] 'Geoffrey Muschamp ... seems to have been worthy, but otherwise unmemorable'.[2] Other stronger views have been expressed by less locally-oriented scholars; for example Saltman described Bishop Roger as 'the sporting type',[3] while David Knowles, vexed by Bishop Richard Peche's escapism in the church's time of peril, wrote icily 'Nor need we delay over Richard Peche, bishop of Lichfield and Coventry ... neither there (sc. Clarendon), nor later ... did he show any individuality of word or act.'[4] This paper, essentially an interim report written after about eighteen months of work on the bishops' *acta* for the British Academy Episcopal Acta project, aims to redress the balance somewhat.

Like the majority of English bishops in the period, those who held this see in the twelfth century owed their promotion primarily to royal service, or at least connections with court. With one exception, Bishop Walter Durdent, who was a monk and prior of Canterbury before his promotion,[5] all were in the royal or episcopal service for much of their careers. All, in their different ways, seem to have realised that the simplest way out of their principal difficulty, shortage of revenue and endowments with which to reward faithful servants, was to gain access to the wealth of a major monastery. In this period it was the monks of Coventry who primarily attracted their attention. Peter, bishop from 1072-85, and responsible for the move to Chester in 1075, about whom little more can be said, had been a

---

1   VCH *Staffs* III, 23.
2   *Ibid.*, 24.
3   A. Saltman, *Theobald, Archbishop of Canterbury*, University of London Historical Studies, ii (London, 1956), 13.
4   D. Knowles, *The Episcopal Colleagues of Thomas Becket* (Cambridge, 1951), 15. At 134 note 2 Knowles cites *Materials for the History of Thomas Becket, Archbishop of Canterbury...*, ed. J. C. Robinson and J. B. Sheppard, 7 vols, Rolls Series (London, 1875-85) v, 176 (*recte* vii, 176) where Bishop Richard is reported hiding in the Welsh Mountains to escape royal officials in 1169 ('...ut ab officialibus tutus sit, secessit in illam partem episcopatus sui quam Walenses inhabitant').
5   *The Historical Works of Gervase of Canterbury*, ed. W. Stubbs, 2 vols, Rolls Series (London, 1879-80), i, 44, 141.

royal clerk,[6] Bishop Robert Limesey, probably the first to try to impose his will on Leofric and Godiva's church c. 1087,[7] had been a royal chaplain.[8] In 1102 Henry I, during the dispute with Anselm, selected him, along with Gerard of York and Herbert of Thetford, to negotiate with Paschal II in Rome.[9] Almost certainly this was the point at which Bishop Robert made his acquisition of the wealthy abbey legitimate: for, according to Prior Geoffrey in 1214/15,

> Abbot Leofwine [II] having died, Bishop Robert obtained custody of the abbey from the king. In time he successfully sought permission from Pope Paschal to move his see from Chester to Coventry. And from then onwards the name of abbot was suppressed and deleted in the monastery of Coventry on account of the episcopal dignity in the same...[10]

A privilege was said to have been granted by Pope Paschal on 18 April 1102.[11]

It is possible that Robert I was in reality always a friend to his monks, though if the list of his abstractions from Coventry printed by the eighteenth-century antiquary Thomas Hearne[12] is true, this may be doubted. It is possible that Lanfranc's censure of the bishop who broke the monks'

[6] *Willelmi Malmesbiriensis monachi de gestis pontificum Anglorum libri quinque*, ed. N. E. S. A. Hamilton, Rolls Series (London, 1870), 66, 308.

[7] This is the conventional interpretation, but the manuscript of Archbishop Lanfranc's letter of rebuke reads *P*, not *R*. Thus it may well have been Bishop Peter who was responsible: F. Barlow, *The English Church 1066-1154* (London, 1979), 62 n. 52 discussing Lanfranc, *Epistolae* no. 29 (in *Opera*, ed. L. Dachery (Paris, 1648) or *Patrologiae cursus completus, series Latina*, ed. J. P. Migne, vol. 150).

[8] *Willelmi Malmesbiriensis monachi de gestis regum Anglorum libri quinque*, ed. W. Stubbs, 2 vols, Rolls Series (London, 1887-9), 386; 388-9; William of Malmesbury, *Gesta Pontificum*, 107, 309-10; *Hugh the Chanter, The History of the Church of York 1066-1127*, ed. M. Brett, C. N. L. Brooke and M. Winterbottom (Oxford Medieval Texts, 1990), 35.

[9] Barlow, *English Church 1066-1154*, 299; Anselm, *Epistolae* (in *Anselmi opera omnia* III-V, ed. F. S. Schmitt (1946-52)), nos. 250, 253, 280, 281; *Eadmeri historia novorum in Anglia et opuscula duo de vita sancti Anselmi et quibusdam miraculis eius*, ed. M. Rule, Rolls Series (London, 1884), 137ff.

[10] '...mortuo abbate Coventrie Lewino, a rege custodiam abbathie obtinuit. Interim a papa Paschale sedem suam a Cestria usque Coventreiam transferri impetravit. Extunc suppressum est et deletum nomen abbatis in monasterio Coventrie propter episcopalem dignitatem in eodem...': London, British Library (henceforth BL) ms. Cotton Ch. xiii, 26 printed in W. Dugdale, *Monasticon Anglicanum*, ed. J. Caley, H. Ellis and B. Bandinel, 6 vols in 8 (edn of London, 1846) (henceforth *Mon. Angl.*) viii, 1242, VI.

[11] *Patrologia Latina*, ed. J. P. Migne vol. 143 col. 95; cf. Bodl. ms. Dugdale 12 p. 438 where the date is given as xiiii Kal' Maii, a.d. MCIIII.

[12] Infra, note 25.

[?muniment] chests and seized their horses and other property was actually directed at Bishop Peter: this is what study of the manuscript should lead us to suspect.[13] It was originally argued by Miss Lancaster, initially convincingly, that it was Bishop Robert who was responsible for initiating the Coventry forgeries on the Westminster model, by which the monks of this church successfully promoted a claim to 'the prior's half' of Coventry, as well as to extensive but entirely spurious judicial and financial rights.[14] I have no wish to enter into the 'forged charters' argument here, save to say, as is well known, that the revisionist view is summarised in the papers of R. H. C. Davis.[15] Miss Lancaster's original argument relied on changes in the style of the house in two bede rolls of the period 1101-13. Because in the bede roll of Matilda, abbess of Caen, of 1113, there is a reference to the Holy Trinity in the monastery's dedication, that is the church of 'the prior's half' of the town, whereas there is none in that of Bruno, the founder of the Carthusians, of 1101,[16] she argued that it follows that the charter of Henry II to Bishop Walter,[17] which mentions Bishop 'Robert' proving his case to these liberties before Henry I's court at Portsmouth, and gaining a charter which has not survived, must refer to Bishop Robert Limesey, and not his successor.

> The inference is that Bishop Robert, having been a royal chaplain and having thus become acquainted with diplomatic and palaeographical forms, was responsible for the original fabrication of foundation charters (now lost), which would have been drawn up as evidence for his case or immediately after his success in the suit before the king at Portsmouth possibly in 1107 or 1111.[18]

It is important to note that the actual forgeries on which any history of Coventry priory has to be based, with their extensive claims to exemption

[13] Lanfranc *Ep* 29: '...arcas eorum fregisti, et equos et omnes proprietates, quas habebant, rapuisti...' (*Patrologia Latina* vol. 150, col. 530) cf. supra, note 7 .

[14] The Coventry forgeries are still best approached via J. C. Lancaster, 'The Coventry Forged Charters: a Reconsideration', *Bulletin of the Institute of Historical Research*, xxvii (1954), 113-40. See also the discussion by F. E. Harmer in *Anglo-Saxon Writs*, 1st edn (Manchester, 1952), 214-24 and *idem*, 'A Bromfield and a Coventry writ of King Edward the Confessor', in *The Anglo-Saxons*, ed. P. Clemoes (London, 1959), 89-103 [both items repr. in *Anglo-Saxon Writs*, 2nd edn (Stamford, 1989)].

[15] R. H. C. Davis, *The Early History of Coventry*, Dugdale Society Occasional Papers 24 (1976); *idem*, 'An Unknown Coventry Charter', *English Historical Review* 86 (1971), 533-45 esp. 540ff.

[16] Lancaster, 'Coventry Charters', 138 citing A. Clapham, 'Three Bede Rolls', *Archæological Journal* 106 Supplt. 40-53, esp. 42.

[17] The great register of Lichfield Cathedral known as *Magnum Registrum Album*, ed. H. E. Savage, *Collections for a History of Staffordshire* 3rd ser. xiv (1926 for 1924), no. 18.

[18] Lancaster, 'Coventry Charters', 138-9.

from episcopal control, in particular the purported licence of Alexander II addressed to Earl Leofric the founder,[19] as well as the alleged privilege granted by the same pope to Edward the Confessor,[20] are highly unlikely to have been drafted by a bishop, whatever his attitude to his monks. Thus the suggestion from Professor Davis that Prior Lawrence played a crucial rôle is highly attractive. The privilege suggests that 'for all time' the house should be 'without harassment from any diocesan bishop'.[21] Given the affinity between their own and the Westminster forgeries,[22] and their dating now on palæographical grounds to 1137 x 57,[23] it seems reasonable to suggest that the monks consulted their brothers when Bishop Roger had departed on crusade, to refashion their charters, building perhaps on the gains of Bishop Robert I. Given that the forgeries were accepted as genuine by King Stephen, in a charter almost certainly issued while he held the town against Earl Rannulf in 1147,[24] this is even more likely.

Of Robert I's other activities I have very little to report. It would appear that he took the usual sort of steps to establish his family on lands of the see. And Bishop Robert was undoubtedly a family man. It is recorded that the mother of his son Richard and Noel, the husband of his daughter, Celestria, were ensconced on the lands of the see.[25]

[19] Stratford-on-Avon, Shakespeare Birthplace Trust Record Office, Gregory Leger Book, p. 19; BL ms. Add. 32100 fo. 114; London, Public Record Office (henceforth PRO) C53/56 m. 8.

[20] Stratford-upon-Avon, Shakespeare Birthplace Trust Record Office, Gregory Leger Book, p. 22; BL ms Add. 32100 fo. 115r; ms. Lansd. 400 fo. 48v; PRO C53/112 m. 3; E164/21 fo.75v; *Mon. Angl.* iii, 191, IV.

[21] 'Per omnia tempora sine vexatione cuiuscunque diocesani episcopi... sit.'

[22] Harmer, *Anglo-Saxon Writs*, 217; J. Tait, 'An Alleged Charter of William the Conqueror', in *Essays in History Presented to R. Lane Poole*, ed. H. W. C. Davis (Oxford, 1927), 163.

[23] T. A. M. Bishop and P. Chaplais, *Facsimiles of English Royal Writs to 1100* (Oxford, 1957), xxii.

[24] The charter is in *Regesta Regum Anglo-Normannorum*, ed. by H. W. C. Davis, C. Johnson, H. A. Cronne and R. H. C. Davis, 4 vols. (Oxford, 1913-69), iii, no. 246 cf. PRO C53/135 m. 5, BL ms. Add. 32100 fo. 116r and *Calendar of the Charter Rolls preserved in the Public Record Office 1341-1417*, 99: the charter is dated 'at Oxford', and although Stephen made his headquarters there from 1141 the reference in it to a precept of Eugenius III makes it definitely from after 1145.

[25] VCH *Staffs* III, 21 based on a note in the Ronton cartulary – BL ms. Cotton Vespasian C xv, cal. 'The Chartulary of Ronton Priory', ed. G. Wrottesley, *Collections for a History of Staffordshire* 1st ser. IV (1883), 264-95 and the transcript 'of an old manuscript in the Bodleian', printed by Thomas Hearne in his *The History and Antiquities of Glastonbury* (Oxford, 1722), 293-4), which I have yet to trace. The latter includes a list of the possessions of the priory abstracted by Abbot Leofwine, Bishop Robert I and Bishop Roger. If it proves to be reliable this manuscript may become the basis of several lost *acta*. In it Bishop

Robert II, whose origins are otherwise totally obscure, seems to have been some sort of royal clerk.[26] According to Wharton he was consecrated by Archbishop Ralph d'Escures at Abingdon on 13 March 1121.[27] Little has been known of his pontificate. Largely because of confusion with his predecessor it is difficult to be certain whether any *acta* were definitely issued in his name. There is in an *actum* of Bishop Walter issued possibly c. 1155 in favour of Trentham Abbey a reference to a customary grant 'which my predecessors Bishops Robert Peche and Roger made to the church of Rocester and neighbouring churches'.[28] Precisely what this grant was can perhaps be deduced from another charter of Bishop Richard to Trentham granting the liberty

> which my ancestor Robert the bishop of good memory granted and confirmed by episcopal authority to the church of Burton on finding them in possession of it – namely that no payment should be given for chrism or holy oil or any other parochial thing and that no man or woman need be sent to the chapter or synod. Instead they shall do justice in their own court provided that they do right.[29]

Note that the word used is *antecessor* not *predecessor*. Although the word *antecessor* can sometimes be used meaning simply 'predecessor', and certainly was employed thus, on at least one occasion, by Bishop Richard himself,[30] in

---

Robert is said to have given away, amongst other things, 'Noel, cum filia sua, Greneberge (sc. Granborough, Warwicks.) et domos Conventr'...matri Ricardi filii episcopi duas virgatas in Franketer...' The Ronton cartulary's largely fictional genealogy of its founder (BL ms. Cotton Vespasian C xv fo. 11r) names Noel's wife Celestria, who it describes as mother of their principal founder.

26   William of Malmesbury, *Gesta Pontificum*, 310-11; *Historia Regum*, 259; Eadmer, *Historia Novorum*, 290.

27   *Anglia Sacra*, ed. H. Wharton, 2 vols. (London, 1691), i, 434 n. g.

28   '...synodalem pensionem et immunitatem ceterarum consuetudinum omnium, quam predecessores mei Robertus Peccm et Rogerus bone memorie episcopi ecclesie de Roucestr' et vicinis ecclesiis secundum ordinem de gentibus remiserunt, ampliorem et liberiorem eis remitemus': BL ms. Harley 3868 fo. 34rb. This source is late – s. xiv[1] – but an original issued by Bishop Richard to Trentham mentions his having seen his predecessor's charter ('...sic eis antecessor noster Gualterius carta sua quam oculis propriis et manibus tractavimus et inspeximus': PRO E326/9005). The date follows by association with a royal charter issued at Northampton, BL ms. Harley 3868 fo. 34rb.

29   '...quam Robertus antecessor noster bone memorie episcopus concessit et pontificali auctoritate confirmavit Bruton ecclesie, quam in ea invenit, scilicet ut non reddat ullam consuetudinem pro crismate vel oleo sancto neque per aliqua re parochiali, nec mittat hominem aut feminam ad capitulum vel synodos sed teneat rectum in curia sua quamdiu se a recto non deficit...': BL ms. Harley 3868 fo. 34va.

30   PRO E326/9005 ut supra, note 28 .

the context at least, an intentional double meaning is possible. Given the existence of Bishop Walter's *actum*, it follows that the charter issued by a Robert, bishop of Chester, on pain of anathema to Burton Abbey, which repeats these terms,[31] must be the product of the pontificate of Robert II, not that of Robert I.[32] It may be further inferred, admittedly on the basis of an extremely limited sample, that Robert II's preferred style and form of address may have been 'dei gratia **Cestrensis** episcopus omnibus archidiaconis suis et omni clero sibi commisso salutem', i.e., stressing the 'of Chester', the form used in this grant and an exactly parallel one to the church of Dinton.[33] This is in contrast to Robert I's 'dei gratia **Coventrensis** episcopus omnibus successoribus suis rite sibi succedentibus et omnibus sancte ecclesie fidelibus salutem', where 'of Coventry' is stressed.[34] Whether this says anything of relevance to the 'forged charters' argument, in that it may possibly indicate Robert I's preference for Coventry, rather than Chester, as the location of his see, I must leave up to you to judge. It is clear that the grant implies some sort of diocesan privilege of exemption from chrism dues for ancient minster churches in the diocese, like Burton and Dinton, which was extended to Rocester and Trentham. The practice of

[31] 'I grant and confirm to the mother church of Burton the privilege which I have discovered there and which it has had since the time of its foundation, that is that no customary payment be made for chrism or holy oil or for any other parochial matter, and that it (i.e., the mother church) need not send any man or woman to chapters or synods, but shall do right by them in its own court for so long as this is done'; '...concedo et confirmo matri ecclesie Burtonensi libertatem quam inveni in ea, et quam habuit ex quo fundata est: id est ut non reddat ullam consuetudinem pro chrismate vel oleo sancte neque pro aliqua alia re parochiali nec mittat hominem aut feminam ad capitula vel sinodos. Sed teneat rectum in curia sua quamdiu se a recto non deficit...': BL ms. Loans 30 fos. 19ra-b.

[32] But note that in Saltman, *Theobald*, 250-1, it is inferred from an [unseen] original charter of Archbishop Theobald, on no obvious evidence admittedly, that it is Bishop Robert I who is meant.

[33] BL ms. Harley 3868 fo. 35vb. In this charter the phrase 'quamdiu se a recto non deficit' is replaced with 'apud se plenam iusticiam faciat'.

[34] *The Cartulary of Worcester Cathedral Priory*, ed. R. R. Darlington, Pipe Roll Society LXXXVI (1968 for 1962-3), no. 265 from Worcester, D&C ms. A.4 (Register I) a s.xiii ms (c.1240). The reference to the church of Wolverhampton being one of the chapels anciently pertaining to the crown – the clause 'Hec quidem ecclesia de Wlfr' una erat antiquitus de propriis regis capellis que ad coronam spectat...' – is potentially suspicious for the early 12th century: it may indicate the charter has been tampered with, but it is otherwise not obviously spurious. Moreover, J. H. Denton, *Royal Free Chapels* (Manchester, 1970), 42 accepted this document at face value, and indeed took it as one of the earliest indications of later attitudes. Although its internal evidence does not make it certain when it was issued, the reference to King Henry I and Queen Matilda (ob. 1115) at least implies a charter of Robert I.

levying chrism fees is known to have been widespread, and probably universal in England.[35] In his discussion of synods, however, Dr Brett suggests that the Burton document I have mentioned is an allusion to a parochial chapel.[36] I feel this is unlikely and that the evidence of the abbey having peculiar jurisdiction over three adjoining parishes – Burton, Abbot's Bramley and Mickelover – is important residual evidence for the pre-Conquest status of Burton, and its having exercised parochial functions.[37] If this were so, it could have been quite a considerable privilege, if the Kentish evidence from the *Domesday Monachorum* of a mediated fee of seven pence from each dependent church[38] were duplicated in this diocese. The accepted foundation dates for both Rocester and Trentham – 1141 x 6 and c.1150 respectively[39] – would seem to conflict with this argument, but for the existence, in both cases, of slight, but nonetheless significant, evidence of their succeeding earlier institutions on their sites. This was of course quite common in the case of houses of Augustinian canons, whether or not in the 12th century they did pastoral work. In the case of Rocester the first grant of the church mentions dependent chapels,[40] whereas with Trentham there are strong indications of a secular minster on the site.[41] Robert II died on 21 or 22 August 1127 and the see probably remained vacant for two years.[42]

Bishop Roger was the nephew of Henry I's treasurer Geoffrey de Clinton, and allegedly bought his promotion in 1129 with the payment of three thousand marks.[43] His career had begun as archdeacon of Buckingham: he was only made priest on 21 December 1129 by Archbishop William, the day before his election and was enthroned, significantly, presumably, in Coventry by Simon, bishop of Worcester, perhaps on Sunday 12 January

35 M. Brett, *The English Church under Henry I* (Oxford, 1975), 164ff.
36 Brett, *English Church*, 159 and note 3.
37 Cf. VCH *Staffs* III, 209. Note also that Archbishop Theobald's charter to Burton, supra, note 32, qualifies the reference to chrism thus: 'id est ut non reddat ullam consuetudinem pro crismate vel oleo sancto neque pro aliqua re parrochiali de parrochia Burton'...'; an obvious reference to an ancient minster *parochia*.
38 Brett, *English Church*, 164.
39 D. Knowles and R. Hadcock, *Medieval Religious Houses. England and Wales*, 2nd edn (London, 1971), 172, 177.
40 VCH *Staffs* III, 247.
41 *Ibid.*, 255.
42 *Anglia Sacra* i, 434 note g.
43 *The Chronicle of John of Worcester 1118-1140*, ed. J. R. H. Weaver, *Anecdota Oxoniensa*, Med. and Mod. ser., pt. xiii (Oxford, 1908), 29; William of Malmesbury, *Historia Regum*, 283; *Henrici archidiaconi Huntendunensis historia Anglorum*, ed. T. Arnold, Rolls Series (London, 1879), 303; *Gesta Stephani*, ed. K. R. Potter, 2nd edn (Oxford Medieval Texts, 1976), 104; *The Historia Pontificalis of John of Salisbury*, ed. M. Chibnall (Nelson's Medieval Texts, 1983).

1130.[44] Even though the author of the *Gesta Stephani* thought him too military a bishop, the fact that Stephen selected him, along with Arnulf, archdeacon of Sées, to defend him at Rome against the charges of the Angevins, suggests that he was considered an able and well-educated clerk. Bishop Roger was also one of the English bishops who went to the Lateran Council of 1139.[45] His interest seems to have been primarily in Lichfield rather than the priory in Coventry. For it was Bishop Roger who seems to have been responsible for transforming the ancient arrangements, which may have dated from the reforms said to have been instituted by Bishop Æthelweard in 822. In the 13th-century account, as well as by Thomas Chesterfield, it is said that Bishop Roger was responsible for setting up a 'modern' chapter, which, unusually for England, was, initially at least, specifically modelled on the arrangements in Rouen: '...he established a college of canons at Lichfield for the first time, for beforehand there were only five priests there each serving their own chapel...'[46] Surprisingly no *acta*

---

[44] 'Rogerus nepos Gausfridi de Clinton Buccinghamnensis archidiaconus ad pontificatum Cestrensem electus xii Kal. Ian. presbiter ordinatur et die sequenti a W. Cant' archiepiscopo consecratur Cantuarie, quem postmodum ex precepto archiepiscopi Simon Wigornensis episcopus Coventrei presulari sede inthronizavit [v Id. Jan. die dominico]': John of Worcester, 29. The addition in square brackets does not appear in the main manuscript but is made in one manuscript of the 12th century (Dublin, Trinity College ms. 502 (E.5.23)). 'v Id. Jan.' cannot be right, since 9 January was a Thursday in 1130, but either an editorial or a scribal slip, misreading two minims as 'v' rather than 'ii', is eminently possible, as in 1130 12 January fell on the first Sunday after Epiphany.

[45] See R. L. Poole, 'The English Bishops at the Lateran Council of 1139', *EHR* 28 (1923), 61.

[46] 'Hic primo constituit collegium canonicorum apud Lichfeldiam, nam antea erat ibi nisi quinque sacerdotes deservientes quinque capellis singuli singulis...': BL ms. Cotton Ch. xiii, 26 printed in *Mon. Angl.* vi, 1243. The reference by Chesterfield to Bishop Clinton's foundation of a number of prebends is printed in *Anglia Sacra* i, 434 and discussed in *The Letters and Charters of Gilbert Foliot*, ed. A. Morey and C. N. L. Brooke (Cambridge, 1967), 172 note 1. There is now a brief section on Saxon and Anglo-Norman Lichfield in M. J. Franklin, 'The Cathedral as Parish Church: the Case of Southern England', in *Church and City 1000-1500. Essays in Honour of Christopher Brooke*, ed. D. Abulafia, M. J. Franklin and M. Rubin (Cambridge, 1992), 183-4. The argument, briefly, is that the five canons mentioned as holding three ploughs in Lichfield mentioned in Domesday Book (*Liber censualis vocatur Domesday Book*, 4 vols. (Record Commission, 1783-1816), i, 247a) correspond to the five mentioned as existing there prior to Bishop Roger's intervention and also to the five prebends of especial dignity whose prebendaries had the duty of serving at the high altar of the cathedral itself (cf. Bishop Hugh's statutes – printed in *Mon. Angl.* vi, 1257 – discussed VCH *Staffs* III, 141). They are thus seen as the lineal successors of Æthelweard's minster's priests. This perhaps explains why the archdeacons at Lichfield never had any ex officio place of

of Bishop Roger in favour of the chapter at Lichfield survive, though there is one in the cathedral cartulary, the *Magnum Registrum Album*, granting the church of Gnoshall, previously held by Bishop Roger himself, to William, archdeacon of London![47] It is known however from two sources, first the bull of Innocent II which discusses that bishop's arrangements,[48] and also from a letter of Gilbert Foliot which refers to a dispute between Simon, one of the canons of Lichfield, and the priory over the church of Honiton (Worcs.), that a charter once certainly existed. In a letter dating either from 1157-8 or 1161-3 Gilbert Foliot mentions inspecting charters of both Bishop Roger and of Archbishop Theobald which mention, to use language more appropriate to later centuries, the collation of Simon to this prebend.[49]

Although no text now survives, it is known from an *actum* of Bishop Gerard Pucelle that Bishop Roger almost certainly issued a charter confirming grants by Earl Rannulf of property in the town,[50] a notion which

precedence (K. Edwards, *The English Secular Cathedral in the Middle Ages*, 2nd edn (Manchester, 1967), 249). An explicit reference to the use of the customs of Rouen at Lichfield occurs in an actum of Bishop Richard Peche to the chapter (Lichfield Cathedral Library ms. 28 (*Magnum Registrum Album*) fo. 88ra, calendared *Magnum Registrum Album*, no. 28): cf. Edwards, *Secular Cathedrals*, 13-19, for discussion of Bradshaw's theory of 'four-square' constitutions derived from Bayeux. On the constitution of Lichfield, with the unusual pre-eminence of the Treasurer over the Chancellor, see *ibid.*, 176 note 1.

47 Lichfield Cathedral Library ms. 28 fo. 127ra-b cal. *Magnum Registrum Album*, no. 169.

48 *Magnum Registrum Album*, no. 454.

49 '...Carthas enim dompni Rogeri dudum Cestrensis episcopi et dilecti patris nostri dompni Cantuar' Teodbaldi inspeximus quibus ecclesiam hanc in prebendam sibi collatam fuisse ante transactionem inter Cestrensem et Couventr' ecclesiam per manum sancte memorie pape Eugenii initam pro certo cognovimus....': *Letters and Charters of Gilbert Foliot*, no. 131. Morey and Brooke (*ibid.*, 172 note 1) point out that the reference to Eugenius is probably a slip for Innocent. Both these *acta* appear to be lost.

50 The text is *recte* '...ipsum locum in quo ecclesia Coventr' sita est cum omnibus suis pertinentiis et cum capellis ad eandem ecclesiam spectantibus videlicet... sicut et carta prefati comitis [sc. Ranulphi comitis] et charta ratificationis et confirmationis pie memorie Rogerii Covintr' episcopi super corroboratione testatur quas et vidimus et coram nobis legi fecimus et propriis manibus contractavimus...': BL ms. Add. 32100 fo. 123r; cf. Lancaster, 'Coventry Charters', 136 note 9. Like those of William Walter's lost roll, this copy was made *c.*1588 for Robert Beale, clerk to the Privy Council and executor of John Hales, who died siesed of the priory's site in 1571 (cf. *ibid.*, 116 note 1). However, it was made from an original, described as being *penes* Mr Arthur Gregory in May of 1588. There is an abbreviated translation of this *actum* in F. Bliss Burbidge, *Old Coventry and Lady Godiva* (Birmingham, 1952), 160-1, but this was made from Birmingham Central Library, Archives Division 297832 vol. II fo. 267r (Bickley's

perhaps contradicts the view of him put forward by Thomas Chesterfield, a canon of Lichfield, as the oppressor of the monks, turning their churches into prebends of Lichfield.[51] That he went on crusade, still an unusual thing for an Englishman,[52] and died there, at Antioch on 16 April 1148, argues against too worldly an interpretation of him.

The connection between Archbishop Theobald and Walter Durdent must always have been close. He was his choice as prior of Canterbury when relations with Jeremiah, the prior the monks of Christ Church had elected in 1137 *sede vacante*, deteriorated, or, as Gervase put it rather more graphically, when 'with the passing of time through the devil's envy and the prompting of the wicked it came to pass that the immense peace and unity of the church of Canterbury was shattered and love transformed into hatred'.[53] It is important to realise the nature of this quarrel, for it is vital evidence for the subsequent interpretation of Bishop Walter's relations with the monks of Coventry. Gervase did not consider Walter a 'bad' prior, unlike his successor of the same name, whose incompetence at estate management was legendary; indeed his description of Durdent was rather flattering: '...Walter Durdent, a man of outstanding religiosity and considerable learning in scripture, ruled as prior of the church of Canterbury at this time...'[54] The argument between the monks and their bishop was about their independence and property: Jeremiah, who had been elected contrary to custom when there was no archbishop, was concerned about the archbishop's project for an establishment at Dover which was a threat both to the monks' endowment and, more importantly, to their position in regard to the election of the archbishop and the supply of benefactions at consecration time for his suffragans. For all Archbishop Theobald's respect for the principle of free election, as the true heir of Lanfranc and Anselm he was never prepared to grant freedom to the monks of his own cathedral monastery. He deposed

---

collections relating to the History of Coventry of *c*.1910), not the original which is now Stratford-upon-Avon, Shakespeare Birthplace Trust Record Office ms. DR 10/258 (printed in *The Early Records of Medieval Coventry*, ed. P. R. Coss, *British Academy Records of Social and Economic History* new ser. 11 (London, 1986), no. 12). A cursory collation of the original with the copy made for Robert Beale suggests that some of the extensions of Bishop 'R.' to parts of *Rogerus* (*Ricardus* is of course also possible, or even conceivably *Robertus*) are made on the copyist's sole authority. The whole matter needs to be checked and will be addressed in *English Episcopal Acta Coventry and Lichfield I.*

51 BL ms. Cotton Cleopatra D ix fo. 72b = *Mon. Angl.* viii, 1241, III.
52 *Ibid.*
53 '...processu vero temporis invidia diaboli et maledicorum suggestione procuratum est ut tanta pax et unitas Cantuariensis ecclesie scinderetur et caritas in odium verteretur...': Gervase i, 126-8.
54 'Gwalterus Durus dens, vir eximie religionis et sacris litteris apprime eruditus, regebat his diebus prioratum Cantuariensis ecclesie...': *ibid.* i, 141.

Jeremiah and, ignoring the judgment by Henry, bishop of Winchester and papal legate, in the former's favour, eventually prevailed against them.[55] When in 1143, the new bishop of St Asaph, Gilbert, was consecrated at Lambeth, rather than as usual at Canterbury, the threat to the monks was manifest: they had no choice but to compromise.

Our knowledge of Bishop Walter's election to Coventry derives from the documentation assembled in 1215 when the monks of Coventry and the canons of Lichfield disputed each other's right to elect their bishop. It is a Coventry account and runs thus:

> The aforesaid Bishop Roger having died and been buried in Antioch, the monks of Coventry were summoned to Leicester by Archbishop Theobald for the purpose of electing the bishop of Coventry. They elected as bishop there W. Durdent, the prior of Canterbury, though the clerks of the diocese, both those of Lichfield and of Chester apparently, objected and appealed to the holy see. Because of the appeal the lord of Canterbury could not receive the elect's profession and consecrate him. But prior Lawrence journeyed to Rome and got the clerks' appeal overturned, the elect was confirmed and consecrated by the lord of Canterbury on the precept of the pope.[56]

The points to note are: Archbishop Theobald's part in the election and the unity of interests between Prior Lawrence and the new bishop at least when it came to safeguarding Coventry's rights against both Lichfield and Chester. The only other account of Bishop Walter's election, that given by Thomas of Chesterfield, a fifteenth-century canon of Lichfield,[57] implies that Stephen intervened and mediated in the dispute. This is not likely in the context of 1148-9, when Stephen had yet to regain his preeminence. Moreover the long gap between Bishop Roger's death and Bishop Walter's consecration

---

[55] On the judgement by Bishop Henry see *English Episcopal Acta VIII: Winchester 1070-1204*, ed. M. J. Franklin (British Academy, 1993), no. 32 and note. Gervase described events as follows: '...ex mandato apostolico in pristinum gradum restitutus est, Walterio, qui ei [sc. Jeremiah] in prioratum successerat, apud Dovoriam interim moram faciente: unde Theodbaldus archiepiscopus Cantuariensis nimia acerbitate commotus, benevolentiam suam avertit a conventu, iurans se nichil in ecclesie sacramentale facturum, quamdiu Jeremias in eadem subsisteret ecclesie...': Gervase i, 127.

[56] 'Isto R. apud Antiocham mortuo et sepulto, vocati fuerunt monachi Coventriae a Theobaldo archiepiscopo Cantuar' apud Leicestriam ad celebrandum electionem episcopi Coventrie qui ibidem W. Durdent, priorem Cant' in episcopum elegerunt, contradicientibus clericis episcopatus tam Lichfeldie quam Cestrie (ut audivit et credit) et ad sedem apostolicam appellantibus pro quorum distuit dominus Cantuar' electum firmare et consecrare. Sed prior Laurentius, Romam profectus, retinuit appellationes dictorum clericorum cassari et electum suum confirmari et a domino Cantuar' per preceptum domini pape consecrari...': BL ms. Cotton Ch xiii, 26, printed in *Mon. Angl.* vi, 1242.

[57] *Anglia Sacra* i, 434.

(between 16 April 1148 and 2 October 1149) is amply explained by the saga of appeals to Rome. Perhaps reflecting this there is unusually on the reverse of Bishop Walter's original profession to the archbishop a narrative of events. According to this Archbishop Theobald, with the assistance of his suffragans Robert, bishop of London, Walter, bishop of Rochester and Nicholas, bishop of Llandaff, consecrated him bishop on 2 October 1149.[58] While the new bishop, in making his profession, described himself as 'elect of Coventry', the narrative, more uncommittedly, mentions him being consecrated 'bishop of the church of Coventry or Chester'.[59] The 1215 account continues

> ...Following his consecration and enthronement at Coventry when he came to Lichfield the doors were closed against him. In consequence he excommunicated them. The same bishop W. brought many evils upon the monks of Coventry. Both Bishop W. and Prior L. were called into the presence of the lord pope and conferred with him. Apostolic concern having intervened, the two made an agreement which included, moreover, the proviso that the episcopal chair would always remain at Coventry and that the prior would have the first voice in the election of the bishop...[60]

Just as it had been at Canterbury the dispute was about the extent of episcopal control of the monks' wealth. Indeed we may presume that this, or rather the comparative poverty of Lichfield, had been the basic cause for the whole saga of changing titles and moving episcopal chairs which characterised the period. The agreement, dated 14 February 1152,[61] put a stop to the practices which characterised the pontificate of Bishop Roger and which were exemplified in Innocent II's bull of April 1139.[62] As a compromise, this arrangement must be taken as a tribute to the negotiating skills of Prior Lawrence. Its most important provisions were that the monks' lands and their right to all the profits from them, both secular and spiritual, were to be protected: no bishop was to change this and anything in the bulls of Pope Innocent or Pope Lucius which caused this was declared invalid. In

[58]   Canterbury, D&C ms. C155/29: printed in *Canterbury Professions*, ed. M. Richter, Canterbury and York Society vol. 67 (London, 1973), no. 94.

[59]   'electus Conventrensis ecclesie', as opposed to 'sacravit...in episcopum Coventrensis ecclesie sive Cestrensis ecclesie': *ibid.*

[60]   'Consecratus et apud Coventriam intronizatus, cum veniat Lichfeldiam clause erant ianue contra eum. Clausis ianuis sic excommunicavit eos. Iste episcopus W. multa mala intulit monachis Coventrie quibus ad presentiam domini pape vocatis, W. episcopus et L. prior et cum eo conparentes, interveniente sollicitudine apostolica composuerunt: confirmato tamen ut semper apud Coventriam haberetur sedes episcopalis et in electione episcopi prior primam vocem habeat...': BL ms. Cotton Ch xiii, 26, printed in *Mon. Angl.* vi, 1242.

[61]   *Magnum Registrum Album*, no. 262.

[62]   *Magnum Registrum Album*, no. 454 = *Papsturkunden in England*, ed. W. Holtzman, 3 vols, Abhandlungen der Gesellschaft der Wissenschaften in Göttingen, phil.-hist. Klasse (Berlin and Göttingen, 1930-52), ii, 157-8.

comparison with Bishop Roger's bull from Innocent II two points stand out: first, the churches and tithes of the monks' vills are no longer to be assigned for the purpose of funding prebends in Lichfield, or as income to the see itself, and second, the monks are to serve their church in the same manner as their brothers at Canterbury, not as at Winchester.[63]

There are other reasons for considering Bishop Walter as something other than just a pious monk. His surviving *acta* demonstrate that he clearly recognised the need to use the endowments at his disposal to support the members of his *familia*. For example he transferred the prebend at Lichfield previously held by William, archdeacon of Chester, to Walter, one of his clerks.[64] Neither was he free from the sin of supporting members of his family, a long-established tradition of the see. Roger Durdent, perhaps the bishop's nephew, bought the land of *Clettul*, probably part of the bishop's manor of Lichfield, with the bishop's consent.[65] Later, in the time of Bishop Richard Peche, Dean William procured the repurchase of this land for 12½ marks and used it to increase the endowment of the Treasurer of Lichfield, who held it in fee of the Dean for 2s. p. a.[66]

The next bishop, Richard Peche, appears to be something of a dinosaur, in that he was almost certainly the son of Bishop Robert II. He had been archdeacon of Coventry, to which office he was presumably appointed by his father, though this is not certain since there are no witness lists attached to any of the putative *acta* of Robert II so far identified by me. The earliest attestation by Archdeacon Richard of Coventry I have been able to trace is c.1140.[67] Although there must have been some objections to his elevation –

---

63 Cf. VCH *Staffs* III, 19.
64 Lichfield, Cathedral Library ms. 28 fo. 131va cal. *Magnum Registrum Album*, no. 186.
65 '...Noverint universitas vestra Reginaldum Durdent consilio et assensu capituli nostri dedisse et concessisse Rogero filio suo et heredibus suis terram de Clettul cum omnibus pertinenciis suis quam emit predictus Rogerus de Hugone de Cestrefeld tempore Walteri bone memorie Coventr' episcopi concessione et assensu eiusdem episcopi et capituli nostri de se et heredibus suis libere et quiete tenendum...': a charter of Dean Richard of Lichfield confirming a lost grant by Bishop Walter – Bodl. ms. Ashmole 1527 (SC 8234) fo. 17r. *English Episcopal Acta II: Canterbury 1162-1190*, ed. C. R. Cheney and B. E. A. Jones (Oxford, 1986), no. 154 is a confirmation of the same lost charter issued by Archbishop Richard. Roger Durdent attested two other *acta* of Bishop Walter: *Magnum Registrum Album*, nos. 126, 582 – the former along with another apparent family member, one Rabellus Duredent, on whom cf. VCH *Staffs* III, 21 note 48.
66 *Ibid.*: i. e. a reference to a lost *actum* of Bishop Richard in the charter of Dean William.
67 *Worcester Cartulary* no. 191 can be reasonably closely dated because of the reference to Ralph, prior of Worcester 1142-3 (D. Knowles, C. N. L. Brooke and V. C. M. London, *The Heads of Religious Houses. England and Wales 940-1216*

the chronicler Ralph de Diceto, writing near the end of the 12th century, in a famous passage,[68] was moved to quote at length from Ivo of Chartres as justification for the consecration of the sons of priests as bishops – according to Thomas Chesterfield at least he was elected with the consent of all, by which he probably meant, with the agreement of both the monks of Coventry and the canons of Lichfield.[69] His was the last episcopal appointment to be made under Archbishop Theobald and it happened when the archbishop was so near to death that the chroniclers were in doubt about the precise circumstances. While the actual profession is made explicitly to Theobald, a point confirmed by Diceto, Gervase says that the archbishop was too sick to perform the ceremony and that it was done instead by Walter, bishop of Rochester.[70] Despite appearances his was a busy episcopate, and my search for Coventry *acta* has so far been most fruitful in his case. Like some of his predecessors he seems to have been particularly concerned with the finances of Lichfield, in particular the deanery, though this may partly have been done at papal command. There are at least ten charters issued by him in the *Magnum Registrum Album*, some in favour of the common fund, some the precentorship and two, specifically, the deanery. One is said to be issued as a result of a papal mandate and the bishop's concern at the exigencies of the church as a result of the recent hostilities, that is the struggles with the Young King c. 1176.[71] He seems to have been a man of conventional piety, remembered as the founder of an Augustinian house to the memory of St Thomas in Stafford, to which he retired shortly before his death on 7 October 1181.[72] One of the two surviving charters issued by him in favour of St Thomas' mentions Henry II as a spiritual beneficiary,[73] but whether this is merely convention or indicative of a real connection with a

---

(Cambridge, 1972), 83): *Magnum Registrum Album* no. 169, in which William archdeacon of London 1132/3-54 (J. Le Neve, *Fasti Ecclesiae Anglicanae 1066-1300*, ed. D. E. Greenway. Vol. i, St Paul's London (London, 1968), 9) is mentioned, may be slightly earlier.

[68] *Radulfi de Diceto decani Londoniensis opera historica...*, ed. W. Stubbs, 2 vols, Rolls Series (London, 1876) i, 305.

[69] *Anglia Sacra* i, 435.

[70] Canterbury, D&C ms. C115/35, printed in Richter, *Canterbury Professions*, no. 101. Cf. Diceto i, 305 and Gervase i, 168.

[71] Lichfield, Cathedral Library ms. 28 (*Magnum Registrum Album*) fo. 217rb cal. *Magnum Registrum Album*, no. 495. Dean Richard succeeded his predecessor in 1175 or 1176: *EEA* 2 no. 155n.

[72] '...in fine vite sue canonicum induit habitum in ecclesia s. Thome martiris iuxta Staffordiam, quam ipse de episcopo fundaverat...': *Anglia Sacra* i, 435. In fact Bishop Richard seems to have completed the pious project of Gerard de Stafford begun 1173-5; cf. Knowles and Hadcock, *Houses*, 146, VCH *Staffs*. III, 260.

[73] '"Chartulary" of the Priory of St Thomas near Stafford', ed. F. Parker, *Collections for a History of Staffordshire* 1st ser. viii (1887) pt. 1, 134.

previous benefactor is uncertain. Note, however, that Thomas Chesterfield suggested that he was elected 'at the command of King Henry'.[74]

Both Gerard Pucelle and Hugh de Nonant began their ecclesiastical careers in Becket's household, though they were prelates of very different nature.[75] The former's time as bishop was short, and, according to Gervase of Canterbury, possibly curtailed by poison,[76] but he had been a man of letters of considerable note. The late Professor Cheney described him as 'a scholarly prelate with a solid grounding in canon law', while to Kuttner and Rathbone he was 'the first English master of canon law of whose career and activities substantial data are at hand...'[77] In fact, since he was probably born in the second decade of the twelfth century,[78] he must have been considered quite an old man by 1183,[79] so perhaps Gervase's rumour should be taken with the customary large pinch of salt. Master Gerard's first career as a teacher of canon law in France had begun before 1156,[80] and he was well known as such both there and in Germany. From 1174 he was principal clerk to the archbishop of Canterbury, Richard of Dover, a monk, but nonetheless one of the new monastic elite, trained in the schools, and thus someone who would know his worth.[81] In the surviving *corpus* of the archbishop's *acta* master Gerard heads the list of witnesses on no less than forty-eight occasions, being eclipsed by the dignity of Benedict the chancellor only four times.[82] Unusually it is known that he had a clerk of his own, a certain R., who attested Archbishop Richard's charter to Burton Abbey of May 1177 x

---

[74] 'Voluntate regis Henrici mediante...,' *Anglia Sacra* i, 435.

[75] *Materials for the History of Thomas Becket* iii, 525 (Bosham).

[76] He was consecrated on 25 September 1183 and died on 13 January the following year. Gervase continues: '...In proximo autem postquam intronizatus est, acerba tactus aegritudine lecto decubuit, et obiit mense quinto ordinationis suae idus Januarii et apud Coventre sepultus est. Erat autem rumor in populo eum interiisse veneno, quod et manifestis secundum physicos claruit indiciis...' (Gervase, i, 307-8).

[77] C. R. Cheney, *From Becket to Langton: English Church Government 1170-1213* (Manchester, 1956), 48; S. Kuttner and E. Rathbone, 'Anglo-Norman Canonists of the Twelfth Century. An Introductory Study', *Traditio*, vii (1949-51), 279-358 at p. 296.

[78] *Ibid.*, 297.

[79] Cf. contemporary attitudes to Bishop Henry of Winchester, born c.1095, in the 1160s.

[80] Kuttner and Rathbone, 'Anglo-Norman Canonists', 297.

[81] On this phenomenon cf. D. Knowles, *The Monastic Order in England*, 2nd edn (Cambridge, 1963), 502ff. The evidence for the archbishop's training is again Gervase: '...de Normannia natus, artium liberalium scholas egressus...' (Gervase, ii, 397).

[82] *EEA* 2, xxxi.

September 1181 as *R. clerico magistri Gerardi*.[83] The archbishop's *acta* testify that master Gerard's legal knowledge and diplomatic skill were frequently in demand: he also became well-known to the monks of Christ Church, who were later to celebrate his obit as they would that of an archbishop.[84] His service to his master obviously merited the premier reward open to an archbishop. Others had been urging his promotion for some time, for example Cardinal Peter of St Chrysogonos, *c*.1178, who wrote to his master, Pope Alexander III, commending Gerard as a master worthy of promotion. This is one of a set of three examples cited by Kuttner and Rathbone, which imply that master Gerard was still active in France as a lawyer, even though presumably he was still in the archbishop's service.[85] It was not until around the end of April/ early May 1183 that Archbishop Richard sent a mandate to the Dean and Chapter of Lichfield, commanding them to send five or six of their seniors, with power to elect, to wait upon him in Normandy, and specifically at Caen on 26 May.[86] This mandate was later used by the chapter to prove its right to elect before Archbishop Stephen Langton in 1223 against the monks of Coventry,[87] but it is interesting to speculate on Archbishop Richard's motives for this decision. The date of Bishop Gerard's election is unknown, except that it must have been after 26 May, and had probably occurred before mid-August, when the archbishop returned to England.[88] Gerard attests as bishop-elect a charter for Missenden Abbey (Cistercian, Bucks.), which was probably issued around this time.[89] The priory here in Coventry was probably in a certain amount of disarray at this time, the long-serving Prior Lawrence having died on 29 January 1179, and not yet been replaced.[90] We are told that Prior Moses was elected the day before

[83] *EEA* 2 no. 63.

[84] BL ms. Cotton Nero C ix fo. 3v, cited in Kuttner and Rathbone, 'Anglo-Norman Canonists', 303 note 47.

[85] The letter of Cardinal Peter is printed in *Patrologia Latina* vol. 200 col. 1370f. Master Gerard witnesses his award to the abbey of Sainte-Geneviève first after the major ecclesiastical dignitaries – Paris, Bibl. Ste.-Geneviève, ms. 1651 (E.l.25) fo. 221r, cited in Kuttner and Rathbone, 'Anglo-Norman Canonists', 302 note 41. It is not known that Archbishop Richard was absent from England in that year; cf. Itinerary, *EEA* 2, 280.

[86] *EEA* 2, no. 156 (from the Lichfield *Magnum Registrum Album*).

[87] Cf. *Magnum Registrum Album*, no. 464 = *Acta Stephani Langton, Cantuariensis Archiepiscopi a.d. 1207-1228*, ed. K. Major (Canterbury and York Society, 1950), no. 61.

[88] Diceto ii, 20 dates this as 11 August. Gervase reports the archbishop at Canterbury by 19 August (Gervase i, 307): cf. Itinerary *EEA* 2 p. 280.

[89] *Ibid.*, no. 167.

[90] *Heads*, 40-1. As the editors of *Heads* pointed out, the reference to a Prior Nicholas *c.* 1179 is almost certainly an error.

Bishop Gerard.[91] Of greater note is the fact that Prior Moses was one of the archbishop's chaplains.[92] For whatever reason it appears that the old Mercian diocese was on the archbishop's mind in May 1183. The appointment of one of his chaplains to the Coventry priorate must indicate both influence, as well as concern. He sent Peter of Blois, another trusted member of his *familia*, to explain the procedure for the appointment of the six Lichfield seniors. The archbishop had sought out the king in Normandy, worried deeply about the many vacant churches in his care; his ostensible reason was the problems being caused by the king's sons.[93] It would seem reasonable to argue that Bishop Gerard would have left his master's suite following his consecration on 25 September, but the fact that the records of his three months or so as bishop that I have so far managed to identify for certain number only two documents, the important Coventry charter I have already discussed,[94] and a second *actum* in favour of Burton abbey,[95] coupled with the fact that he attests two *acta* of Archbishop Richard as bishop,[96] suggest that this may not in fact have been the case. Obviously there are problems of identification with documents issued by a Bishop 'G.' of Chester, Coventry or Lichfield, particularly those found in cartularies, for it is reasonable to expect that steps to avoid this difficulty would be taken in originals issued by Bishop Geoffrey.[97] It would seem that Bishop Gerard was more eclectic in his choice of style than his successor-but-one: thus an *actum* purporting to be issued by a Bishop 'G.', 'dei gratia Coventrensis ecclesie minister' starts with a reasonable probability of being an *actum* of Bishop Geoffrey, and *vice versa*. Thus it is likely that an *actum* of Bishop 'G.' addressed to Ivo, archdeacon of Derby, was issued by Bishop Gerard, not Bishop Geoffrey.[98]

91   *Heads*, 41 citing BL ms. Cotton Roll xiii, 26. The inference there that this was in January 1183 cannot be right, even if we read *recte* 1184, because of the archbishop's election mandate in the Lichfield *Magnum Registrum Album*.

92   He attests thirteen of the archbishop's charters: *EEA* 2, nos. 64-5, 69-70, 84, 92, 112, 144, 160, 163, 170, 221-2.

93   '...propter dissencionem filiorum domini regis, quam in proximo per dei misericordiam mitigabimus...': *EEA* 2 no. 156.

94   Supra, note 50.

95   BL ms. Loans 30 fo. 19ra-b.

96   *EEA* 2, nos. 54, 96.

97   Evidence to the contrary exists. Bodl. ms. Douce Charters a.1.69 (SC 22008), an original actum of Bishop 'G.', 'dei gratia Coventrensis ecclesie humilis minister' to Bretton Priory, must have been issued by Bishop Godfrey according to the argument infra.

98   PRO E326/8941. The date of Archdeacon Ivo's death is not certain, but after 21 June 1198, i.e. the date of Bishop Geofrey's consecration, is extremely late. A similar argument can be applied to BL ms. Harley 3868 fo. 3v, an actum of Bishop 'G.', 'dei gratia Coventr' episcopus' to Wombridge priory, which also has anunusual dating clause – cf. infra, note 21.

Bishop Hugh, whose attempt to impose his will on the monks of the priory I will discuss further later, and who did not always enjoy the favour of the establishment, certainly began his career high in Henry II's favour. A scion of an important Norman ecclesiastical family,[99] he owed his initial advancement to the patronage of his uncle, Arnulf, bishop of Lisieux.[100] He seems to have been sent to Canterbury for his education: he is first noted in the historical record in Becket's entourage in 1164.[101] He went into exile with Becket, but was reconciled to the king in 1170. He probably owed his promotion to the see to his successful diplomatic mission on the king's behalf to Pope Lucius in 1184. The long gap between his election and consecration (3 years: 1185-8) is probably explained by another mission to Rome on the king's behalf, this time seeking permission for the crowning of John as King of Ireland. He arrived back in Dover along with the Cardinal Deacon Octavian, apparently charged as papal legate with the crowning, on Christmas Eve 1186. Although it is known that they spent the feast at Canterbury and the New Year in London, there is no evidence in any of the chroniclers that this ever took place.[102]

The general loss of prestige as a consequence of the Cistercian boom, to say nothing of the expansion of the contemplatives, the Carthusians, and, to some extent, the Premonstratensians, promoted hostility between bishops and monastic chapters. The new generation of bishops, trained in canon law, of which Bishop Hugh and Archbishop Baldwin were a part, could see no place for the monastic chapter, which markedly constrained their freedom of action, at least when compared with the patronage available to their brothers with secular chapters. In October of 1189 the simmering passions in the most important of the cathedral monasteries, Canterbury, came to a head.[103] Bishop Hugh's moves against his monks began almost immediately. According to Gervase of Canterbury he felt it totally improper for there to

---

99 See the genealogical table in *The Letters of Arnulf of Lisieux*, ed. F. Barlow, Camden 3rd ser. (London, 1939), xi.

100 Bishop Arnulf seems finally to have set up a group of jurisdictions around Gacé (Dépt. Orne), close to the place from which his nephew took his toponym, for him including the deanery of Gacé, the prebend of Croisilles in his cathedral and the archdeaconry of Lisieux, though at first he seem to have been content with giving him a different prebend, that of Chapelle Hareng, nr. Thibouville (Dépt. Eure). See *ibid* no. 134 on Chapelle Hareng, and p. 201 n. c on Gacé). Rather bitterly, in two letters written when they had fallen out in the late 1170s, Bp Arnulf describes how he educated and provided for his nephew: *ibid* nos. 133, 138.

101 *Materials for the History of Thomas Becket* iii, 57, 525. See Bosham's character sketch, *ibid.*, 525-6.

102 Gervase i, 346 and *Gesta regis Henrici* ii, 4.

103 On Canterbury see Knowles, *Monastic Order*, 314-22, 325-7.

be monks in English cathedrals; the bitterness of his animosity was indicated by the oath imputed to him by the chronicler.[104] According to William of Newburgh he exploited the divisions within the community and finally broke into the precinct by armed force.[105] It would appear that some form of fracas took place in which Bishop Hugh himself received some injuries: Gervase dated this incident as 9 October 1189,[106] whereas Richard of Devizes alluded to it thus:

> Hugh... lodged a complaint against his monks of Coventry, who had laid violent hands upon him, spilling his blood before the altar. He had, however, expelled the majority of the congregation from the church before the confrontation...[107]

According to Gervase, he invaded the claustral buildings, made the prior flee and expelled the monks, destroying part of the structure. More important, he broke into the cupboards and burned certain charters and privileges.[108] The monk Geoffrey, who became prior in 1215/6, and was presumably present, described the incident much more graphically:

> ...in the aforesaid ejection, so sudden and unexpected, all the muniments the monks had were utterly destroyed, apart from the confirmation of Walter and the other Bishops of Coventry which were kept by their adversaries [sc. the canons of Lichfield] and are still retained by them...[109]

For a time a secular chapter was set up:[110] opinions were mixed on the success of the short-lived community[111] and the monks must have managed

104 Bishop Hugh to King Richard: '"Domine rex, si vultis mihi credere, infra duos menses in nulla sede episcopali in regno vestro erit aliquis monachus, quia iustum non est" et adiecit, "monachi ad diabolos"' (Gervase i, 470; *Epistolae Cantuariensis*, ed. W. Stubbs, Rolls Series (London, 1865), no. 329).

105 'Denique inter priorem et monachos discordias serens vel nutriens... occasione captata, manu armata expulit universos': William of Newburgh in *Chronicles of the Reigns of Stephen, Henry II and Richard*, ed. R. Howlett, Rolls Series (London, 1884-9) ii, 394.

106 Gervase i, 461.

107 'Hugo... querelam deposuit super monachis suis de Covintre, quod manus in eum violentas iniecerant, et sanguinem suum suderant coram altari. Maximam etiam partem congregationis ante querelam exputerat de ecclesia, etc...': *The Chronicle of Richard of Devizes of the time of King Richard the First*, ed. and transl. J. T. Appelby (Nelson's Medieval Texts, 1963), 387.

108 'Omnia etiam ecclesie almaria confregit cartas et privilegia quedam igne concremavit...': Gervase i, 461.

109 'In qua eiectione, tam repentina et inopinata, omnia deperdita erant instrumenta ecclesie Coventrensis, super confirmatione W. et aliorum episcoporum Coventre in manus adversariorum suorum, et sic successoribus adhunc retenta...': BL ms. Cotton Ch. xiii, 26, printed in *Mon. Angl.* viii, 1242, VI.

110 Gervase i, 489.

111 Cf. *Giraldi Cambrensis Opera* IV, ed. J. S. Brewer, Rolls Series (London, 1861)

to retain some form of corporate existence, for in the autumn of 1194 Prior Moses sued in the royal court for novel disseisin.[112] In January 1197 the monks were restored. Bishop Hugh was by this time lying terminally ill in Normandy, ironically repentant and clad in the habit of Bec.[113] He died finally on Good Friday 1198, in the words of the admittedly slightly biased Winchester annalist, after 'a long illness and unbearable suffering followed by a well-deserved death'.[114]

Bishop Geoffrey Muschamp, the last of the Anglo-Norman bishops, was like the majority of his predecessors in that he owed his promotion to royal favour. Within less than three months of Bishop Hugh's death, on 21 June 1198, he was being consecrated at Canterbury by Archbishop Hubert.[115] This was undoubtedly due to King Richard's favour, but the reason for this was more a reward for his turncoat behaviour towards his original patron, Geoffrey Plantagenet, the king's half-brother and archbishop of York, than his service to the king. According to Roger de Howden, when in 1194 Archbishop Geoffrey made his peace with the king for the sum of two thousand marks, he confessed that in 1189, at the death of Henry II, and while still royal Chancellor, he had fraudulently affixed the Great Seal to documents causing the appointment of Geoffrey as archdeacon of Cleveland and two others to canonries of York.[116] By September 1194 Geoffrey the archdeacon had fallen out with his erstwhile patron, for he was one of the delegation which went to Rome to seek papal letters nullifying the archbishop's letters of excommunication and sequestration of the fruits of benefices.[117] The three falsely appointed office holders were sentenced to deprivation but the Pipe Rolls show they were allowed to buy back their offices.[118] Moreover, Howden records the story of how Geoffrey Muschamp

---

112 [*Speculum Ecclesie*], 64-8 and *William of Newburgh* ii, 393ff.
Rotuli Curiae regis..., ed. F. Palgrave, 2 vols. Record Commission (London, 1835) i, 3, 66-7. It is true, however, that Moses is there styled 'Moses qui fuit prior Conventr'...'

113 *Rogeri de Wendover liber qui dicitur flores historiarum...*, ed. H. G. Howlett, 3 vols, Rolls Series (London, 1886-9) i, 274; Gervase i, 552; Giraldus iv, 70-1.

114 '...post diutinam languorem et poenam intolerabilem miseram vitam merita morte terminavit': *Annales monastici*, ed. H. R. Luard, 5 vols, Rolls Series (London, 1864-9) ii, 67.

115 *Chronica Rogeri de Houedene*, ed. W. Stubbs, 4 vols, Rolls Series (London, 1868-71) iv, 45; Diceto ii, 162-3.

116 Houeden iii, 274.

117 *Ibid.* iii, 272. The other members of the delegation were Hamo the dean of York, and master William Testard, archdeacon of Nottingham. They arrived back from Rome *paulo ante festum sancti Michaelis* and published their letters on 29 September.

118 *The Great Roll of the Pipe for the Seventh Year of King Richard the First, Michaelmas 1195 (Pipe Roll 41)*, ed. D. M. Stenton (Pipe Roll Society, 1929), 91.

received the chrism and Holy Oil at Southwell, from the bishop of Whithorn, the only remaining bishop of the province, and threw it into a dungheap,[119] thus showing that he continued in office, even if it says nothing for his piety. In assessing him as Bishop of Coventry I have no quarrel yet with the judgement of the VCH given at the start of this paper;[120] his *acta* give signs of the sort of administrative work to be expected of a bishop c.1200. I have no wish to comment further at this stage, except perhaps to note that the practice of dating *acta*, either by pontifical or incarnation year, does not seem to have taken root in this diocese in his time.[121]

I will close this unavoidably provisional statement at this point. It is to be hoped that it is clear now that the Anglo-Norman bishops of this see are not quite as uninteresting as was once thought, even if I have painted a picture of almost unremitting oppression of the monks of Coventry.

[119] Houeden iii, 286.
[120] Supra, note 2.
[121] Cf. *EEA* 8 etc.

The Priory in the Later Middle Ages
R. N. SWANSON

The dissolution of St Mary's priory in 1539 consigned to oblivion an institution which had been central to Coventry's existence for almost five hundred years. Many may bemoan the architectural loss and the destruction of a rich liturgical and spiritual tradition; for historians the dissolution had even more disastrous repercussions. More than the buildings and monks disappeared; so did the archives. Given those losses, and the priory's anomalous status, it is hardly surprising that Coventry is usually ignored in discussions of the medieval monastic cathedrals. A brief exculpation in a footnote, an apologetic mention in a sentence, is enough to acknowledge its existence before moving on to those cathedrals which provide more abundant evidence.[1]

What was actually lost in 1539? The blunt answer is that no-one knows; yet much must once have existed. It is reasonable to presume a range of records very like those available for the other pre-Reformation Benedictine monastic cathedrals of Norwich, Durham, Ely, Worcester, Canterbury, Winchester, and Rochester. From these a quite daunting amount of material survives, still relatively under-studied.

The Coventry material has been lost almost entirely, some of it only relatively recently.[2] The records were presumably widely dispersed when the priory was dissolved, and their immediate fate was not recorded (although some passed to the families which acquired the properties). The surviving scraps are an insufficient basis on which to construct the history of the house. These gleanings do dissolve some of the shadows, but they remain a meagre record of a major house.

What, then, is to be made of Coventry priory in the later middle ages? A survey of some three centuries in a brief space could only be cursory at the best of times: in the absence of an extensive documentary base that becomes unavoidable. However, a number of specific issues can be addressed to shed some light on the priory and the contexts in which it operated, even if not to the extent that might be desired.

The most tangible of those contexts was the immediate one of Coventry itself. The priory's part in Coventry's economic and constitutional

---

1   B. Dobson, 'The English Monastic Cathedrals in the Fifteenth Century', *Transactions of the Royal Historical Society* 6th ser. 1 (1991), 154; J. Greatrex, 'The English Monastic Cathedrals and the Rule of St Benedict', *Regulae Benedicti Studia* 3-4 (1975), 89 note 1.

2   Two Cartularies and the Pittancers' Rolls cited in W. Dugdale, *Monasticon Anglicanum*, 6 vols. in 8 (London, 1849), iii, 185, have been lost since that edition was prepared.

development was obviously great, and requires further exploration. But the priory's urban context will not be examined here; nor will its role in national secular life and politics. The emphasis will be on other features of the priory's existence: its internal monastic organisation; its status as a cathedral and the resulting relationship with the diocese and diocesan authorities; and the wider ecclesiastical context, how Coventry fitted into the totality of the English church. It may not be possible to put much flesh on a skeleton which is itself vestigial, but there is enough to allow a partial appreciation of an institution which had an important role in the medieval Midlands.

***

Although it was a major house, the community at Coventry was not large. Supposedly established with a complement of twenty-four monks in 1043,[3] in 1256 there is mention of the prior and thirty monks.[4] The fourteenth-century total may have fluctuated, with reports of many deaths from plague in the 1360s;[5] but the fifteenth century offers a fairly static picture. A document of 1409 named twenty-six monks,[6] a figure seemingly replicated in 1478.[7] There may have been a slight drop later, with only seventeen names appearing on a certificate in 1496;[8] but the position recovered within a generation. In 1518 twenty-three monks were named.[9] That figure was said to be 'complete', which suggests a formal limit on the numbers the house would accept. Only nineteen were listed in 1521, to whom should be added four who were absent studying. The final report of Blythe's visitations, in 1524, lists twenty-one.[10] The number of novices in 1518 – six – suggests that the house and the monastic way of life had not lost their appeal. That three or four were at university in 1521 again suggests no major loss of momentum.

Regardless of numbers, the house had to be organised. Coventry, like most major monasteries, was a significant economic machine. In 1535 the

---

3   W. Page, ed., *Victoria County History* (hereafter *VCH*), *Warwickshire* II (London, 1908), 52.

4   H. R. Luard, ed., *Annales Monastici* I (London, Rolls Series, 1864), 379.

5   *Calendar of Entries in the Papal Registers relating to Great Britain and Ireland: Papal Letters* (vols. I-XV, London, 1893-1955; vols. XV-, Dublin, 1978- in progress) (hereafter '*CPL*') IV, 39, 47.

6   LJRO, B/A/1/7, ff. 207r.-208r. (also in LJRO, D30/I, f. 80v.).

7   J. C. Russell, 'The Clerical Population of Medieval England', *Traditio* 2 (1944), p. 190 n.m. No source is given for the figure, but the date coincides with the pittancers' rolls cited by Dugdale (above, note 2).

8   C. Harper-Bill, ed., *The Register of John Morton, Archbishop of Canterbury, 1486-1500*, II, Canterbury and York Society (hereafter 'CYS') 78 (1991), no. 374.

9   P. Heath, ed., *Bishop Geoffrey Blythe's Visitations, c.1515-1525*, Collections for a History of Staffordshire (Publications of the William Salt Archaeological Society) (hereafter 'SHC'), 4th ser., 7 (1973), 15-17.

10 Heath, *Blythe's Visitations*, 85-7, 115-17.

total income was put at over £700, derived from a combination of pensions, rectorial incomes, lands urban and rural, and other resources. The house had to make payments in turn, and ensure its own continuation and the fulfilment of its spiritual and other obligations. To ensure that, the system of obedientiaries functioned here as elsewhere. Tasks were separated off, with their own revenues. The *Valor Ecclesiasticus* records those who had their own endowments following division of the monastic revenues, with the prior, chamberlain, treasurer, steward, and kitchener enjoying independent incomes. They were not the full total of obedientiaries. The visitation material and the chapter list of 1409 identify others – pittancer, infirmarer, precentor, aqueductor, succentor, refectorer, cellarer, almoner, hospitaller, master of novices, subsacrist, penitentiary, keeper of St Mary's chapel, sacrist. Things were almost at the stage where there was one office per monk (and if James Pope had not combined the offices of sub-prior, sacrist, pittancer, and infirmarer in 1518, probably would have been).[11] Presumably these, too, had their own incomes and accounts to maintain; but their income may have been derived from charges on other obedientiaries rather than independent endowment, and therefore would be unrecorded in the *Valor*.

Such divisions could cause administrative problems. In 1518 the prior claimed to have inherited a debt of £800 from his precursor, and in 1521 to have had to spend £50 because of the irresponsibility of some of the obedientiaries. Administrative problems might also arise from other sources. Although the bishop was also technically the abbot, just what were his powers in the house? This issue also confronted other monastic cathedrals, producing a variety of solutions. At Worcester the bishop appointed the sacrist, potentially an agent within amongst the monks; whilst at Carlisle the compromise worked out between the monks and Bishop Silvester de Everdon allowed the bishop the appointment of the sub-prior and cellarer.[12] Whether anything similar happened at Coventry (beyond episcopal approval of the prior's appointment, which may have been merely technical) is not known. If it did, it may have had a de-stabilising effect within the house.

The visitation evidence indicates, however, that internal order was maintained, with no sign of major internal discord. The report of 1518 is so bland as to be complimentary: there is no sign of the abuses which are almost instinctively associated with late-medieval monasticism.[13] However, in 1521 there are signs of minor abuses, and of some discord within the community.

---

11 For Pope, Heath, *Blythe's Visitations*, 16.
12 J. Greatrex, *Monastic or Episcopal Obedience: the Problem of the Sacrists of Worcester*, Worcestershire Historical Society, Occasional Publications, 3 (1980); H. Summerson, 'The King's Clericulus: the Life and Career of Silvester de Everdon, Bishop of Carlisle, 1247-1254', *Northern History* 28 (1992), 81. See also D. Knowles, *The Monastic Order in England* (Cambridge, 1966), 626-7.
13 Heath, *Blythe's Visitations*, 15-17.

The prior may have been under the influence of laymen, and possibly not telling the truth about grants of livery and salaries. Nevertheless, abuse was not significant, and partly due to external influences and the presence of outsiders within the house. One monk actually complained that there were too many scholars, whom the house could not afford. Maybe the impact of Coventry city's contemporary economic collapse was also taking its toll: the pittancer's office was said to have lost money because of the vacancy of tenements.[14] The visitation report for 1524 again shows little to suggest deep decay. However, the novices were being instructed by a secular chaplain, and there are hints that not all was well. Thomas Coventre certainly seems to have been a thorn. He had assumed the office of notary public without the prior's authorisation, and a state of enmity had arisen between them so intense that Coventre was reported as having said 'I pray God I may say *De profundis* for his [the prior's] soul before I depart'.[15]

Thomas Coventre's behaviour is a reminder that these men were individuals, not a mindless collectivity. The extant material reinforces this. Individual monks appear in scattered sources receiving a variety of minor licences and dispensations. Appointments as penitentiaries and licences to hear confessions may integrate them within the diocesan structure.[16] Dispensations to become priests below the canonical age for promotion may reflect a shortage of priests within the house.[17] Some of the monks were dispensed to acquire benefices, possibly not always with authorisation from the prior.[18] Less disruptively, others were licensed to choose their own confessor, while prior Richard Crosby was granted a portable altar.[19]

The information about the house's internal arrangements and spiritual activities is relatively meagre, except for the notable jurisdictional clashes with the burgesses of Coventry.[20] But the internal system provides one of the main frameworks for the priory's existence. A second framework is provided by the diocese, and by the priory's cathedral status.

***

14   Heath, *Blythe's Visitations*, 85-7.
15   Heath, *Blythe's Visitations*, 115-17.
16   LJRO, B/A/1/3, f. 115v.; B/A/1/6, f. 135r.; B/A/1/7, ff. 142r., 153r., 195r., 201v.; B/A/1/13, f. 132r.
17   *CPL* IV, 39, 47; *CPL* XII, 670.
18   *CPL* II, 371; *CPL* V, 190; *CPL* XV, 324, 413, 451; *CPL* XVI, no. 541; W. A. Pantin, ed., *Canterbury College, Oxford* III, Oxford Historical Society, n.s. 8 (1950), 116.
19   *CPL* V, 218; *CPL* VI, 353, 382.
20   A. and E. Gooder, 'Coventry Before 1355: Unity or Division? The Importance of the Earl's Half', *Midland History* 6 (1981), 1-38. See also J. Röhrkasten, 'Conflict in a Monastic Borough: Coventry in the Reign of Edward II', *Midland History* 18 (1993), 1-18.

The constitutional oddity of the bicephalous – at times possibly tricephalous – bishopric of Coventry and Lichfield is perfectly illustrated by the naming of the parties representing the diocese in a charter of 1400. Here John Burghill, bishop of Chester [sic], the dean and chapter of Lichfield, and the prior and convent of Coventry, all on the one part, act to resolve a boundary dispute at Sallowe (Derbyshire) caused by a change in the course of the river Trent.[21] The bishop had to act with his two cathedrals, and that Coventry priory was one of them obviously affected the house. The role of the priory qua cathedral has to be distinguished from its position as a major monastic house, which accidentally was the *locus* of an episcopal *cathedra*. There is a difference, exemplified in the activities of many of the other major Benedictine houses throughout the country.

The priory's status within the diocese was constantly evolving as constitutional relationships were defined and established. In this process, the thirteenth century seems to have been most important and the main period of conflict with the bishop, largely as the aftermath of the uncertainties of the twelfth. Conflict seems to have arisen chiefly from attempts to differentiate between the various rights of those seeking to divide the spoils of the pre-Conquest bishopric: the bishop and the two cathedral bodies. As in other monastic cathedrals, the twelfth century saw the almost-final stages of the division of the endowment between the house and its nominal abbot.[22] Nevertheless, some matters remained undecided.

The legacy was not simply uncertainty about electoral procedures for the episcopate; there was also heated conflict over possessions. The primary focus of dispute was the church of St Michael at Coventry itself, where the bishop claimed the patronage against the priory, while Lichfield's canons claimed revenues. The dispute originated in the twelfth century, and rumbled through the early thirteenth. Under Bishop Alexander de Stavensby the dispute had so soured relations that in 1238 it was agreed to deposit a crucial charter at Combe abbey, to be 'signed out' by bishop or priory when needed. A resolution by Bishop Hugh de Pateshull broke down: eventually the matter was settled in 1248, after arbitration. The priory was recognised as the patron (confirmed by a fine in the royal courts), but was obliged to offer compensation to the bishop and the secular chapter.[23]

21 Oxford, Bodleian Library (hereafter 'Bod'), MS Ashm. 1527, f.78r.-v.

22 Knowles, *Monastic Order*, 625-6. For Durham, F. Barlow, *Durham Jurisdictional Peculiars* (Cambridge, 1950), 4-10; for Carlisle, Summerson, 'The King's Clericulus', 80-1.

23 For the original charter (of earl Ranulf III, dated 1192), see P. R. Coss, ed., *The Early Records of Medieval Coventry*, Records of Social and Economic History n.s. 11 (London, 1986), 20-1; G. Barraclough, *The Charters of the Anglo-Norman Earls of Chester, c.1071-1237*, Record Society of Lancashire and Cheshire 126 (1988), no. 219. For the dispute see W. B. Stephens, ed., *VCH, Warwickshire* VIII (London,

The priory necessarily acted in a variety of capacities within the diocesan structure. Occasionally a prior acted as vicar general for an absent bishop, but if this was jointly with a secular cleric it is difficult to tell who was actually organising the administration.[24] The priory's most immediate contact with diocesan business came at the time of episcopal elections, when its role as co-chapter with Lichfield came to the fore.

The relative importance of the two chapters began to emerge as contentious in the late twelfth century. Bishop Hugh de Nonant's attempt to transform the monastery into a secular college – which presumably would have been the sole electoral body, supplanting Lichfield as well as the priory – had come to naught, but showed the anomalies of diocesan bishops who were only nominally abbots of their electing houses. Lichfield's slow emergence as a formally capitular body also created tensions: when the see was still officially that 'of Coventry', where did these upstarts fit in? Yet the Lichfield canons had established their claims, the evolution of a *modus vivendi* being a relatively slow process.[25]

After initial conflict, the relationship between the priory and the secular cathedral over elections seems to have mellowed. Conflict was at its fiercest in the convent's attempt to elect their prior Geoffrey as successor to William de Cornhill in 1222, ignoring any claims of the canons of Lichfield to participate in the election. This was apparently backed up by a bull of Honorius III, presumably recently obtained. However, the Lichfield canons would have none of this. In a flurry of appeals to the papacy, archbishop Stephen Langton annulled the Coventry election, and in the end Alexander Stavensby emerged as bishop.[26]

1969), 346; M. W. Lambert, 'The History of the Benedictine Priory of St Mary, Coventry', in B. Hobley, 'Excavations at the Cathedral and Benedictine Priory of St Mary, Coventry', *Transactions of the Birmingham and Warwickshire Archaeological Society* 84 (1967-70), 59-60; also H. E. Savage, ed., *The Great Register of Lichfield Cathedral, known as Magnum Registrum Album*, SHC 1924 (Kendal, 1926), nos. 238-400 (the agreement to deposit the charter is no. 500).

[24] R. A. Wilson, ed., *The Registers or Act Books of the Bishops of Coventry and Lichfield, Book 4, being the Register of the Guardians of the Spiritualities during the Vacancy of the See, and the First Register of Bishop Robert de Stretton, 1358-1385: an Abstract of the Contents*, SHC, n.s. 10/II (1907), 70-1, 105-6; R. A. Wilson, ed., *The Registers or Act Books of the Bishops of Coventry and Lichfield, Book 5, being the Second Register of Bishop Robert de Stretton, A.D. 1360-1385: an Abstract of the Contents*, SHC, n.s. 8 (1905), 3-5.

[25] The quarrels are summarised in *VCH, Warwickshire* II, 54; Lambert, 'History', 60, 62.

[26] Summarised in Savage, *Magnum Registrum Album*, no. 464; see also K. Major, ed., *Acta Stephani Langton, Cantuariensis Archiepiscopi, A.D. 1207-1228*, CYS 50 (1950), nos. 61, 64.

Presumably the Lichfield canons feared that if the Coventry monks did monopolise the election, they would eventually make Coventry the sole cathedral. The outcome of the papal appeals seems not to be recorded, and disputes continued in the later thirteenth century; but in the long run the two bodies did have to compromise and co-operate. In 1248 it was agreed that they should be considered of equal weight in an election, even if there was a disparity of numbers, and this was confirmed in 1255.[27] Subsequent evidence shows the monks and the canons negotiating on procedural arrangements after a bishop's death, seeking and receiving permission to elect from the crown during a vacancy, and making arrangements for the election, which was sometimes actually held at the priory.[28] Admittedly election was rare in the later middle ages, and especially in the thirteenth century was often subjected to external pressures, notably from the king.[29] After 1300 most bishops were appointed by papal provision (which realistically usually meant government decision). There were still some real elections, as in 1386 and the choice of Walter Skirlaw.[30] The monks, however, seemingly accepted that any hope of elevating one of their own number was forlorn. The last such attempt was made in 1321, with the candidacy of prior Henry de Leycester. This, as in 1222, accompanied a dispute between the two bodies on electoral arrangements, with the monks acting unilaterally when agreement on the numbers to participate in the election could not be reached; as in 1222 it came to nothing, with Roger Northburgh gaining the see by papal provision.[31] However, Northburgh's appointment did not immediately end the dispute. The Lichfield canons appealed to Rome, initiating a lengthy but obscure and possibly inconclusive process. Appointments of proctors to deal with the appeal against Leycester's election are entered in the chapter acts into the 1330s; doubtless the Coventry monks had parallel representation – and expenses – at the curia.[32]

With regard to direct relationships with the bishops, there is little to comment on. Personal links are rarely documented, although there is a hint that the prior and Bishop Walter Langton were co-conspirators in extortions at the turn of the thirteenth and fourteenth centuries.[33] The existence of the Lichfield chapter diminished the priory's overall role within the diocesan

27 Savage, *Magnum Registrum Album*, nos. 240, 24, 589.
28 Luard, *Annales Monastici* I, pp. 377-9; LJRO, D30/I, ff. 3v., 4v.-5r., 86v.
29 M. Howell, *Regalian Right in Medieval England* (London, 1962), 94.
30 Edmund Stafford was also put forward as a candidate: LJRO, D30/I, f. 5r. [not noted in J. Le Neve (ed. B. Jones), *Fasti Ecclesiae Anglicanae, 1300-1541*, X: *Coventry and Lichfield Diocese* (London, 1964) (hereafter 'Le Neve'), p. 2].
31 Le Neve, p. 1; Bod, MS Ashm. 794, f. 1v.
32 Bod, MS Ashm. 794, ff. 1v., 5v., 16r.-17r., 29r.-30v., 47r.
33 A. Beardwood, ed., *Records of the Trial of Walter Langton, Bishop of Coventry and Lichfield, 1307-12*, Camden society 4th ser., 6 (1969), 290-1.

structure. The bishops evidently drew most of their administrative staff from the secular clergy who could be satisfied with posts in the secular cathedral; when resident within the diocese, the bishops seem mainly to have been around Lichfield – certainly within Staffordshire rather than Warwickshire – and treated Lichfield as their prime cathedral. The appearances may be deceptive, the result of an imbalance in the source material; but this seems unlikely. The priory's diocesan role cannot have equalled that of other monastic cathedrals, in dioceses where the monastery was the sole cathedral church.

The day to day administrative relationship thus seems rather dry, the priory being almost marginalised within the diocesan structure. But the bishops did not totally ignore their second cathedral, or its inhabitants; although as they were rarely monks, and their main residences were elsewhere, direct contact was limited except at visitations (and even those might be conducted by proxy). As a Benedictine house, the priory was, like other such houses, subject to the bishop's visitatorial jurisdiction. Visitations did occur, throughout the period, although there is little detailed evidence before the pontificate of Geoffrey Blythe. In the thirteenth century, the process of visitation and its costs obviously caused some discord. A compromise of 1283 gave the bishop the option of receiving 10 marks for procurations, or taking procurations in kind.[34] This was upheld in later visitations: at the *sede vacante* visitation of 1414, for instance, procurations were taken in kind,[35] but cash payments appear in other accounts.[36]

The truth is that the bishops had little need for the second cathedral. As a community of monks, the priory perhaps needed the bishop more than the bishop needed it. With the failure of Hugh de Nonant's scheme to replace the priory by a secular college, and the bishops' increasing identification with Lichfield, the priory's diocesan role became almost peripheral. But the monks still needed a bishop, if only to ordain them. The palace at Coventry was apparently rarely used, although its existence was a constant reminder of the priory's status. Even if not the base for a diocesan bishop, the priory could still provide lodgings for a suffragan, like the *camera* occupied by the bishop of Killaloe in the 1430s.[37]

Where the priory had more impact was in its explicitly constitutional claim to be a co-defender of the rights of the see. The bishop and the two cathedral chapters were technically one body, despite de facto separation of their resources, and all three might unite as one party in a charter affecting

34 Savage, *Magnum Registrum Album*, no. 643.
35 E. F. Jacob, ed., *The Register of Henry Chichele, Archbishop of Canterbury, 1414-43*, CYS 42, 45-7 (1938-47), iii, 299.
36 Harper-Bill, *Reg. Morton* ii, nos. 40a, 429a.
37 London, British Library (hereafter BL), MS Harley 1279, ff. 123v.-124v.

the property rights of the see.[38] This also meant that the priory (with the secular chapter of Lichfield) had to approve all episcopal actions which affected the see's resources, from leases to appropriations of benefices to appointments of minor episcopal officers. This is the type of record which would be entered in any register of the common seal (such as the one that survives for Winchester).[39]

Evidence of such actions by the priory is scattered widely in the sources, confirming that this was a regular aspect of its diocesan role.[40] However, it is impossible to say whether that assent was positive, or merely rubber-stamping. Since only approval had to be recorded, there is naturally no evidence that the priory (or, for that matter, the chapter of Lichfield) ever refused to endorse an episcopal act which was thereby negated; although there was at least one action which secured papal ratification notwithstanding that approval from the two chapters had not been obtained.[41] This co-responsibility for the oversight of the see's properties is also recognised by a commission of archbishop Walter Reynolds of Canterbury which mandated the prior of Coventry to act with two canons of Lichfield to investigate charges of dilapidations brought by Bishop Northburgh against his predecessor, Walter Langton.[42]

The need for approbation and oversight of episcopal acts by the two cathedral bodies also sometimes served as a protective screen for the bishop. In 1369, during a dispute with Edward III, Bishop Stretton protested that he could not alienate an advowson without the approval of both capitular bodies.[43]

Institutionally, the priory's cathedral status was recognised by its being the site for the bi-annual diocesan synods at Easter and Michaelmas. Here, as elsewhere, evidence for synodal activity is extremely sparse. While there were synods in the twelfth and thirteenth centuries, their location is rarely stated. Generally they may be presumed to have occurred at the cathedral which, before 1200, would be explicitly Coventry; but other places are also

---

38 Above, note 21.

39 J. Greatrex, ed., *The Register of the Common Seal of the Priory of St. Swithun, Winchester, 1345-1497*, Hampshire Record Series 2 (1978).

40 For such confirmations, see e.g. R. R. Darlington, ed., *The Cartulary of Darley Abbey*, 2 vols. (Kendal, 1945), 613, 630-4; LJRO, B/A/1/1, ff. 11v., 14v.; Birmingham Reference Library, 435125, mm. 2d., 3r. Unless the copying of confirmations was selective, Coventry may have been the sole confirming body until well into the thirteenth century, which again suggests its gradual eclipse by Lichfield.

41 *CPL* XI, 377-8.

42 LJRO, B/A/1/3, f. 105v.

43 Wilson, *Reg. Stretton, Book 4*, 129-30.

named.[44] Fifteenth-century evidence does show synods being held at Coventry, and presumably in the cathedral.[45] In addition to this diocesan role, the cathedral also seems to have been a focus for the archdeaconry. Archidiaconal synods are recorded as occurring there in October in 1408 and 1413, in terms which suggest that was the regular practice.[46] Another gathering may have been held earlier in the year as well, to match the pattern for diocesan assemblies.

Other priory actions had only minor impact on the diocese, although they deserve to be noted. For any religious house, a major concern would have been the exercise of patronage to the benefices of which it held the advowson, and particularly those benefices appropriated to it. Here Coventry was exceptional in holding the patronage of two prebends – Ufton Decani and Ufton Cantoris – within the secular body at Lichfield, an arrangement which is apparently unique.[47] The significance of the prebendal appointments should not be overstated: these were by no means wealthy offices. The *Valor Ecclesiasticus* of 1535 valued them at a mere 53s. 4d. each,[48] so whatever attractions they held were not immediately financial.

Coventry priory's integration into the patronage relationships of the late medieval church was not limited to the two Lichfield prebends. Several other benefices in the diocese (and others) were also in its gift. Here the disappearance of the priory's archives is a real loss, for they would probably have elucidated much of the mechanics whereby individuals secured particular appointments. Even in their absence, there is no reason to suppose that Coventry evaded the pressures of third parties which appear at Durham and other religious houses, as laity and prelates sought to persuade the priory to give its patronage to their nominees, in return for favours, or at least in return for not incurring hostility.[49] Unfortunately, the nature and extent of such relationships here cannot even be surmised.

---

[44] C. R. Cheney, *English Synodalia of the Thirteenth Century* (rev. ed., Oxford, 1968), 18-20.

[45] Stafford, Staffordshire County Record Office, B1734/3/2/4, m. 11d.; LJRO, B/A/21/123984, mm. 16d.-17r.; London, Public Record Office, SC6/Henry VII/1846, m. 19r.; SC6/Henry VIII/7154, m. 9r.; SC6/Henry VIII/7155, m. 12d.

[46] LJRO, B/A/1/7, ff. 208v., 209r.

[47] Le Neve, 61-4, consistently refers to the appointments as collations, which they were not.

[48] *Valor Ecclesiasticus* iii (London, 1817), 131.

[49] R. N. Swanson, *Church and Society in Late Medieval England* (Oxford, 1989), 69; R. Donaldson, 'Sponsors, Patrons, and Presentations to Benefices – Particularly Those in the Gift of the Priors of Durham – During the Later Middle Ages', *Archaeologia Aeliana* 4th ser., 38 (1960), 169-77; see also E. M. Halcrow, 'The Social Position and Influence of the Priors of Durham, as Illustrated by their Correspondence', *Archaeologia Aeliana* 4th ser., 33 (1955), 81-6.

The evidence is clearer for the depredations on the priory's patronage made by more institutionalised alienations. The crown was obviously one such actor, because of the rights acquired during the vacancy of the priory; but the priory's patronage was also liable to attack from within the ecclesiastical structure. This essentially involved action by the papacy. From the fourteenth century, papal reservations and provisions cut into the patronage exercised by ecclesiastical bodies, and Coventry was no exception. Some specific provisions and reservations are noted,[50] and there may well have been further claims by the process of *forma pauperum* provisions, which were issued in their thousands in the fourteenth century but with no central record at Rome. As these did not involve episcopal institution, they are quite elusive.[51]

Further invasions might result from other papal action. In 1345 Bishop Northburgh received papal licence to collate to a benefice in the priory's gift in order to augment his own meagre patronage.[52] Papal envoys might also exercise rights of provision.[53]

The priory's integration into diocesan patronal arrangements had its own consequences. While the monks may have been the nominal patrons, they were presumably subject to the same pressures as other ecclesiastical patrons. These led to the alienation of rights of next presentation, although either the Coventry livings were of little relative importance, or the monks withstood such importuning, as there is little sign of such grants before the threat of dissolution loomed. Nevertheless, the few grants which appear do complicate matters. As the priory presented to the two Ufton prebends, the composition of the chapter of Lichfield could be affected, and was. In 1434 the presentation to Ufton Decani was exercised by Sir Robert Babthorp;[54] a grant of 1536 made to a vicar choral of Exeter conjointly with two laymen was

---

[50] W. E. Lunt and E. B. Graves, eds, *Accounts Rendered by Papal Collectors in England, 1317-1378*, Memoirs of the American Philosophical Society 70 (Philadelphia, 1968), 152, 200; *CPL* II, 370-1; *CPL* III, 101, 156, 300; *CPL* XII, 63-4. For petitions concerning benefices in the priory's gift, W. H. Bliss, ed., *Calendar of Entries in the Papal Registers relating to Great Britain and Ireland: Petitions to the Pope, vol. I, A.D. 1342-1419* (London, 1896), 26, 330, 368, 488 (those at 572-3 can be discounted, as the pope addressed was considered an antipope in England).

[51] C. Tihon, 'Les expectatives in forma pauperum, particulièrement au XIVème siècle', *Bulletin de l'institut historique belge de Rome* 5 (1923), esp. pp. 57-93. For discussion in another diocese, A. D. M. Barrell, 'The Effect of Papal Provisions in Yorkshire Parishes, 1342-1370', *Northern History* 28 (1992), 92-109.

[52] *CPL* III, 176.

[53] Lunt and Graves, *Accounts of Papal Collectors*, 137; Bliss, *Calendar of Papal Petitions*, 305-6.

[54] LJRO, B/A/1/9, f. 30v.

149

unspecific about which of the two prebends it affected.[55]

Other such grants pose problems. St Michael's and Holy Trinity, Coventry, were each alienated at least once. However, the case of Holy Trinity suggests that the priory retained some influence over the eventual outcome. The grant was made in 1411 to the bishop [John Burghill] and two others, but Robert Umfrey was the sole survivor when the grant was actually implemented in 1422. The presentee, Nicholas Crosby, was already prebendary of Ufton Cantoris (a benefice in the patronage of the prior and convent), and held a chantry in Coventry of which the priory was also patron.[56] His surname suggests a relationship with the prior, Richard Crosseby, so that the whole arrangement may have been in some way collusive. The grant of next presentation to St Michael's, implemented in 1441, requires less comment, but still offers food for thought. One of the two joint recipients was the prior of Stone who, coincidentally, had frequently acted as vicar general in the 1430s:[57] did Coventry priory make a habit of alienating its advowsons to the diocese's administrators for their own reasons?

Even though there were few grants of next presentation, this does not prove that Coventry was firmly in control. More elusive than grants of next presentation are alienations of the right of nomination, which would not affect the priory's formal participation in the administrative processes of institution, but would eliminate its control over the nomination, and would probably be totally invisible in the formal record in the episcopal register.

Just who the priory promoted to its benefices, and why, remain matters for further analysis, insofar as that can be provided. One case is worth mention. In 1422 Master Gregory Neuport was instituted to Copson's chantry at Coventry.[58] This was stated at the institution to be in accordance with the recently approved provincial constitution to encourage the promotion of graduates within the church.[59]

While patronage was an important area of activity, the priory also had its own jurisdictional role. As a cathedral body, it is unsurprising that the prior and convent exercised a peculiar jurisdiction, one of those fragmentations of diocesan unity which are all too easily overlooked in the structure of the late medieval church. What is surprising, however, is its small scale. Only in one parish does it appear that the convent exercised archidiaconal jurisdiction, at Priors Hardwick.[60] Although the bishop retained rights of institution, the

---

55 BL, Cotton charter v.27.
56 LJRO, B/A/1/9, ff. 7v.-8v.
57 LJRO, B/A/1/9, f. 40r.-v. For the appointments as vicar-general, *ibid.*, ff. 30r., 33r., 34v., 36v., 39r.
58 LJRO, B/A/1/9, f. 9r.
59 Jacob, *Reg. Chichele* I, pp. clii-clix, III, 72-5.
60 BL, MS Add. 32100, f. 118r.

Official of the jurisdiction carried out inductions. However, the small size of the peculiar sometimes allowed the formalities to be ignored: on several occasions the induction mandate was addressed (at least, as registered) to the archdeacon of Coventry or his Official.[61] Nevertheless, the prior and convent presumably stood on their rights, with one entry in the episcopal register noting that the issue to the archdeacon was 'badly and erroneously done', because the registers had not been checked.[62] The jurisdiction presumably also gave the prior and convent the right to hold their own courts within the parish, putting Priors Hardwick on a par with the small parochial jurisdictions found in other dioceses.[63]

While Priors Hardwick is the only parish where the priory's peculiar jurisdiction is explicit, there is evidence for other jurisdictional rights. The manor of Packwood was also a peculiar, even more obscure than Hardwick. The concession of archidiaconal jurisdiction over the *nemus* of Packwood was confirmed by Bishop Roger de Meuland;[64] but as this was not a parish, there are no institutions in the later episcopal registers, and consequently no formal statement of its jurisdictional isolation. In the *Valor Ecclesiasticus* it appears as a stipendiary curacy, although treated parochially.[65] Its post-Reformation history confirms its peculiar status, the manor having its own probate jurisdiction and in 1816 its lord being said to appoint his own Official and registrar.[66] Presumably the priory, or perhaps the prior (this being a priory manor), did likewise.

The most obvious place for the priory to have a peculiar jurisdiction would be in Coventry itself, and there are some signs that it did. Although the bishop had visitatorial rights over Coventry priory, the prior and convent were to a certain extent autonomous within the cathedral. The extent of that autonomy is rarely revealed, but does seem to have extended over the secular clergy employed within the church. In 1364 Bishop Stretton sent a mandate for an exchange of benefices to the prior, which would allow the then vicar of Hardwick to receive the chantry of Holy Trinity within the priory.[67] The format of the mandate, and of the prior's response, suggests that episcopal jurisdiction extended only over the vicarage, not the chantry: institution to that seems to have been firmly reserved to the prior. This picture seems to be

---

61 See e.g. in LJRO, B/A/1/10, ff. 22r., 26v., 29r., 31v.

62 LJRO, B/A/1/11, f. 10v.

63 R. M. Haines, *The Administration of the Diocese of Worcester in the First Half of the Fourteenth Century* (London, 1965), 17-24.

64 R. N. Swanson, 'The Rolls of Roger de Meuland, Bishop of Coventry and Lichfield, 1258-95', *Journal of the Society of Archivists* 11 (1990), 38 n. 5.

65 *Valor Ecclesiasticus* iii, 82.

66 J. S. W. Gibson, *Wills and Where to Find Them* (Chichester, 1974), 136; *Valor Ecclesiasticus* iii, 511.

67 Wilson, *Reg. Stretton, Book 4*, 33-4.

confirmed by its virtual replication in an exchange of 1397.[68] Presumably therefore the authority of the prior and convent over the clergy acting within their church paralleled that exercised by the dean and chapter at Lichfield over the vicars choral and chantry priests. Moreover, this authority was clearly restricted to the priory church: the chantry of St Clement established next to the cathedral was firmly under archidiaconal jurisdiction.[69] The jurisdictional situation is rendered even odder by the fact that the priory was not itself parochial, but fell within the bounds of Holy Trinity.[70]

Perhaps the strangest arrangements operated with regard to the church of St Michael and its dependent chapelries. Although the vicarage was within the jurisdictions of the bishop and the archdeacon of Coventry, with the former authorising institutions and the latter responsible for inductions;[71] for the lesser clerical posts within the parish the position was seemingly different. The wording of the ordination of the vicarage implies that the priory had jurisdictional and correctional rights within the chapelries and over the clergy, although evidence of its exercise is elusive – the most suggestive evidence being that there appear to be no institutions to the chantries in the episcopal registers. The format of exchanges for these chantries suggests that the jurisdictional arrangements gave the priory powers identical to those exercised within the cathedral.[72] With the chapelries the status of the priests as stipendiaries made the posts donatives anyway, so the priory could hire and fire at will. In 1399 the priory secured papal approval for the appropriation of the vicarage as well, converting the parish into a secular donative. This presumably would have further diminished the right of the bishop and archdeacon, but it did not go through.[73]

The absence of extensive documentation precludes detailed assessment of the powers exercised by the priory in these cases, although the clerical population affected was not inconsiderable.[74] If one will (of 1361) is sufficient foundation for an argument, the priory may also have exercised a probate

[68] LJRO, B/A/1/6, ff. 12v.-13r.

[69] E.g. Wilson, *Reg. Stretton, Book 4*, 55-6.

[70] *CPL* IV, 403.

[71] E.g. R. N. Swanson, ed., *The Register of John Catterick, Bishop of Coventry and Lichfield, 1415-1419*, CYS 77 (1990), no. 51.

[72] LJRO, B/A/1/12, ff. 9r., 21v.-22r.

[73] *CPL* V, 190.

[74] The 1406 poll tax on unbeneficed clergy and chantry priests listed 22 clerics under St Michael's, Coventry, with 13 at Bablake chapel, plus the chaplains of the chapelries: London, Public Record Office, E179/15/72. In 1533 there was a curate and 14 other clerics at St Michael's, and 7 at Bablake, plus the chaplains of the chapelries: BL, MS Harley 594, ff. 118r., 119r. (I owe this reference to Dr T. N. Cooper.)

jurisdiction over part of Coventry; but exactly which part is unclear.[75]

Turning to more spiritual issues, the priory's role as cathedral must have given it a claim on the alms of the diocese's inhabitants. Evidence from other cathedrals – although, admittedly, usually secular cathedrals – suggests that the fabric funds were supported by a diocese-wide fraternity which issued or sold indulgences as a means of encouraging contributions.[76] This may also have applied with some of the monastic cathedrals, although the evidence is so far inconclusive.[77] In a diocese with two cathedrals, the arrangement may have been slightly different. Lichfield certainly did have a fraternity, of St Chad, which issued indulgences and privileges, and offered participation in the masses and psalters recited by several religious houses.[78] Whether Coventry matched this is not clear. It may be significant that Coventry is not among the religious houses which offered masses for members of the St Chad fraternity at Lichfield; but that may merely reflect discord between the two rather than an independent fabric arrangement. Twice under Bishop Northburgh (1322-1358) questorial licences were registered for the priory which referred to grants by his predecessors and hinted at an annual round of the diocese.[79] Further possible corroboration is provided in a fifteenth-century bidding prayer, which ambiguously mentions Coventry between the Lichfield fraternity and the members of local parish guilds.[80]

[75] A Descriptive Calendar of Ancient Deeds in the Public Record Office V (London, 1906), A.11564.

[76] J. C. Colchester, ed., Wells Cathedral Fabric Accounts, 1390-1600 (Wells, 1983), 6, 10, 17, 22-3, 29, 36 (see also expenses at 11-12, 18-19, 24-5, 30-1, 38-9); A. M. Erskine, ed., The Accounts of the Fabric of Exeter Cathedral, 1279-1353, Devon and Cornwall Record Society, n.s. 24, 26 (1981-3), ii, p. xi. For questors for the fabric of York Minster, J. Raine, ed., The Fabric Rolls of York Minster, with an Appendix of Illustrative Documents, Surtees Society 35 (1858), 221.

[77] The references to a 'confraria' and 'briefs' in the sacrists' rolls of Worcester seem suggestive: S. G. Hamilton, ed., Compotus Rolls of the Priory of Worcester of the XIVth and XVth Centuries, Worcestershire Historical Society Publications (Oxford, 1910), p. 63 (but cf. p. xxi, which gives a different explanation of the confraternity, which I think unconvincing); J. M. Wilson, ed., Accounts of the Priory of Worcester for the Year 13-14 Henry VIII, A.D. 1521-2, Worcestershire Historical Society Publications (Oxford, 1907), p. 36. I have noted nothing similar in the printed obedientiary rolls of Winchester or Durham, and confess that the appearance under the sacrist's account is rather odd.

[78] R. N. Swanson, ed., Catholic England: Faith, Religion, and Observance before the Reformation (Manchester, 1993), 218-21; M. W. Greenslade, ed., VCH Staffordshire III (London, 1970), 150, 158.

[79] LJRO, B/A/1/3, ff. 20v., 103v.

[80] E. Calvert, 'Extracts from a Fifteenth Century MS', Transactions of the Shropshire Archaeological and Natural History Society 2nd ser., 6 (1894), 106.

Of course, the priory's prime function was devotional. Exactly how it operated as a devotional machine is nowhere recorded – there is nothing for Coventry to match the post-Dissolution memories for Durham.[81] However, there are signs of the contribution to devotion within the region. The monastery held a number of relics, among them an arm of St Augustine of Hippo.[82] It is unlikely that the arm of an ancient African bishop, even if a Father of the Church, stimulated major devotion. In the *Valor Ecclesiasticus* the only cult linked with the priory is that of St Modwen, whose chapel at Offchurch was under the priory's oversight, producing revenues of £10 per annum.[83] Within the house Marian devotion was doubtless encouraged, partly by possession of a relic of the Virgin's milk, with the chapel of St Mary being sufficiently important to have its own keepers among the monastic obedientiaries. Whether this devotion matched the urban cult of St Mary of the Tower is debatable. The priory's major attraction was the shrine of St Osburga. Devotion to her was certainly being encouraged in the early fifteenth century, with her Nativity being made a double feast within the archdeaconry of Coventry (but significantly not the diocese as a whole) in the episcopate of John Burghill. That would have stimulated pilgrimages; but there is no sign of the scale of the devotion, or of any indulgences being granted to add to its attraction.[84] On the other hand, Pope Boniface IX in 1391 had granted the priory the indulgence of the Portiuncula – one of the supreme indulgences of the medieval church – for visitors on the Feast of the Exaltation of the Holy Cross and the two following days, which presumably did stimulate offerings.[85]

***

Beyond the diocese, the house had to fit into other contexts and structures. These created further relationships with other bishops, other religious houses, with the crown, and with the papacy. Often, the separation of the individual strands is a fairly arbitrary exercise. This is well illustrated by aspects of the links with the crown, where the priory's status may have caused complications within the explicitly diocesan context. Coventry was one of the monastic houses (and the sole cathedral priory) which the crown claimed by escheat during vacancies because of its increasingly anachronistic obligations of feudal knight service.[86] The crown's appointment of keepers

---

[81] J. T. Fowler, ed., *Rites of Durham*, Surtees Society 107 (1902).

[82] *VCH, Warwickshire* II, 52.

[83] *Valor Ecclesiasticus* iii, 50.

[84] C. Phythian-Adams, *Desolation of a City: Coventry and the Urban Crisis of the Late Middle Ages* (Cambridge, 1979), 21, 171.

[85] *CPL* V, 243. For the indulgence, see *Dictionnaire de théologie catholique* XII/ii (Paris, 1935), cols. 2603-9.

[86] H. M. Chew, *The English Ecclesiastical Tenants-in-Chief and Knight Service*,

during the vacancies provided an opportunity for the monarch to gain temporary control of the priory's ecclesiastical patronage; it also meant that the appointment of the next prior became a matter of some sort of politics. How much the kings actually sought to influence the elections is unknown, although the necessary licences and approbation would have to be sought. A side-effect of that situation was that the kings gained a slightly greater influence over appointments to the cathedral chapter at Lichfield. During the vacancies of the priorate, presentations to the two Ufton canonries (if vacancies occurred) fell to the crown. This might also cause problems. In 1404 the appointment of Hugh Holbach to Ufton Cantoris by the prior was followed by a writ of prohibition *ne admittatis* because Henry IV claimed the patronage for his own candidate (even though the previous vacancy of the priory had occurred in 1399).[87]

For the house as a whole, perhaps the most immediate of these additional contexts was provided by its Benedictine links, the priory being obviously affected by the development of the order. From the initial autonomy of the foundation, the increasing concern to make the separate houses part of a greater agglomeration necessarily imposed changes. With the establishment and reinforcement of an overarching Benedictine Order in 1215 and 1336, the priory was integrated into the formalities of a structured disciplinary system, participating in the intra-order visitations and the regular chapters general.[88] Visitation has left few traces, save for acknowledgement of its occurrence (and sometimes mention of the prior as a visitor for other houses).[89] As for the chapters-general, again there is little information beyond the fact that Coventry played a part. That role, and presumably therefore the influence within the English branch of the Benedictine structure, may have been increasing as the centuries passed. The chapters of the late fifteenth and early sixteenth centuries were held fairly regularly at Coventry, and so presumably under the auspices of the house.[90]

---

[87] *especially in the Thirteenth and Fourteenth Centuries* (Oxford, 1932), 164-5.
For the succession to Ufton Cantoris, Le Neve, 61-2. The writ is cited at LJRO, B/A/1/7, f. 11v.

[88] On the constitutions, Knowles, *Monastic Order*, pp. 373-4; D. Knowles, *The Religious Orders in England* (3 vols., Cambridge, 1948-59), ii, 3-7; W. A. Pantin, ed., *Chapters of the Black Monks*, Camden Society Publications 3rd ser., 45, 48, 54 (1931-7). See also Lambert, 'History', 69-71.

[89] Pantin, *Black Monks* ii, 169, 242-3, 250-1 (general visitations within the diocese, e.g. *ibid.* ii, 9, 16, presumably covered Coventry as well); I. H. Jeayes, 'Descriptive Catalogue of the Charters and Muniments Belonging to the Marquis of Anglesey Sometime Preserved at Beaudesert but now at Plas Newydd, Isle of Anglesey', *SHC* 1937 (Kendal, 1937), no. 696.

[90] Pantin, *Black Monks* iii, 116-17, 217, 219. For the prior's attendance at chapters held outside Coventry, *ibid.* ii, 96, 137, 152-3, 183, iii, 33.

Associated with the house's size within the Benedictine system was the requirement for monks to receive a university education. The evidence of this for the Coventry monks is nothing like that available for Norwich, Durham, and perhaps other cathedral monasteries.[91] Assiduity may also have fluctuated: in 1426 it was complained that Coventry had not produced a scholar for two years.[92] The evidence of Blythe's visitations confirms that monks were being educated at university then,[93] and two 'scholars' had been named among the monks in 1409.[94] The precise mechanics are less clear. The monks might be expected to attend Gloucester College, Oxford, for which the evidence is meagre. At Canterbury College, Oxford, the fact that one of the chambers was known as Coventry chamber may confirm regular university attendance, at least initially.[95] However, the Coventry monks seem to have deserted Canterbury College by 1490, presumably being accommodated elsewhere.[96] In 1521 Thomas Leke complained of the cost of supporting the students,[97] although the *Valor Ecclesiasticus* commissioners discounted the 40s. a year claimed by the house for supporting a monk at university as a tax-deductable expense.[98]

***

In other activities, the scant evidence may not adequately reflect the priory's importance. The prior clearly had a role in the proceedings of the Canterbury provincial convocations; but that is rarely documented.[99] Overall, however, the accumulation of evidence shows the priory's continued vitality, and the reality of its integration into many areas of possible influence and activity, ecclesiastical and secular. Both poles combine in the occasional nominations to collect clerical taxes, an onerous responsibility which the house probably resented.[100] In the wider ecclesiastical sphere, the prior occasionally acted as a papal judge delegate, determining conflicts such as that between Burton

91   J. Greatrex, 'Monk Students from Norwich Cathedral Priory at Oxford and Cambridge, *c*.1300 to 1530', *English Historical Review* 106 (1991), 555-83; R. B. Dobson, *Durham Priory, 1400-1450*, Cambridge Studies in Medieval Life and Thought 3rd ser., 6 (Cambridge, 1973), 342-59.

92   Pantin, *Black Monks* ii, 172, 174.

93   Above, note 10.

94   Above, note 6.

95   W. A. Pantin, ed., *Canterbury College, Oxford* IV, Oxford Historical Society, n.s. 30 (1985), 93.

96   Pantin, *Canterbury College* iv, 95.

97   Heath, *Blythe's Visitations*, p. 86.

98   *Valor Ecclesiasticus* iii, 51.

99   For one instance of participation in convocation proceedings, Jacob, *Reg. Chichele* iii, 36-8.

100   E.g. LJRO, B/A/1/7, ff. 203r.-204v.; B/A/1/9, f. 178v.

abbey and its reluctant tithe-payers in the 1320s.[101] The appointment suggests that the papacy considered the prior suitable for such tasks; more importantly, given the processes by which judges delegate were nominated, it shows that the house was still considered important within a local context.[102]

Sometimes the positions were reversed. Coventry's interests also embroiled it in legal issues, some of which required resort to papal judges delegate. In 1286, for instance, there was a case concerning tithes at Hampton Lucy.[103] While the imbroglios between the priory and the burgesses of Coventry have gained considerable attention, they were not the sole front on which the house had to act in its own defence. The priory was among the monasteries to which the crown claimed the right to nominate a pensioner or corrodian, although this obligation was disputed. In the 1390s Richard II's nomination of a corrodian was strongly resisted: in this case the fight was apparently successful, although nominations continued later.[104]

***

In addition to all this, there was the priory's involvement in secular affairs, which cannot be investigated here. But even when confining attention to ecclesiastical matters, it is clear that the areas in which the priory acted spread widely, across Coventry, across the archdeaconry, beyond the diocese, even to Rome. The haystack within which the evidence must be sought gets larger at each level; the rewards seem to decrease accordingly. But the range of activity is striking. The archival losses mean that, for the present, any full assessment of the priory's activities in the late middle ages is elusive. However, although Coventry priory may have been consigned to oblivion, it cannot be totally ignored. This was a major medieval monastery, which impinged directly on life in the city for several hundred years. It also affected people beyond Coventry, with its integration into patronage networks, its status as the diocese's co-cathedral, its role in the Benedictine structure, and its place in the national and international structures of state and church. The surviving evidence of that activity gives a clouded picture; but that must not be allowed to diminish the priory's standing in late medieval England. When dissolution came, what was lost was more than just a monastery, it was an important constituent of religious and institutional life in the Midlands, and beyond.

---

[101] Jeayes, 'Descriptive Catalogue', nos. 427, 433, 435. For other cases, *CPL* I, 134-5; H. R. Luard, ed., *Annales Monastici* iii (London, Rolls series, 1866), 286.

[102] J. E. Sayers, *Papal Judges Delegate in the Province of Canterbury, 1198-1254* (Oxford, 1971), 109-18.

[103] BL, MS Add. 32100, ff. 90r.-113v.

[104] BL, MS Add. 32100, ff. 73r.-76v. On corrodians, see *VCH Warwickshire* II, 55-6; Lambert, 'History', 64-5, 69.

The Dissolution of St Mary's Priory, Coventry
J. J. SCARISBRICK

The profound religious changes of the sixteenth century which we call the Reformation brought to Coventry more than a fair share of uncertainty, upheaval and destruction. In the first place, the city lost the four communities of religious who had played a conspicuous part in its daily life for generations: the two friar houses – Franciscan and Carmelite – the Charterhouse and, of course, the Benedictine priory whose arrival in the city about 950 years past this volume of essays commemorates. The Benedictines formally surrendered to the royal officials on 15th January 1539 and were dispersed forthwith, and if the year 1043 relates to dedication rather than foundation, then the monks completed half a millennium of residence in the city (see Hunt, this volume). The fall of the Carmelites (Whitefriars) also brought down the chapel and shrine of Our Lady attached to it; similarly St Anne's chapel, belonging to the Carthusians, fell with their priory. In 1545 Coventry's St John the Baptist hospital, which could accommodate between 24 and 30 poor people and travellers overnight, and had a staff of five sisters, was suppressed. Two years later the attack on guilds and chantries began in earnest. Coventry boasted one of the most prestigious religious guilds, Trinity Guild, in the country. This lost its lands, its chapel (St John's Bablake) and eleven priests. St John's Bablake was eventually restored to worship in 1608 after 50 years of desolation, but another guild chapel of St Nicholas eventually disappeared, as did St George's, the chapel of the shearmen tailors by Gosford Gate and Corpus Christi Guild. All the other guild and chantry chapels were then ripped out of the two parish churches, Holy Trinity and St Michael's, and their landed endowments confiscated, as had been the lands of the monks and friars.[1]

Then, in 1552, with the final abolition of the Catholic mass and its replacement by the Protestant form of worship, the rich medieval heritage of chalices, pyxes and paxes, chasubles and copes, censers, bells and processional crosses, and all the rest of the equipment of Catholic worship belonging to those two mighty parish churches, could be seized. The smashed chalices, the jewels, silver and gold thread stripped from the vestments, the silk and satin copes and rich candlesticks would have been loaded onto carts for delivery to the royal coffers, even as altars were pulled down, statues and stained glass windows hammered, and wall-paintings whitewashed.

---

[1] For all this see M. Knight, 'Religious Life in Coventry, 1485 to 1558' (unpublished PhD thesis, University of Warwick, 1986). I am much indebted to this learned dissertation.

All this had taken place in a mere 15 years – 1538 to 1553. We must (of course) be careful not to overstate the social and other consequences of these upheavals. But the two monastic houses – Benedictine and Carthusian – had been distributing annually to the poor and needy the equivalent in today's money of several £10,000s, the Carthusians alone providing a formidable amount in bread, beer and grain at the priory gates. That hospital dedicated to St John which went down in 1545 was no mean resource, as we would say today, and must surely have been missed. True, those other two great institutions, Ford's Hospital and Bond's, survived. But for a while there was a serious threat that the latter would collapse because the head of the Bond family tried, unsuccessfully as it eventually proved, to have it suppressed in order to recover his grandfather's endowment for himself. Royal spoliation was doing this sort of thing to people. It was setting a bad example – or encouraging subjects to get in first.

A further consideration: the religious houses had been centres of consumption and employment. The shrines of Our Lady and St Osburg (in the cathedral) had presumably been attracting pilgrims and alms, and been good for innkeepers and souvenir shops. The guilds had been patrons of the arts and, with their pageants and plays, both tourist attractions and employers of craftsmen – professionals as well as humbler folk. Furthermore, all these changes came hard on the heels of a major, longer-term economic crisis in the city's history. Coventry already had enough problems by the 1530s not to need any more.

Finally, Coventry was to suffer a further and unique loss. The cathedral which those Benedictines had previously staffed was shut down and eventually largely destroyed. Like its second, Coventry's first cathedral was the victim of man-made desecration.

To understand how this came about, we must remind ourselves that ten medieval English cathedrals had been in the care of monks, rather than deans and chapters, i.e. communities of secular priests. The monastic cathedral, whose daily round of public prayer and worship was carried out by regular clergy, was an institution almost unique to England. To complicate matters further, there were two dioceses in England which, as a result of mergers, were 'double' dioceses, that is, had two cathedrals each, one staffed by monks and the other by a secular dean and chapter, but only one bishop. These were Bath and Wells and Coventry and Lichfield, each of whose bishops had a *cathedra* in two mother-churches and was nominally the abbot of his monastic cathedral community.

When Henry set about suppressing the religious orders an interesting question arose. What would happen to those cathedrals which had for centuries been served by monks, like Canterbury, Ely or Worcester? The answer eventually was this: they would be formally dissolved and their

159

buildings and lands surrendered to the crown, but then reconstituted as secular cathedrals – with their endowments considerably slimmed down by a gracious head of the Church. So, like the rest of the medieval cathedrals (such as Winchester, London or York), they would be staffed henceforth by deans and canons. At the same time, six large Benedictine abbey churches, including those of Gloucester, Peterborough and Westminster, were spared destruction and turned into the secular cathedrals of new sees, often with minimal displacement of personnel – though once again the crown failed to hand back to these new institutions all their previous endowments.[2]

But what about those especially anomalous Benedictine communities of Bath and Coventry which were twinned with secular cathedrals yet had but a single bishop? There were three possibilities. The king, as supreme head of the newly constituted Church of England, could have separated these ecclesiastical twins and reconstituted the two monastic churches as independent secular cathedrals of new sees. Or he could have simply 'secularised' them and left their bishops in the extraordinary position of having two secular cathedrals. Or he could relieve the two sees of their 'surplus' cathedrals by closing them down and seizing their buildings and endowments, which is what he did. The head of the Church and Defender of the Faith made these two cathedrals redundant.

By a series of accidents, Bath's survived and survives. Coventry's did not. So Coventry has the unenviable distinction of being the only city to have lost its medieval cathedral. And what it lost we lost: a fane as breathtaking perhaps as Norwich, Worcester or Gloucester which for centuries had echoed to the daily round of chant and public prayer, had hosted Parliament (with the result that, most unusually, the prior had acquired a seat in the Lords) and received at least five royal visits in recent decades.[3]

It is not clear exactly when, how or by whom the destruction was done. The monks were expelled on 15th January 1539. Two royal agents were in the city in the following July with the express purpose of pulling down (presumably with the aid of gunpowder) the cathedral and the Carmelite church, but stayed their hands when they heard there might be a change of government mind in response to local pleas – of which more shortly.[4] Household goods would have been sold off as soon as the monks departed and perhaps the buildings 'defaced', that is, made uninhabitable and secure against intruders by removing stairs and maybe some roofing, and blocking

2 See M. D. Knowles, *The Religious Orders in England*, iii, *The Tudor Age* (Cambridge, 1959), chap. xxxi.

3 Between 1495 and 1516 Coventry Priory had also hosted the triennial meetings of the English Benedictine chapter. So Knowles, *op. cit.*, 10. Curiously, Knowles paid little attention to the later fate of the two 'twinned' Benedictine cathedrals of Coventry and Bath.

4 *Infra*, 166.

up doorways. But otherwise they were apparently left intact. They seem to have still been standing six years later. This is the only reasonable interpretation to be put on the following fact: in July 1545 the crown, as we shall see, sold to two gentlemen the whole site of the priory, together with a watermill, stables, the hopyard, orchard and gardens, malthouse, kilnhouse, slaughterhouse and porter's lodge, and all the other outbuildings and waterworks of the former monastery; but there were reserved to the king and his heirs all the lead, bells, iron and glass in and on (*in et super*) the church, belfry, cloister, chapels and other monastic buildings, and all the stone thereof.[5] The clear implication is that all these buildings were still standing.

What had happened? Had there been a loss of nerve? Had even a Henry VIII shrunk from a blasphemy so provocative as felling a cathedral? Perhaps. And what happened next? We cannot know. But it is possible that the priory was never subjected to any swift act of demolition. Like Bath Abbey (perhaps) it may have simply been abandoned, having also first been 'defaced'. Unlike Bath's church, which was subsequently rescued by local initiative, was Coventry's left to the elements and casual looting to take their toll of a silent, derelict victim? If so, that perhaps explains why the two western towers were still intact in 1655, when the vicar of Holy Trinity refurbished them and built himself a residence nearby, and why a guesthouse was not demolished until 1820 and the bishop's palace not until the 1850s.

Whether the end came swiftly or by slow attrition, the fact remains that the Reformation cost Coventry its medieval cathedral; and this unique loss requires further scrutiny.

Alas, we cannot know much about the spiritual and material condition of the priory on the eve of its suppression. No episcopal visitation records survive and the reports of the royal agents who carried out a whirlwind visitation of religious houses in 1535 have disappeared. But since those visitors' findings were often luridly prejudiced and always have to be treated with circumspection, perhaps we have not suffered a serious loss. Thirteen monks signed the surrender and eleven were granted pensions (the prior, Thomas Camswell, receiving a generous £133 13s. 4d. a year for life – a huge douceur). We cannot be sure that every member of a community was present at the surrender or that all those present actually signed. There is a further problem – and one not peculiar to Coventry: there do not seem to be as many hands on the document as there are signatures. To put the same thing another way: some of the signatories seem to have provided more than one signature, and this cannot have been due to illiteracy.[6] Be all that as it may, if

5   Public Record Office [hereafter PRO], Patent Rolls (C66), 770, mm 12-13, summarised in J. Brewer, J. Gairdner and R. Brodie (eds), *Letters and Papers ... of Henry VIII* [hereafter *L.P.*], xx, i, 1335 (51). Unless otherwise stated, all L.P. references are to documents, not pages.

there were no more than thirteen inmates at the end, the priory had certainly shrunk badly since its heyday. Whitefriars boasted more (fourteen) and even the Franciscan house, never more than a modest establishment, had eleven.

We are told that there were only small quantities of plate and jewels to be seized for the crown at the suppression and little in the way of rich vestments, apart from fourteen copes of 'tissue' (cloth of gold or silver) and two pieces of 'old work'.[7] The priory had for some time been reported as in serious debt. But, as every mortgaged householder today knows, indebtedness is not necessarily proof of decadence or profligacy; and anyway, a major cause of the priory's difficulties was that the prior, recently appointed, owed the crown his first fruits, that is, the equivalent of the whole of his first year's income.[8] Tough royal taxation rather than mismanagement was the major problem.

The official valuation of the Church, the *Valor Ecclesiasticus* of 1535, had recorded a gross annual income of £748 for the priory, which may have been a considerable undervaluation, and anyway suggests that the community was adequately endowed. It was the largest single property-owner in the city and had lands scattered across five nearby counties. But by the standards of a St Albans or a Westminster, this was a house of no more than middling wealth. Even the typically bizarre collection of relics confirms this judgement: the head of St Osburga (a seventh-century virgin saint whose cult had never matched that of a Hilda or Etheldreda), set in a shrine of copper and gilt only; St Cecilia's foot; arms of four saints, including Justin, Jerome and Augustine; relics of Becket, St Catherine and the three kings of Cologne; a piece of Our Lord's tomb and part of the true cross.[9] A modest collection.

No doubt the priory was still an accepted part of the life and culture of the city – even if not a very highly revered one. The Benedictine community was probably 'jogging along' – like many others – in a rather uninspired way. By the later 1530s it was probably seriously demoralised and increasingly resigned to the fate that was overtaking religious communities throughout the land. As elsewhere, there was a rush of sales and leases by the monks, and

---

6   The document is in the PRO, Augmentations Office Deeds of Surrender (E322), 61. I confess to being baffled by the matter of the signatures thereto. There are two discrepancies between the names on the surrender document and those on the pension list (*L.P.*, xiv, i, 601): a Winfred Cellar on the first becomes Humfrey Colar on the second (which is no major problem for us) and a John Eccleshall appears for the first time on the second list. Either he was one of the two Johns who signed the surrender but was now giving his placename rather than patronymic, or he did not sign the surrender and should be added to the total complement at the time. I incline to the former explanation.

7   *L.P.*, xiv, i, 183.

8   *L.P.*, xiii, i, 1298; xiv, i, 183.

9   *L.P.*, xiv, i, 69.

maybe even hiding of more precious possessions. Thomas Camswell's brother Michael did particularly well during the weeks immediately before the royal agents moved in.[10] And after the failure of that great protest against the religious changes (especially the attack on the monasteries), namely, the Pilgrimage of Grace – one of whose leaders fled to Coventry to hide[11] – the chances of large-scale resistance to the royal programme were slim. Thomas Camswell was obviously a key figure in the story of the priory's demise. He had been prior a mere ten months, having been elected in March 1538. Though the monks had gone through the traditional motions of a free election, in fact he was a royal nominee – or rather, a nominee of the king's chief minister, Thomas Cromwell. We can be fairly sure that a number of monastic elections on the eve of the Dissolution were rigged by the government in order to ensure the appointment of governors who would hand over their houses without fuss. Sometimes a stubborn abbot might be forced to resign in order to clear the way for a 'voluntary' surrender to the royal agents. This happened at Evesham and St Albans, for example. Was Camswell's election another example of such manipulation? Some have assumed so. But there is a difficulty with this theory, for, though appointed thanks to Cromwell's intervention, Camswell's suit had been pressed in the first place by a third party, one Sir Francis Bryan, whose involvement in the affair is inexplicable.[12] Cromwell had simply done Bryan a favour by securing Camswell's appointment. In the event, Camswell proved compliant and handed over his house without much demur, but he does not seem to have been involved in any conspiracy.

Even so, it may not be easy to feel benevolent towards him. Before passing sentence, however, we do well to recall that by January 1539 religious houses were tumbling thick and fast across the land and that any informed head of one of the dwindling number of survivors would have had a strong, debilitating sense that English monasticism was doomed. Furthermore, Camswell would have had to face the fact that the penalty for obstinacy was death, death by hanging. That was the fate of the three Benedictine abbots of Glastonbury, Reading and Colchester, hanged at their abbey gates in 1539 because they had been stubborn. On the other hand, compliance could earn a huge pension for life. Camswell chose the latter – John London, one of the royal officials in charge of the surrender, insisting that the prior's handsome pension was not so much a reward for services rendered as an encouragement to others to follow his example.

---

10 *L.P.*, xiii, ii, 1153; xiv, i, 3; xvii, i, 550.
11 Namely, Thomas Kendall, vicar of Louth and prime mover of the rising in Lincolnshire in October 1536. Why he should have sought sanctuary in Coventry is not known.
12 *L.P.*, xiii, i, 30, 1298.

The same Dr London remarked laconically on 21st January 1539 that he had despatched the monks of the priory, the Charterhouse and Coombe Abbey 'with much ado'.[13] Would that he had told us what that 'ado' was. Had there been scuffles and noisy protest – even physical resistance by the monks? We do not know. However, we do know that there was indignation in high places at what was taking place.

A week before the priory succumbed, the mayor and aldermen of the city had written to the bishop of Coventry and Lichfield, Rowland Lee, begging him to plead with the king's council for the continuance of the cathedral.[14] The bishop complied. Four days later he had written in the strongest terms to Cromwell. That cathedral, he claimed, was his 'principal see and head church'. It should be converted into a secular cathedral like Lichfield – so that he might keep his title (*viz* bishop of Coventry and Lichfield) and the city continue to enjoy the benefit of it. Lee had apparently talked to Cromwell about all this some time previously and so went on to remind the minister of the 'loving answer and comfort' that he had received then. A bargain had evidently been struck. Cromwell had promised Lee that his cathedral would survive – or so Lee thought.[15]

For some time there had been talk that the crown intended to convert some of the larger monasteries into 'colleges', i.e. communities of secular clergy traditionally dedicated to saying mass for their founders and perhaps doing some teaching as well, but which for a zealous Protestant like Latimer, bishop of Worcester, would primarily be centres for teams of preachers. Perhaps prompted by this, shortly after the dispersal of the monks of his cathedral, Rowland Lee returned to the fray and proposed that Coventry priory be set up as a college of learned preachers.[16] He even suggested that it could also provide lodging where pensioned abbots of the neighbourhood (those of Kenilworth and Coombe, for instance) could spend their last days. Whether he meant that the church would remain a cathedral is not clear; perhaps he had given up hope on that score and was presenting this as an alternative scheme.

Meanwhile the corporation had weighed in. Seven days before the priory was suppressed, the mayor and aldermen wrote to Lee begging him to appeal to the king's council to secure the continuance of the cathedral, 'the lack and

13 *L.P.*, xiv, i, 113.
14 *Ibid*, 34.
15 *Ibid*, 57.
16 *Ibid*, 183. Hugh Latimer had had an interest (unexplained) in the Coventry election of 1538 which gained Camswell the priorship. Since he was at that time urging the case for the conversion of Great Malvern into a new-style college, it is possible that he proposed to Cromwell a similar adaptation for Coventry. See G. E. Corrie (ed.), *Sermons and Remains of Hugh Latimer*, Parker Society, 20 (1845), 386-87, 389, 410-11.

decay whereof shall be not only a great defacing of the said city but also a great hurt and inconvenience to all the inhabitants there in time of plague, the friars churches there being already suppressed'. There could be 'such alteration and use as may stand with his grace's pleasure', that is, the king could demote it to a secular college and strip many of its assets, or even reduce it to a mere parish church and seize all its endowments – but let the church be spared.[17] In July 1539 there was a further desperate appeal to Cromwell from the recorder of the city – a letter pleading that the royal officials who had returned to Coventry to oversee the 'razing and pulling down of the churches of the late priory and white friars' be bidden to halt.[18] As we have seen, this appeal was apparently successful. The building seems to have escaped complete demolition.

So there had been stout opposition, including vigorous effort by the city fathers. This is interesting, because, of course, Coventry had been a notorious centre of Lollardy, that native English anticlerical, anti-sacramental, biblical movement which was particularly hostile to monks and friars, images and pilgrimages. We might have assumed that one of the reasons why the Reformation bit so deeply in Coventry was the presence in the city of a strong anti-Catholic tradition. Recent work, however, has suggested that Coventry's Lollards were a small and dwindling sect on the eve of the Reformation and that the prevailing religious mood of the city was strongly orthodox.[19] One has only to read Thomas Bond's provisions for his hospital, for instance, with its astonishing regime of prayer and penance for the inmates, to encounter late-medieval piety at its most intense. Furthermore, there is some evidence that John Bond, son of the founder and an MP for Coventry in the Reformation Parliament, was an opponent of the attack on the English Church and English allegiance to Rome, and was associated with a dangerous group of MPs who included Sir George Throckmorton (MP for Warwickshire), members of Thomas More's circle and the brother of John Fisher.[20] In 1547 Coventry's MPs led resistance to the bill for the suppression of chantries and religious guilds, and even forced the government to retreat. The bill passed only because the opposition was bought off.[21]

On top of all this we have the corporation putting up a fight to save the cathedral. No doubt Coventry had its share of anticlericalism and

17 PRO, State Papers (SP1), 142, ff. 25-6 (*L.P.*, xiv, i, 34).
18 PRO, State Papers (SP1), 152, f. 250 (*L.P.*, xiv, i, 1350).
19 As Knight convincingly argues in the thesis cited in n. 1 above.
20 His name appears in an intriguing list of MPs drawn up in 1533 which was very probably a tally of opponents of the regime compiled by the government. See S. T. Bindoff (ed), *The History of Parliament. The House of Commons, 1509-1558* (1982), i, 10-11.
21 J. J. Scarisbrick, *The Reformation and the English People* (Oxford, 1984), 66-8 tells this story.

disaffection. We know, for instance, that one Henry Over, who had been sheriff in 1538, earned golden praise from the royal agents for the enthusiasm with which he had aided them during the suppression of the religious houses in the city, in contrast, they noted, to 'most of his neighbours'. He was 'a lively, politic man', said John London, so the latter had given him the job of guarding the suppressed houses against 'unruly poor people' bent on looting, and of despatching the plate to London for the king's use.[22] But Over, as we are told, was unusual. The picture that emerges is still one of a community conservative in its religious habits and with leading citizens ready to speak out against change.

Why, then, did the corporation not take more active steps to save the cathedral? When the recorder sent that letter to Thomas Cromwell in July 1539 about halting the demolition of the cathedral and the Carmelite church, he asked that they be spared until the city council had had time 'to wait' on Cromwell to know 'the king's pleasure for the redemption of the said two churches' and their appurtenances within the city walls. In other words, the city fathers were thinking of trying to rescue the buildings by buying them from the crown, and were possibly going to send a deputation to Cromwell to negotiate a deal. Their suit, the recorder assured Cromwell, would be 'no more to have stand and remain but only the two churches to make parish churches, without the which the city is half undone, having but two parish churches within all the city', which two churches (St Michael's and Holy Trinity) could not at one time 'contain all the people there by a great number'.[23] As far as we know, however, no such delegation was sent and no offer made. So, despite the recorder's forthright statement, Coventry did not do what the inhabitants of Tewkesbury, Pershore, Malmesbury and Romsey, for example, did. They did not put up the necessary cash.

They did not do so probably because they could not afford to. But maybe that is not the whole explanation. In 1542 the famous benefactor, Sir Thomas White – a rich London merchant – came forward with a magnificent donation of £1,000, with which the corporation bought up a large number of properties in the city that had belonged to the priory, but not the priory church and its associated buildings. These were presumably on the market. The crown had offered Bath Abbey for 500 marks (£333 13s. 4d.) and might have settled for a similar amount for Coventry.[24] Moreover, the city did purchase Whitefriars church as well as the site and remains of Greyfriars.

That they did not buy, or attempt to buy, the cathedral also was not necessarily because they did not care or were irreligious. Perhaps they still could not afford to do so, despite White's gift. They might have acquired the

---

22 *L.P.*, xiv, i, 150.
23 PRO, State Papers (SP1), 152, f. 250 (*L.P.*, xiv, i, 1350).
24 Bath surrendered on 27th January 1539 – only twelve days after Coventry priory.

building for £333, but if it was to be reconstituted as a collegiate church, let alone a secular cathedral, it would have had to be adequately endowed to support the dean and chapter, the organist and choir, and all the rest of the large staff required by such an institution. Since the crown was driving fairly tough bargains, to acquire lands and properties which could generate the necessary revenue would have required an enormous capital outlay. The alternative was to buy back the priory church and use it as simply a parish church with a much smaller staff, which is what the recorder in July 1539 said was in view. But could one justify having a third parish church on that large mound in the centre of the city – a mere stone's throw from Holy Trinity and St Michael's, both massive fanes? Here was a serious rub. When appealing to the crown for the continuance of the cathedral the corporation had been able to argue only that, with the two friary churches gone, the cathedral would be the only place where victims of the plague could be segregated for worship.[25] This was not an impressive argument.

In truth, there was no clear pastoral need for the building, despite what the recorder asserted. Had Henry offered the former Benedictine cathedral on very generous terms, the city would presumably have accepted. But if it were available only at the going market price, that was another matter. Perhaps the city fathers expected the king to act graciously and make a generous offer; if so, they were naive. No such offer was forthcoming. So instead, they acquired only Whitefriars church, which made much more pastoral sense since it was some distance from St Michael's and Holy Trinity.

The priory had owned properties all over Warwickshire (as names like Priors Marston and Priors Hardwick remind us) and four neighbouring counties, as well as being a major landlord in the city. The crown started leasing and then selling these possessions quickly. The co-operative Henry Over and Michael Camswell, the last prior's brother, were picking up leases of former properties as early as 1539.[26] From 1540 the sales began in earnest, with the manors of Wasperton and Honnington being sold in April of that year, and a manor in Leicestershire in the following month.[27] More possessions of the former priory were sold in the next years. Then in June 1545 came that massive deal which has already been mentioned. For nearly £1,000 the crown parted with some 200 properties in Coventry formerly belonging to the priory, together with monastic outbuildings and the site of the priory proper (but not the buildings thereon). It sold to two dealers acting on behalf of a certain John Hales – who also acquired the building and site of

[25] PRO, State Papers (SP1), 142, f. 25 (*L.P.*, xiv, i, 34).

[26] *L.P.*, xv, pp. 559 and 564; xvii, 556 (21); xxi, i, 1383 (89). Over also made considerable purchases via professionals acting as agents/speculators in ex-monastic properties. So Knight, *op. cit.*, 293.

[27] *L.P.*, xv, 611 (26), 733 (12).

St John's Hospital allegedly to provide for a new free grammar school.[28] Hales was a mystery man, a maverick. He and the corporation were to be locked in controversy for twenty-seven years. Suffice it to say here that, thanks to his purchase in 1545, Hales had become a considerable power in the city, rivalling the corporation, and that the story of the school was a saga in itself. In the midst of trying to hold its own with Hales, the corporation was also soon doing battle with the crown over the lands belonging to the former Trinity Guild, which had been promised as a gift in 1547 but which were not acquired (and then at a high price) until 1552. Only at Hales's death in 1572 was the school finally set up; two years later, the corporation acquired the site of the priory and its former possessions within the city walls for £400 from the heir of John Hales's deceased brother. The city fathers were at last masters of their own house.[29]

We know nothing about what happened to the former inmates of the monastery. Perhaps some of them bought capacities, that is, licences to continue as secular clergy, and acquired benefices in or around the area. Or perhaps Thomas Camswell and his brethren disappeared into retirement to enjoy substantial pensions and lived more or less happily ever after. But what did it feel like to walk out of one's past in that way and to disown so rich an inheritance? How many consciences were troubled from time to time, one wonders? And what did the mass destruction of sacred and beautiful things and the radical breach with the past do to the soul of the whole community of Coventry, lay as well as clerical? A city already deeply wounded by economic dislocation had also undergone a profound psychological and spiritual trauma.

---

28 *L.P.*, xx, 1335 (39) and (51).
29 All this story is well told by Knight, *op. cit.*, 302-9. Hales had earlier sold considerable ex-priory properties to that same Henry Over whom we have already seen as a major beneficiary of the suppression of the priory. As well as eventually acquiring all of Hales's 'haul', the corporation had in 1542 bought the reversion of ex-priory possessions, including two pools (i.e. ponds) and numerous messuages in and around the city (plus the remains of Greyfriars), leased to Over in 1540. *L.P.*, xvii, i, 556 (21).

The Theatre of the Soul – Liturgy Then and Now: Worship in Coventry's Priory Church

MICHAEL SADGROVE

The Church of Osburga and Godiva

In one sense, we can say virtually nothing about the worship of the Benedictine community of St Mary at Coventry. No service books have come down to us, no liturgical texts of any sort, no Coventry customary. Apart from a single poignant chalice and paten in pewter, no liturgical artifacts survive to tell their story – the ornaments, images, vestments that belonged to the ceremonies of this great monastic church. Finally, so little is left of the building itself that even to attempt to reconstruct its liturgy on the basis of the ground-plan is fraught with difficulty. Like the building itself, its worshipping life is lost to us almost without trace.

For instance. The priory church was dedicated 'in honour of God and St Mary His Mother, of St Peter the Apostle, of St Osburga the Virgin, and of all Saints'. We can, I think, assume that the priory contained the shrine to St Osburga, the eponymous foundress of Coventry's first religious house, destroyed by the Danes, it is said, in 1016. Her legend seems to have been increasingly cherished and nurtured by popular piety during the later middle ages. So her shrine 'in copper and gylte'[1] would have been a notable place of devotion in the Priory, and a significant source of income as the goal of pilgrims. As late as 1410, a synod of the Archdeaconry acceded to the request that her birthday should be solemnised annually as a major feast of the priory. We can guess that the members of the refounded community would regularly have processed to the shrine and offered prayers there, perhaps at the conclusion of one of the choir offices. Richard Morris conjectures that it may have been situated on the south side of the church.[2] A position near the east end, somewhere in the quire, is another possibility, like the shrine of St Cuthbert at Durham Cathedral. If we knew exactly where, we could begin to reconstruct at least some of the processional movements that would have formed a key part of the liturgy at Coventry.

Osburga was not of course the only woman to feature in the priory's calendar. It seems that Coventry's other, more famous lady, Godiva herself, acquired increasing prominence in the priory's folk-memory as the middle ages wore on. Mass on the anniversary of her death, 10 September, 'Dame Goodyves daye', was attended each year by the members of the Cappers' Guild.[3] According to William of Malmesbury, both Leofric and Godiva had

---

[1] F. Bliss Burbidge, *Old Coventry and Lady Godiva* (Birmingham, n.d.), 120.

[2] See Richard Morris' paper in this volume.

[3] Charles Phythian-Adams, *Desolation of a City: Coventry and the Urban Crisis of the*

169

been buried near the west end of the church they had founded 'in ambabus porticibus', which Brian Hobley, following Joan Lancaster, takes to mean 'matching side-chapels on the north and south sides of the (Saxon) church'.[4] This is presumably evidence for altars sited beneath or near the north-west and south-west towers, and it would have been here that the annual obit mass was celebrated. Indeed, the priory may have played an active part in shaping the legend of Godiva's ride, the earliest form of which dates from the early 13th century. It has been pointed out that the story, bringing together the themes both of fertility (her nakedness) and taboo (Peeping Tom), may be a Christianised version of an ancient pagan myth with its attendant springtime rituals.[5] It is not impossible that the monks used their foundress's name and virtue in an attempt to get rid of pagan survivals by baptising them into their own religious system.

The Priory's Liturgical Inventory

Meagre in the extreme are any other references of a liturgical kind in documents of the period. We know of a bishop's *cathedra* in the quire; of the Holy Rood for which Trinity Guild made payments for 'bourdes, nayles, jemowes (hinges), vestments, boyling and burnyshing the silver vessels, dying or steyning the altar coverings or curtains'. We also know of altars to St Mary, St John the Baptist, St John the Evangelist, St Katherine, the Holy Trinity, King Edward the Confessor, Edmund, Archbishop of Canterbury, All Saints, and the Holy Cross (which may have been an altar on the nave side of the rood screen, as it was in other foundations).[6] To each of these altars, a procession would have been made at Lauds and Vespers on the feast of its patron, and probably on other occasions as well.

Dugdale tells us that one pound of incense per annum was supplied to the priory by the Cluniac house at Daventry.[7] An inventory from the time of the dissolution lists the relics contained in the priory as follows: 'The arm of St Augustine of Hippo, purchased by Archbishop Ethelnoth, when he visited Rome, for 100 talents of silver, and one talent of gold; a part of the Holy Cross; relics of St Thomas à Becket, St Cecilia, St James, St George, St

---

Late Middle Ages (Cambridge, 1979), 171.

4   Brian Hobley, *Excavations at the Cathedral and Benedictine Priory of St Mary, Coventry* (Oxford, 1971), 51.

5   On folk elements in the story of Godiva's ride, see VCH, *Warwickshire*, VIII, 242ff; and Joan Lancaster, *Godiva of Coventry* (Coventry, 1967), 61ff. (a chapter written by H. R. Ellis Davidson).

6   Hobley, *op. cit.*, 73; David Parsons, *Liturgy and Architecture in the Middle Ages* (Leicester, 1989), 7-8.

7   Hobley, *op. cit.*, 56, citing W. Dugdale, rev. William Thomas, *The Antiquities of Warwickshire* (1730), 159.

Justine, St Jerome, St Andrew, St Lawrence, St Syboyne, St Katherine; a barrel of mixed relics; two bags of relics; a piece of Our Lady's Tomb; and Our Lady's milk in silver gilt.' To this is added, with Protestant wit, by one of the Henrician commissioners, Dr London, 'And among these relics your Lordship shall find a piece of the most holy jawbone of the ass that killed Abel.' The commissioners also plundered 'from the sacrist's treasures of the great cathedral church of Coventry fourteen copes of tissue, and two of old work for the King's use'.[8]

The Rule of St Benedict and the Regularis Concordia

All this tells us no more than we could have conjectured about the priory's worship: that in its proliferation of altars, its elaborate ceremonial and its thriving cult of the saints, it was typical of its age. To progress further in trying to reconstruct its liturgical life, we must fall back on what we know about other, comparable, institutions. We must of course be careful not to read back into the earlier period of the community's life practices that belong to a later era. The pre-Conquest foundation of the abbey in or around 1043 was more distant in time, and perhaps in ethos, from the dissolution in 1539 than the dissolution is from our own day. The scale of liturgical change over that time must not be under-estimated. The decreasing role of the laity in monastic life during this period, for instance, is one development that would have had significant, and visible, liturgical implications. Fortunately, although the local detail will be missing, there is enough material from other sources at our disposal to help us paint a reasonably accurate picture of worship in the priory church, enough at least for us to glimpse how the community both understood the place of worship in its corporate life, and how it expressed that ideal in practice.

Whether in monastic foundations like Coventry, or secular cathedrals like its partner at Lichfield, liturgy was the building's *raison d'être*. It was the centre of the life of the community, whose object was 'the perpetual celebration of divine worship by a body of men set apart for the purpose'.[9] This had always been envisaged in the *Rule of St Benedict*, which saw worship to be the principle around which the whole of the rest of life was to be organised. Worship imparted *stabilitas*, coherence. Hence the centrality of the choir offices, the *opus Dei* or work of God, celebrated by the community's twenty-four monks night and day. The focus of the offices lay in the psalms, which Benedict required to be recited in their entirety during the course of each week. In most Benedictine foundations, although the pattern varied with the latitude and the time of year, the working day began at 1 or 2 am

---

8   Egerton MS 2603, fol. 26; cited VCH, *Warwickshire*, II, 58.
9   Kathleen Edwards, *The English Secular Cathedrals in the Middle Ages* (Manchester, 1967), 56.

with Vigils and Lauds, working through the offices of Prime, Terce, Sext and
None, concluding with Vespers in the early evening and Compline at about 7
pm. The winter day would have begun somewhat later. But whatever the
exact timetable, the offices would have punctuated the Priory's daily life with
these rhythmical points of prayer, reflection and devotion. We can safely say
that by far the most time-consuming element of the monks' waking hours
was the recitation of the offices. It was for this that the priory, like all the
Benedictine foundations, primarily existed.

This is underlined in another key text which, like the *Rule of St Benedict*,
is crucial to our understanding of the life of the monastery. This is the
important document known as the *Regularis Concordia*. It was drawn up
towards the end of the tenth century, so that when St Mary's Abbey was
founded in 1043, it would have been in existence for around 60 or 70 years.[10]
It is associated with the name of St Dunstan, the great reformer and
refounder of monasticism following the Danish raids that had so damaged
monastic life in England at the turn of the millennium. The aim of the
Concordia is to reinstate monastic life in England along the lines already
established across Europe. It makes some interesting concessions to the uses
of the English, for instance in allowing the lighting of fires in cold weather,
and encouraging bell-ringing at festivals. It draws attention to the role of the
king and queen as the royal patrons of monasticism, and enjoins on the
community that they be prayed for at choir offices, a tradition that passed
straight into Cranmer's *Book of Common Prayer* and thus into modern times.
What is significant in this text, and very Benedictine in spirit, is the heavy
emphasis laid on the role of monks as guardians and celebrants of the liturgy.
They are to be liturgical people above all else.

Processions In and Around the Priory
One liturgical detail of direct relevance to Coventry is the mention of
processions at festivals. It is taken for granted in the text that processions
around the church, with stations at the various altars, is part of the daily
liturgical routine. In addition, however, the *Concordia* seems to envisage that
the monastic 'great' church will be the head of a family of churches nearby,
and that the route of certain liturgical processions (e.g. at Candlemas or Palm
Sunday) will take in, not only the monastic enclosure, but the neighbouring
churches as well. The arrangement of a parish church hard by the walls of a
great monastic foundation is familiar to us from other medieval towns, but it
cannot have been more striking than at Coventry. According to one text,
which records the visit to the priory of King Henry VI in 1457, there was a

10   David Knowles, *The Monastic Order in England: a History of its Development from
     the Times of St Dunstan to the Fourth Lateran Council 943-1216* (Cambridge, 1949),
     31ff; T. Symons, ed., *Regularis Concordia* (London, 1953).

'mynster durre that openeth into Trynite chirchyarde', through which the royal party came.[11] The attempt to find this door (which, if it was used for a royal procession, must have been of some size) in the excavations of 1965-67 failed. Earlier reconstructions of the priory showed it in the south wall of the nave near the south-west tower, and directly opposite the north porch of Holy Trinity, the prior's church in the city.[12] The door may more likely have been located in the south transept of the priory, especially if this was where Osburga's shrine was located. Either way, we can safely posit 'procession ways'[13] crossing and circulating the churchyard, the arena which was in effect the ecclesiastical centre of the city, and around which the priory and the two parish churches were grouped. Along these the clergy and the congregations of all three churches would have processed at the great festivals with lights, banners, incense, and, in later years, the blessed sacrament. As Phythian-Adams demonstrates, ceremonial occasions like these would have had an important civic dimension to them, especially, as we shall see, when the festival of Corpus Christi came to Coventry.[14]

We are fortunate that the record of one such ceremonial occasion has been preserved. This is the meeting of the triennial general chapter of the Benedictines, which from 1498 to 1519 met alternately at Westminster and Coventry, a fact that demonstrates the prestige enjoyed by both the city and its priory at this period. The Leet Book records the civic service that marked the first meeting in July 1498:[15]

> This yere the Chaptur of blak munkes was kept at Coventre about the visitacion of our Lady. And many of them came on the Seturday at night, & some on the Morowe & taried there vnto Wensday: at which day they had a general procession. And they came forth at the south durre in the Mynstere & toke their wey thurgh the newe bildyng downe the Bailly-lane. And the Maire & his Brethern in their scarlet Clokes with all the Craftes in theire best arraye stode vnder the Elme in Saynt Mighelles Chirchyard. And all the pensels [pennons] of the Cite before them; which pensels there went before the Crosse, & the Maire with his Brethern & the Craftes stode styll till the presidentes cam whom the Maire toke by the handes & welcomed them to town, & so folowed the procession; which procession went down the Bailly-lane, & so forth as is vsuelley vsed on seynt George day; & so into the Priory; and there was a solempne sermon seyde, where the Maire there satte

11   Hobley, op. cit., 92 n. 7, citing M. Dormer Harris, ed., The Coventry Leet Book (Early English Text Society, old series 134 [hereafter EETS, o.s.]).

12   See, for example, VCH, Warwickshire, VIII, 126.

13   Phythian-Adams, op. cit., 162.

14   Charles Phythian-Adams, 'Ceremony and the Citizen: the Communal Year at Coventry 1450-1550' in Peter Clark and Paul Slack (eds.), Crisis and Order in English Towns 1500-1700: Essays in Urban History (London, 1972), 76.

15   David Knowles, The Religious Orders in England (Cambridge, 1959), III, 10.

betwixt both presidentes, & after sermon doon they departed every man to his loggyng & som with the Maire to dyner, as dyvers of them did before.[16]

This is the most vivid glimpse we have of a liturgical event in the priory. It is as if, for the brief space of a summer's morning, the veil of obscurity surrounding the daily life of the priory is lifted, and we are in touch with the human beings who peopled it.

The Offering of Life

In 1102 (the generally accepted date), the abbey became a monastic cathedral under Bishop Limesey. As a diocesan church, albeit progressively eclipsed by the secular cathedral at Lichfield, its liturgy would inevitably have acquired particular prominence. Again, we can only conjecture how its diocesan status affected the daily liturgical routines of the priory. There may be a parallel in nearby Worcester, also a monastic cathedral. Although the foundations at Coventry and Worcester were never historically linked in the middle ages, these were without doubt two of the most prestigious monastic houses in the midlands. The rich array of liturgical texts that has survived at Worcester perhaps offers a glimpse of the kind of liturgical world inhabited by the canons of Coventry. The Worcester *Antiphoner* and *Gradual* are 13th century texts that embody much older material, some of it pre-Conquest. The highly developed forms of chant found in these books make them vital sources in the study of plainsong and its development. We may conjecture that Coventry similarly would have engaged in the quest for increasingly elaborate liturgy, both in its music and ceremonial.

The status of St Mary's, then, as a cathedral priory, would have reinforced the symbolic function of the community's worship, which was to demonstrate that all of life belonged to God, beyond the cloister as well as within it. And this brings us to the very distinctive theological understanding of life that characterised the middle ages. No medieval man or woman would have questioned that religion lay at the heart of human existence, or that worship was a person's first and fundamental duty. The differentiation between 'sacred' and 'profane', familiar to us, would have meant nothing at that epoch. And if particular men and women were called to a distinctive, 'religious' life of prayer and worship, such as at the abbey founded by Leofric and Godiva, then what such people did, they did on behalf of all. Their vocation, in a theological sense, was the vocation of all human beings.

The Celebration of Mass

There was one place, above all other, where the medieval mind found an icon that held up to it its entire world. That icon was the Mass.

16 Hobley, *op. cit.*, 71, citing M. Dormer Harris, ed., *The Coventry Leet Book* (EETS, o.s., 134).

At the centre of the whole religious system of the later middle ages lay a ritual which turned bread into flesh – a fragile, small, wheaten disc into God. This was the eucharist: host, ritual, God among mortals. In the name of the eucharist some of the most humbling, and the most audacious, claims have been made: that God and humans could meet and unite, mix and merge, that a disc of baked wheaten dough could embody the saving body of Christ, that the lives of men and women, of cities and nations, could be encompassed, redeemed, transformed or forsaken through it. [17]

The Mass had become a world-symbol, 'the centre and source of the whole symbolic system of late medieval catholicism'.[18] Not only did it make visible the drama of the world's redemption in Christ. It also encapsulated everything else in the world-order medieval people took to be God-given: the hierarchies of creation (embodied in the powerful myth of the great chain of being), of society (men and women in their social relations with one another), and of the church. The Mass, as the supreme act of the Church, stood for the good-ordering of things, cosmos in the midst of chaos, stability (to use the Benedictine word again) in a confusing and frightening world.

We do not know how the Mass was celebrated at St Mary's. Many of the great churches of England were developing local 'uses' during the middle ages, notably at Salisbury, Hereford, Lincoln and York. So prestigious was the Use of Sarum, for instance, that neighbouring dioceses in the south of England adopted it for their own, and by the time of the Reformation, it was enjoined upon the entire southern province. The distinctiveness of each 'use' did not primarily lie in deviating from the text of the western eucharistic rite as it had developed over nearly a thousand years. It lay rather in the evolution of a local ceremonial, as well as in the texts of 'propers' belonging to festivals enshrined in the calendars or sanctorales of each place. Hints of the latter exist, as we have seen, in the cult of Osburga at Coventry. As far as the eucharistic rite itself is concerned, it is probably more correct to speak of local 'dialects' or 'accents' of the one Latin Rite, rather than of rites altogether different from one another.[19] Whether there was a 'Coventry Use' we cannot say. More likely, the priory followed the use of one of the other cathedrals of middle England, Hereford, perhaps, or Lincoln, whose diocese at that time marched with Coventry and Lichfield. By the early 16th century, in all probability, it would have conformed to the Use of Sarum.

It is not too much to say that the offering of the Mass, whether in cathedral, monastery or village church, was seen as the summit of human experience this side of the grave. And so no limit was set on the investment

[17] Miri Rubin, *Corpus Christi: The Eucharist in Late Medieval Culture* (Cambridge, 1991), 1ff.

[18] Eamon Duffy, *The Stripping of the Altars: Traditional Religion in England c.1400-c.1580* (New Haven, 1992), 110.

[19] Gregory Dix, *The Shape of the Liturgy* (London, 1943), 585.

of time, money and human resources to ensure that the Mass was offered as splendidly and effectively as possible. Eamon Duffy has shown how parish inventories at the time of the Reformation testify to the panoply of liturgical goods possessed by even quite modest communities for the celebration of Mass: altar books, vestments, jewelled vessels, lights, bells, veils, houseling-cloths, hanging pyxes, frontals, towels, censers, chrismatories, paxbreds, Easter sepulchres... the list is endless.[20] We have already caught a very partial glimpse of the inventory of the priory church. It was not the wealthiest of houses, but its list of liturgical possessions would have been impressive. Unfortunately, little of it has survived.

An important development in late medieval practice is the rise of the chantries. These were foundations specifically endowed for the purpose of offering Mass for the soul of the departed benefactor. Sometimes, the endowment provided for the erection of a chantry chapel inside the church itself, together with funds to pay the stipend of a priest and the costs of the liturgy (principally the altar lights). More commonly, a priest would be endowed to say Mass at one (or more than one) of the existing altars, and this seems to have been the case in the priory. Copstone's chantry was founded in around 1291, and a chaplain was paid 100 shillings to celebrate Mass daily at the altar of St Edward. Leicester's chantry of 1328 was staffed by two secular priests who, in 1534, were being paid £4 per annum by the prior.[21] Duffy shows how the wills of prosperous late-medieval people reveal their intense preoccupation with death and the destiny of the soul in the endowment of chantries.[22] But in respect of chantries, the priory church probably stood in some contrast to its busier parochial neighbours of St Michael's and Holy Trinity. In both parish churches, we know of an abundance of chantries, and priests to serve them. At the priory, the small number of the chantries we know about suggests a more restful liturgical atmosphere. As is well known, the chantries were much criticised by the Lollards in the late 14th and early 15th century, a time of some unrest in centres such as Coventry where Lollardy was strong. We can at least say, however, that underlying the chantry system was an important theological instinct: that even the boundaries between life and death could be transcended by the faith and worship of the Church.

The Cult of Mary
The opulence of late medieval religion, and the sheer scale of society's investment in it, as exemplified by the chantries, can easily be misconstrued, particularly when it is contrasted, as it often is, with the squalor and

20 Duffy, *op. cit.*, 478ff.
21 Hobley, *op. cit.*, 72-73.
22 Duffy, *op. cit.*, 299ff.

meanness of so much of medieval life. What we need to understand is the underlying theological motivation that maintained the medieval system of worship for nearly a thousand years. We can perhaps best sum this up by saying that it was a thoroughly *sacramental* world-view, a vision of life in which everything was potentially a symbol or metaphor of some truth about God and the human condition. This view of things rests on the theological assumption that God is involved with the stuff of creation, which is what is meant by incarnation.

This helps to explain why the cult of Mary played so prominent a part in medieval worship. In Coventry, this is symbolised by a touching reference in the will of Lady Godiva herself. William of Malmesbury records that she bequeathed to the abbey (as it still was at her death in 1067) a 'rich chain of precious stones, directing it to be put round the neck of [the statue of] the blessed Virgin Marye, so that they who came for devotion there should say as many prayers as there were gems'.[23] Godiva was as well known for her devotion to Mary as for her own beauty and her charity towards the poor. Hence the primary dedication of the abbey to St Mary. Hers was, however, typical of the piety of the late Saxon period, with its intense and intimate preoccupation with the Blessed Virgin. Late medieval Christianity in England directly inherited this love of the Virgin Mary, and, by implication, a love of the infant Jesus. Throughout the life of the abbey and priory, the annual cycle of the Marian feasts – the Conception, Birth, Annunciation, Visitation and Assumption – would have elicited ceremonial at its most splendid, with the obligatory processions, and prayers at various stations. This would also have been true of the feasts associated with the Nativity of Mary's Child – St John Baptist's Day, Advent, Christmas, Epiphany and Candlemas. No doubt the iconography of the church reflected this devotion, with Godiva's jewelled rosary as an early witness.

In the later middle ages, however, the figure of Mary would have been prominently associated with a quite different image. This was the Great Rood, at the foot of which she would be depicted standing, together with St John. The erection of roods in churches reflects a new emphasis in late medieval religion, an increasingly popular devotion to the crucified Jesus. Poems such as *The Dream of the Rood*, and prayers at the elevation of the host like the immensely popular *Anima Christi* (late 14th century), testify to the significance the passion was acquiring in the devotional imagination of the middle ages. Such laity as worshipped in the priory's long nave would have seen the elevated host surmounted by the figure of Christ on the cross, much as, in Coventry Cathedral today, it is Christ in Glory on Sutherland's tapestry that gives the eucharist context and meaning. (It is interesting to see how this late-medieval preoccupation with the cross was directly inherited at

[23]   VCH, *Warwickshire*, II, 58.

the Reformation. Cranmer's communion rite of 1552, for example, is focused on the cross to the virtual exclusion of every other aspect of the saving history, including the incarnation and the resurrection. The late-medieval devotional *response* to the Mass has become the actual *content* of the reformed service.)[24]

The Corpus Christi Celebrations

One event, perhaps more than any other, gave to this development tremendous impetus. Its importance for medieval Coventry cannot be overestimated. This was the establishment of the new feast of Corpus Christi, which by 1318 was being celebrated throughout Europe, nowhere with more enthusiasm than in England.[25] By 1343, there was a liveried Corpus Christi Guild in Coventry, whose responsibility was to organise the elaborate procession on one of the city's major festival occasions.[26] Corpus Christi was, in essence, a feast of the passion, celebrating the sacramental presence of Christ in the eucharist as the priceless gift of Christ bequeathed to the church at his death. Observed on the Thursday after Trinity Sunday, and therefore near midsummer, it was inevitable that it would attract ceremonies that had been associated with that time of year since pagan times. The procession of the blessed sacrament in a richly decorated casket, with a canopy above supported by prominent laymen, would, very possibly, visit each of the city's holy sites in turn, accompanied by the guilds and members of the city hierarchy.

This illustrates how, to the medieval mind, it was impossible to separate sacred from secular as two realms of existence. The movement of the Corpus Christi procession from altar to market place is a vivid enactment of the flow from liturgy to life and back to liturgy again that marked the middle ages. Indeed, celebrations such as this should properly be seen as liturgical ceremonies that, through the power of the eucharist, consecrated the entirety of civic life and, in an important way, acted out its nature as a society.

The same instinct for dramatisation is found in the mystery plays that grew up in Coventry, as in York, Chester and other places, around the Corpus Christi celebrations. Here too, we are talking about ceremony rather than theatre in the modern sense: a taking into the street of the church's story that already belonged to, and was being acted out in, the liturgy of the eucharist. It is not surprising, therefore, that the passion features so prominently in the plays. It is not clear how directly the priory was involved

---

[24] Richard F. Buxton, *Eucharist and Institution Narrative: a Study in the Roman and Anglican Traditions of the Consecration of the Eucharist from the Eighth to the Twentieth Centuries* (London, 1976).

[25] Miri Rubin, *op. cit.*, passim.

[26] Phythian-Adams, *op. cit.*, 119.

in the production of the plays themselves, though it is significant that the Corpus Christi Guild that was so influential in promoting them belonged to the prior's half of the city. We know that the plays survived the dissolution of the priory by about 40 years. But then they, too, inevitably succumbed to Protestant reform. Theirs was a world of myth and ritual that was anachronistic in the text-dominated 16th century. Without Mass and Corpus Christi procession to give them context, their death was inevitable.

The Theatre of the Soul

Why was the nave of the priory so long? Not in order to accommodate worshippers: Holy Trinity was founded by the priory for that. Surely we are talking about a *processional space* – a kind of stage on which the priory community could act out its theatre, the theatre of movement, sound, colour and light that was the liturgical procession.

Peter Brook has coined the phrase 'holy theatre' to describe the stage as a sacramental place where the invisible can be made visible and tangible, where the language is not primarily that of words, but rather the exacting speech of actions, sounds, of 'word-as-part-of-movement'.[27] Calling attention to the origins of theatre in religious ritual, he writes (in 1968) about the 20th-century Coventry Cathedral and its liturgy:

> In Coventry ... a new cathedral has been built, according to the best recipe for achieving a noble result. Honest, sincere artists, the 'best', have been grouped together to make a civilized stab at celebrating God and Man and Culture and Life through a collective act. So there is a new building, fine ideas, beautiful glass-work – only the ritual is threadbare. Those Ancient and Modern hymns, charming perhaps in a little country church, those numbers on the wall, those dog-collars and the lessons – they are sadly inadequate here. The new place cries out for a new ceremony, but of course it is the new ceremony that should have come first – it is the ceremony in all its meanings that should have dictated the shape of the place, as it did when all the great mosques and cathedrals and temples were built. Goodwill, sincerity, reverence, belief in culture are not quite enough: the outer form can only take on real authority if the ceremony has real authority.[28]

It is clear, from what we can reconstruct of the worship of Coventry's priory church, that ceremony lay at the heart of its life. The procession, the Mass, the cult of saints, the Corpus Christi celebrations all spoke of the coherent, symbolic universe in which the people of medieval Coventry lived. The instinct to ritualise is perhaps one of the distinguishing marks of the middle ages, when compared to the modern period where the equivalent instinct is to verbalise. The medieval insight, for which Coventry priory once stood in all its glory, is that the liturgy is something *performed* before it is

[27] Peter Brook, *The Empty Space* (London, 1968), 47ff.
[28] *Ibid.*, 50-51.

something *said*. The primary liturgical command of the New Testament is to 'do this in remembrance'. The preoccupation with rubrics, that is, with performance, with the concrete, with praxis, was the attempt to do justice to that incarnational way of viewing the world. The belief was that people learned, we could almost say absorbed, faith by participating in the liturgy. We do not have to endorse every medieval practice to recognise the importance of that insight.

The vivid liturgy of the middle ages, what I am calling 'the theatre of the soul', now feels to us, the more we study it, like another country, the past where, L. P. Hartley reminds us, they do things differently. The priory whose scant remains we are celebrating this year belonged to a culture far removed from our own. In some respects, its belief system and spirituality may indeed feel like a different religion altogether.[29] It is not for us to make judgments about the comparative value of the medieval vision as compared with ours; but it is questionable whether, in terms of liturgy at least, we have gained more than we have lost.

---

[29] Dennis Nineham, *Christianity Mediaeval and Modern* (London, 1993), especially the conclusion. See also Eamon Duffy, *op. cit.*, for a detailed study of the different worlds of pre- and post-Reformation liturgy as it was practised at the parish level.

'The Road that Leads to Salvation': Benedictine Spirituality for Today

HEATHER M. WALLACE

Over the last two days we have heard of Leofric and Godiva, of kings, bishops, abbots and priors; we have discussed building lines and made informed guesses about doors and pillars and shrines and chantry chapels; we have heard of Helmsley's hole, of Shelton, Tickner and Hobley, but we have heard very little about the men who, for whatever reason, took their vows in the abbey church and gave their lives to God.

In a Benedictine House, following the precepts and the Rule of St Benedict, the monks made their vows of *stabilitas*, conversion of life and obedience to God and their abbey, not to an order. They expected to stay in their abbey for the rest of their lives.

When we planned this Symposium it seemed right that we should remember those men and consider what relevance the Rule of Benedict has for today.

I take my title from the last paragraph of the Prologue to the Rule of Benedict.[1]

'Do not be daunted immediately by fear'. Already we see the humanity of Benedict; you can feel the alarm bells ringing in the minds of the young novices. 'Do not be daunted immediately by fear and run away from the road that leads to salvation. It is bound to be narrow at the outset. But as we progress in this way of life and in faith, we shall run on the path of God's commandments, our hearts overflowing with the inexpressible delight of love.'

'Do not run away from the road that leads to salvation'. But of course we do. Those few words sum up most of our attempts at growth in our spiritual lives. We run away from getting to grips with prayer, with Bible reading, with new forms of worship, with people with funny ideas or funny habits (take that as you will).

If we get through Lent in one piece we live off our virtue for the rest of the year and yet those of us who have attempted, albeit in a small way, to follow a Lenten rule have found it rewarding and life-changing.

'It is bound to be narrow at the outset' says Benedict. The trouble is we seldom get past that narrow bit!

The subtitle of my talk is 'Benedictine Spirituality for Today'. Interest in Benedict and his Rule continues unabated. Many books, commentaries and pamphlets have been written over the years. The most well known

1   All quotations from the Rule of Benedict are taken from *RB1980* (Collegeville, Minnesota, 1981).

Benedictine in this country today is perhaps Cardinal Basil Hume, and his book *Searching for God* is full of Benedictine insights.

We must not view the monks of the Abbey of St Mary through rose coloured spectacles. Yes, they followed the Rule of St Benedict; but they were also human beings of their own time, and the community of monks, the number of which fluctuated through the centuries, reflected the age in which they lived.

But reading the Rule today links us to those men and those who had gone before and in interpreting the Rule for today we are following their path.

I begin with a quotation that I came across in the Benedictine convent at West Malling in Kent. It comes from *The Great 1000 Years*, by Ralph Adam Cram.

> You may know a crescent epoch from one that is decadent by this test – if its tendency is centripetal rather than centrifugal. If scattered units are being gathered up into greater wholes instead of the reverse process then great fortunes lie beyond and the future has much to give.
>
> If on the other hand things once united and consistent are resolving themselves into their component parts; if a church is disintegrating into sects, a philosophy into personal following, society into classes and subclasses each fashioning for itself its own aggressive propaganda and its own scheme of offence and defence; if literature and the arts are ceasing to be a great popular voicing and are becoming the personal idiosyncrasies of over-differentiated egoists; and if finally the human personality itself is breaking up into its component parts so that each person lives not a dual but a multiple life (his religion, business, philosophy, politics, domestic life all separated by inviolable frontiers) then you may know that an epoch is drawing to its close and if you are wise you will look all around for the signs of a new day, the grey dawn of which must be visible along the hills.

That quotation has stayed with me for all of what must be twenty years since I first read it. It seems very relevant to me at this point of the twentieth century as we search the skies for signs of a new day. Perhaps it has always been so. I have just finished reading Barbara Tuchman's account of the fourteenth century, *A Distant Mirror*; I was both saddened and cheered. Saddened because like the story of the twentieth century it was a story of war, of greed and famine and epidemic – the Black Death in place of AIDS. A century of selfishness and self delusion, of intrigue and corruption. But I was cynically cheered in a way – perhaps the twentieth century isn't so bad after all. Perhaps this is the way it has always been and to imagine otherwise is to live in Never Never Land. Perhaps the Rule of Benedict has survived 1500 years and still has relevance because human nature and conditions for all our so called progress hasn't changed, but that in each succeeding generation there have been enough people prepared to believe in that new day and look for the dawn.

We must remember that for many centuries those in authority or in the corridors of power were religious from the great monasteries who each day heard a chapter of the Rule (hence Chapter House) read out so that it permeated their subconscious. David Knowles in a paper he gave here at Coventry Cathedral at the 'Vision of Europe' conference in 1967 puts it like this:

> For many centuries almost all the writers and very many of the most distinguished bishops and royal councillors and administrators had heard every day, year in year out, a section of the Rule read in chapter, and had as novices learnt it by heart as the guide of their lives. We could be sure, even if we had not the evidence of countless quotations, explicit or hidden, in the writings of the time, that the Rule was ever present in their conscious or subconscious mind. We can scarcely be wrong in supposing that the peculiar qualities of the Rule – its simplicity, its moderation, its humanity – must have moulded their outlook and judgment, and through them, the outlook and judgement of countless individuals in the higher levels of thought and action in the medieval centuries.

We are all too aware of our world and its fragmentation, but what of the time of Benedict? His dates are reckoned to be c.480-547 or even later. I am no historian able to unravel the happenings of 1500 years ago but it is obvious that the upheavals of the fifth century had rocked the civilised world. Just the names of those who invaded Italy have a barbaric ring to them: Alaric the Goth, Attila the Hun, Gaiseric the Vandal. The world of Benedict was as uncertain as ours is today. The church was torn by schisms and it is quoted that there was not a sovereign or ruler who was not either an atheist, a pagan or a heretic.

And so, what about Benedictine spirituality for today? I could spend the short time I have this morning examining various chapters of the Rule – the chanting of the psalms, the 12 steps of humility etc, the vows of Stabilitas, Conversio Morum and Obedience – and discuss their relevance for today but as I have said there are many books available that do just that. And so I decided to concentrate on just one aspect. As I read the Rule I was very conscious of the men for whom Benedict wrote and the men and women down the centuries who have lived by it.

In Mark chapter 10 we read the story of the young man who asks 'What must I do to inherit eternal life?' At the end of the story Jesus tells him: 'Go sell what you own... then come follow me'. Then there follows one of the saddest verses in the gospel – 'When he heard this, he was shocked and went away grieving, for he had many possessions.'

Jesus calls us all in different ways to do things for him; it is difficult to obey his call and I expect that we have all 'gone away grieving' at some time or other. Benedict felt that God was calling him out of the chaos that was Rome to live the life of a hermit and this he did for three years. But in fact God was calling him to experience community; to work at community and to draw up a blueprint for living in community within the framework of the *opus dei* – the work of God.

Of course there had been monasteries and rules of life before the time of Benedict. In my days as a teacher, teaching music history, I was always aware that the great names – Handel, Bach, Mozart, Haydn, Beethoven – were the composers who clothed the hard work of lesser composers with genius – they put the icing on the cake of others' endeavours.

So with Benedict. He relies heavily on a contemporary rule, the Rule of the Master. Large chunks of the Rule of Benedict are taken from the Rule of the Master but the difference is that Benedict comes over as a man who was aware of the need for compassion. He manages to breathe humanity and an understanding of the difficulties of relationships into his Rule. He was aware that young and old find it difficult to co-exist, that rules must be elastic enough to encompass all who have bravely answered the call 'Come follow me'. And so Benedict wrote, for the twelve small monasteries each of about twelve men, about community.

One of the frightening statistics of the late 20th century is the number of single parent families and people living alone. This is not to say that single parents can't do a good job or that people shouldn't live alone but it is frightening because of the loneliness of their lives. It becomes too easy to lose faith in oneself, to look inwards, to feel that you are on the scrap heap.

The need for community today, of real community, is one of the challenges that the church needs to meet.

Scott Peck in his book *The Different Drum*[2] quotes from a book by Keith Miller, *The Scent of Love*,[3] which suggests that the reason why the early Christians were such phenomenally successful evangelists was not because of their gifts of speaking in tongues or teaching or even evangelising but because they had discovered the secret of community – outsiders had only to observe how they spoke to one another, interacted, cared for one another. They gave off the scent of love which attracted others to join.

The secret of community. What is community? It certainly does not mean a group of friends that all get on together from the same social class with the same accents who've been to the right schools and speak the same language. A community is a group of people all of whom have something to offer one another, all of whom must be enabled to make that offering, a

[2] Scott Peck, *The Different Drum* (New York, 1987).
[3] Keith Miller, *The Scent of Love* (Waco, Texas, 1983).

group who feel secure enough to be able to disagree, who can be honest and open and who have the common bond of wanting the best for each other.

Too many of us shy away from real community. We make do with what Scott Peck calls pseudo-community which has as its essential dynamic conflict avoidance, the ignoring of individual differences, the speaking in generalisations.

In this age of isolation we need to think about Benedict's teaching on community. The need to care for one another in all areas of our life as Benedict did for his monks, the need to create community across the generation gap and the social class in such a way as allows for communal caring and personal freedoms within the parameters of accepted structures. So let us look at the Rule of Benedict, or as much of it as time allows, from the point of community.

The *Prologue* begins with the words 'Listen carefully, my child' (the inclusive translation gives this rather than the literal translation 'son') 'attend with the ear of your heart'.

I spent quite a lot of time this summer with young children. They love you with unfailing trusting love. Every day for them is a new day, every day the slate has been wiped clean. The tears and tantrums of yesterday have faded. One three-year-old consistently muddled up yesterday with tomorrow. 'Do you know what we did tomorrow?' – the future reflected in the past.

But they can also hate you as only a child can when the answer is no. They feel real pain, they cry and storm and so cause the adult pain but through that pain comes the acceptance of a parameter of how far they can go – of what is acceptable and what is not – and so the child grows. As adults too we have to be ready to experience pain in order to grow. Benedict knew this. He knew that everyone needs discipline, discipline of self, discipline to a group, discipline to accept what at first seems impossible to achieve. Perhaps we can learn from Benedict the need for commitment; perhaps the church today is too willing to be liberal in its requirements. Perhaps it makes it too easy for us. In the chapter on receiving a new brother Benedict makes it clear that the Rule has to be spelt out. 'If you can keep it come in, if not feel free to leave.' Perhaps our insistence on personal freedom, freedom of the individual, is to blame for many of our social ills.

'Listen carefully, my child, attend *with the ear of your heart*'. What a wonderful phrase: 'the ear of your heart'. When in doubt let your heart rule your head. And this means love. We all need to love and to allow ourselves to be loved and true community allows for this. In Chapter 4 – there are seventy-three chapters, by the way, all fairly short – 'the Tools for Good Works', Benedict begins 'First of all love the Lord God with your whole heart, your whole soul and all your strength and love your neighbour as yourself.' This is the first of seventy-three tools mentioned in Chapter 4. Love permeates the Rule. But it is love that is controlled and structured. 'Trusting in God's help he must in love obey', 'Meet a guest with all the courtesy of love.' 'A kind word is better than the best gifts.' 'See how the Lord in his love shows us the way of life.'

Perhaps Chapter 72 is our blueprint for community love:

> Just as there is a wicked zeal of bitterness which separates from God and leads to hell, so there is a good zeal which separates from evil and leads to God and everlasting life. This, then, is the good zeal which monks must foster with fervent love: They should each try to be the first to show respect to the other (Rom 12:10), supporting with the greatest patience one another's weaknesses of body or behavior, and earnestly competing in obedience to one another. No one is to pursue what he judges better for himself, but instead, what he judges better for someone else. To their fellow monks they show the pure love of brothers; to God, loving fear; to their Abbot, unfeigned and humble love. Let them prefer nothing whatever to Christ, and may he bring us all together to everlasting life.

Throughout the Rule there is insistence on concern for one another, for civility – it is interesting that Scott Peck's new book *A World Waiting to be Born*[4] deals with the need for the world to return to civility.

There is much in the Rule about the Abbot, his role, how to choose him, what sort of qualities he should possess, but it is also clear that Benedict believes in communication and consultation and in true community this doesn't mean a rubber stamping of decisions already taken but real discussion, real communication. Yes, it takes longer; but so often the people most affected by decision making get left out in the decision process.

In Chapter 3 we read, 'As often as anything important is to be done in the monastery the Abbot shall call the whole community together and himself explain what the business is; and after hearing the advice of the brothers, let him ponder it and follow what he judges the wiser course. The reason why we have said all should be called for counsel is that the Lord often reveals what is better to the younger.'

A community respects every member and values their contribution. Misfits fit, the lonely are accepted, the eccentrics enjoyed. Everything that Benedict writes is backed by quotations from Scripture; all of life must be God centred. This particular chapter ends with a quotation from the Apocrypha, 'Do everything with counsel and you will not be sorry afterward' (Sir 32:19).

I think that too often we want to opt out of decision making; we want to leave it to others and then complain when decisions are made we don't like. Scott Peck again: 'A community cannot exist if the members depend on a

[4]   Scott Peck, *A World Waiting to be Born* (New York, 1993).

leader to lecture them or to carry their load.' A community must be aware that all have responsibilities and commitments to others.

I have said that Benedict's advice is controlled and structured and one of the aspects of community that we shy away from is the fear of being too involved or having no time for ourselves, no time of silence and quiet, no shutting the door, no taking the phone off the hook without feeling guilty. We do need to be able to escape at times from others who invade our space.

Chapter 22: 'Monks are to sleep in separate beds' – think back to all those historic houses you have visited, to conditions in the sixth century, to peasant life – and that sentence is quite revolutionary. Put in modern terms it says that we need our personal space – need room for us. There is no need to have a guilt-trip. Of course Benedict may have had the chastity of his monks in mind when he wrote that but it still remains that they were allotted a portion of personal space – their own bed. And we need to safeguard our space.

Benedict, conscious of the rule of hospitality ('All guests who present themselves are to be welcomed as Christ'), is also conscious that the rhythm and peace and silence of the monastery must be preserved so as not to destroy what the guest has come to find. In her book, *Seeking God – The Way of St Benedict*, Esther de Waal puts it this way:

> Time and space must always be kept so that the monk can encounter God. A proper care and love of myself is something I must preserve at all costs, even in the face of the subversive claims that I hear so many people making about how they never spare themselves and how they never count the cost in what they do for others. Endless people encountered, a mass of entertaining, constant coming and going, countless numbers of people and at the end of all this activity St Benedict faces us with two very simple questions: Did we see Christ in them? Did they see Christ in us?

> For if we are really to receive everyone as Christ that means that we must respect each as made in the image of God and not in the image of ourselves. And this particular piece of idolatry is all too easy.

Chapter 15 is entitled 'The times for saying Alleluia' and Benedict's message is: say it every day except in Lent. Alleluia – the shout of praise dating back to earliest Jewish and Christian liturgies.

There is a New Zealand prayer I have used on occasions:[5]

> PRAISE
> I've been looking for a suitable word
> to praise you, Lord. Something enthusiastic
> but not too formal, the sort of happy shout
> a child gives to its mother.
> I've tried Hallelujahs, Glorias and Hosannas,

---

5   Joy Cowley, *Aotearoa Psalms* (Wellington, NZ, 1989).

but really, what I'd like is a word
from my own language, a word that is me.
If I were a bellbird, I'd fill my throat
with ecstatic song. Or, as a lamb,
I could fling myself into spring dance.
As a mountain stream I would spill out
inarticulate babblings of joy.
And if I were the sea, my waves would explode
in a thunder of love for you.
Lord, you overwhelm me with your great goodness.
Praise should not be difficult and yet
I can't find the exact word. Perhaps
it doesn't exist, though if it does,
I'm sure that it sounds like 'Yippee!'

Are we people of joy? Do we praise God and each other? Do we shout yippee?

What a difference it would make to the communities we belong to, to our daily life, our relationships, if we echoed St Augustine, 'We are an Easter people and Alleluia is our cry!'

We belong to many different communities but it is the church community where we must look for signs of the new day where we must be enabled to reach out with the 'scent of love'. And remember Benedict was a layman – it is the job of the laity to take the lead, we can't leave it to the clergy.

The Bible is Benedict's text book; every chapter is backed up with biblical quotations and Benedict imparts a sense of urgency. If our faith has any relevance to our lives and our contribution to the world we live in, it is time we took it seriously.

Chapter 5:

Let us get up then, at long last, for the Scriptures rouse us when they say: It is high time for us to arise from sleep (Rom 13:11). Let us open our eyes to the light that comes from God, and our ears to the voice from heaven that every day calls out this charge: If you hear his voice today, do not harden your hearts (Ps 95:8). And again: You that have ears to hear, listen to what the Spirit says to the churches (Rev 2:7). And what does he say? Come and listen to me, sons; I will teach you the fear of the Lord (Ps 34:11). Run while you have the light of life, that the darkness of death may not overtake you (John 12:35).

Seeking his workman in a multitude of people, the Lord calls out to him and lifts his voice again: Is there anyone here who yearns for life and desires to see good days? (Ps 34:12). If you hear this and your answer is 'I do,' God then directs these words to you: If you desire true and eternal life, keep your tongue free from vicious talk and your lips from all deceit; turn away from evil and do good; let peace be your guest and aim (Ps 34:13-14). Once you have done this, my eyes will be upon you and my ears will listen for your prayers; and even before you ask me, I will say to you: Here I am (Isa 58:9). What, dear brothers, is more delightful than this voice of the Lord calling to us? See how the Lord in his love shows us the way of life.

No, the monks of the priory church were not paragons of virtue; they were people just as we are, but their days were built round the daily offices and the Mass and every day they heard a chapter of the Rule. Their lives were centred on God, detached, if only slightly, from the world around them.

We too need to centre our lives on God and look for the 'grey dawn . . . visible along the hills'.

The Celebration of the 950th Anniversary of the Founding of the Abbey Church of St Mary: Sermon preached at Festival Eucharist Sunday 12th September 1993 Coventry Cathedral

MICHAEL MAYNE

Words from the Rule of St Benedict, chapter 43: 'Let nothing be preferred to the service of God.'

This weekend many of you are celebrating the 950th anniversary of the founding of your cathedral just twenty-four years before Edward the Confessor built Westminster Abbey. If I feel a shade fraudulent in this setting, it is because if you ask historians what the links were between the Benedictines of Westminster and the Benedictines of Coventry the answer is a resounding silence. Indeed, the only link I can find between Coventry and Westminster is in one Richard Neale who, as Dean of Westminster in 1605, befriended the young George Herbert, then a scholar at Westminster School, and who became Bishop of Lichfield and Coventry in 1610. Neale complained that he had been beaten so often at Westminster that he never learned any Latin, but that did not prevent him from playing a dizzy game of preferments which was all ladders and no snakes. Launching himself from the Deanery of Westminster, in 22 years he successively became Bishop of Rochester, Bishop of Lichfield and Coventry, Bishop of Lincoln, Bishop of Durham, Bishop of Winchester and finally Archbishop of York – not bad going, even by Stuart standards. The other link between us, of course, is that your former Provost, Colin Semper, is now a most treasured member of the Abbey team of clergy.

In a week that has contained its predictable stories of violence and bloodshed and genocide, a good number of you have come to Coventry to study the monastic life of the Middle Ages. Those who judge that an irrelevance, a form of escapism from the horrors that nightly fill our screens, might have said the same of those who, during the Wars of the Roses or the Black Death, escaped into the relative calm and order of the monastic life. Others of us would claim that those who down the centuries have sought to follow a religious Rule, like that of St Benedict, and live in monastic communities – Eastern or Western, active or contemplative – are like those who seeing a pearl of great price, or a treasure hidden in a field, renounce everything in order to achieve it; and that their way of life could not be more relevant to the values by which we are called to live in 1993. For what the best of them have glimpsed and striven for is the Kingdom of God; and what they have attempted, by a life of obedience, humility and prayerful silence, is to show what it means to be a human being created in God's image as well as to demonstrate what a true community under God might be.

The Benedictine Rule, that under the abbot ordered the life of the monasteries of Coventry and Westminster, saw daily life as all of a piece: worship *and* daily work *and* feeding the hungry, clothing the naked and welcoming the stranger were inseparable, and could not be divided into that which is of God and that which is not. Prayer penetrated life, and daily life and work was not so much interrupted by, as contained within and stitched together by, the seven daily Offices and the daily Mass, from Matins at 2 a.m. to Compline just before sleep: those seven Offices that Cranmer later so brilliantly condensed into our Matins and Evensong. They were the golden thread that bound together this wise and adaptable Rule.

So the monks' chief work was the doing of the *Opus Dei*, the work of God: that is to say, the singing of the divine Offices and the performing of the Eucharist. This is why the great monastic abbeys and churches were built: in order that the worship of God, the singing of the psalms, the reading of the scriptures and the celebrating of the Eucharist, might be done not just with care and devotion, but aided by all the richness of architecture, all the subtlety of colour and ceremonial, all the beauty of words and music, of which we human beings are capable when we approach God – or, rather, when we invite God to approach us.

St Benedict was a man who understood the mystery and complexity of a human being. Like all great spiritual teachers he recognized the deep sense of incompleteness and yearning within each of us. We have a need for that which transcends us: that which is beyond and other than ourselves and which creates in us a sense of awe. For many, believers and non-believers, that may come through music or theatre or art or nature; but Christians believe that all these are pointers to the One who is the source of all beauty and truth and in whose likeness we are made. The God who has revealed himself as Christ-like and in whom alone lies our true fulfilment.

Now what a great building like yours or mine can do is to take you out of yourself; to arouse in you this sense of awe and wonder; and to feel awe is to begin to worship. Week by week tens of thousands come into the Abbey, thousands come into this cathedral, people of all faiths and none, people who have eyes to see and those who are spiritually blind; and there will be among them many who are hurt and damaged.

My point is simply this: *Anyone may come at any moment* into this space; and through music or architecture or word or liturgy God may touch them, speak to them, take them briefly out of themselves so that they glimpse some spark of truth, or become aware of their own mystery, as they never have before.

Which is why in the end the only reason for the existence of our churches, great or small, is what the Rule of St Benedict calls the *Opus Dei*, the work of God, the daily round of prayer and psalms and canticles and the reading of scripture, the daily taking and blessing and breaking and sharing of the Eucharistic bread, for all these things speak, in the place that is here and the moment that is now, of the eternal truths of God and our encounter with him in Christ.

That is why for us at Westminster nothing is more important, for example, than the corporate silence with which we start each day; or the singing of Evensong on a weekday evening in winter; or the daily lunch-time Eucharist in the nave with the tourists flowing all around you. All are part of the *Opus Dei*, and everything else we do is secondary to that. And, costly though it sometimes is, it must be done with attentive care.

I can think of many points where this has a direct relevance to the daily evidence of our inhumanity; I offer you just one. Once you dismiss the mystery of each human being made in the divine image; once awe and wonder count for nothing; once our sense of the holy and the transcendent are denied; then life becomes cheap and it becomes possible to shatter with a single bullet those most miraculous objects, the human brain and the human heart, with scarcely a second thought.

By our daily round of prayer and worship, the doing of the *Opus Dei*, we stand with those who affirm night and day that God is worthy of our love and praise, and that every living soul, made in God's likeness, is of infinite value in his sight.

The Middle Ages are Over
ROBERT JEFFERY

At the end of this symposium my mind has turned to the following poem by
R. S. Thomas:

> Make my voice sharp
> So it may rise to the clerestories
> And pierce the ear
> of the great God. And make
> my sword to enter
> into the bowels of God's foes.
>
> Forget it. The Middle Ages
> are over. On a bone
> altar, with radiation
> for candle, we make sacrifice
> to the god of quasars
> and pulsars, wiping
> our robotic hands clean
> on a disposable conscience.[1]

I am a person who is never happy in a new place until I have discovered its
roots. I need to know how we have got to where we are. When I first moved
to Worcester, I read the Dean & Chapter's Minutes for the previous fifty
years. It gave me real insights into the present position. You discover also
how things came to happen. For instance, the origin of the ending of daily
Choral Matins lay in the introduction of National Insurance. The employer
of people first thing on a Monday morning had to pay the insurance stamp.
The Dean & Chapter did not want to do that!

So we do need to look at our roots – but let us not be romantic about the
past. None of us would like to have lived in the Middle Ages. People then
may be just like people today, but the way life was organised was very
different. Life was very firmly ordered and corporate. We have seen how
there was much struggle for power. We cannot avoid the fact that religion
and the Christian faith was used to suppress people and keep them in their
place. This was even true of some forms of devotion.[2] It was a society where
most people lived most of their time in one place. People only travelled any
distance for war, crusade and pilgrimage and even then they did so with great
danger.[3] Life was very cohesive and introverted in each community.

---

[1]   Reprinted by permission of Bloodaxe Books Ltd. from *Counterpoint* by R. S.
      Thomas (Newcastle, Bloodaxe Books, 1990).
[2]   M. R. Miles, *The Image and Practice of Holiness* (London, 1988).
[3]   J. Sumption, *Pilgrimage* (London, 1975) and J. G. Davies, *Pilgrimage, Yesterday*

I doubt if we would understand their form of Christianity and they would not understand ours. Just as this world was structured, so was heaven and hell; God, angels and saints all in their order in heaven, the devil, demons and tortured souls in hell. This world was the place where God and the devil fought for human souls. This world was a battlefield. The Church was God's key instrument in this battle.[4]

So in Church and society we see the same pattern and interacting on each other. Just as feudal lords fought for power and territory so did bishops. Tradesmen and merchants traded, soldiers fought and the serfs remained serfs.

There was one very big difference in the Church's understanding of its role. There was no sense of, or need for, mission. They understood the Great Commission of Jesus at the end of St Matthew's Gospel as relating only to the Apostles and not going on any longer. In any case there was no need. A Christian nation was a Christian nation. There was nowhere to go in mission and people did not travel anyhow. They could see no need for a Decade of Evangelism![5]

The essence of Church life lay in Christian Presence. The Church was a sign of God's presence in the world – a way of getting in touch with the things of God. We have seen how this became focused in the Mass, in the act of consecration which re-enacted the incarnation.[6] Nor did they express their Church life the way we do. There was no sense of a corporate sharing in the eucharist, which is the fruit of the Liturgical movement of this century. People made their confession and went to communion once a year; otherwise they made sure they were present in the Church for the elevation of the Host in the Mass. They often gained indulgences by saying extra prayers like the *Anima Christi*[7] while the Host was elevated. Pilgrimages, festivals, processions and plays were part of the regular structure of life and helped to provide an integrated society and gave identity to community.

People's devotions were very simple, often relying on easily repeated prayers. The communication of the faith in an illiterate society depended on the visual aids of ceremonial, mystery plays, wall paintings and devotional objects. The saints were a main focus of faith. People did not read the Bible, they heard stories from the Bible and the stories of the saints. Many medieval paintings make no distinction between saints and biblical characters and they

---

and Today (London, 1988).

[4] For the medieval world view, see D. Nineham, *Christianity Medieval and Modern* (London, 1993) and also J. Huizinga, *The Waning of the Middle Ages* (Harmondsworth, 1991).

[5] The first to apply the Great Commission to his own time was Martin Bucer in *Von der varen Seelsorge* in 1538.

[6] Miri Rubin, *Corpus Christi* (Cambridge, 1991).

[7] R. M. C. Jeffery, *Anima Christi* (Darton, 1994).

are often mixed up together. The saints were the means of getting in touch with heaven, hence the devotion to relics. Here was a tangible contact. Relics also helped to give places identity and significance.[8] They were also an important source of income and attracted pilgrims and tourists to holy places. Worcester Cathedral was rebuilt out of the proceeds of pilgrims coming to the shrines of St Oswald, St Wulfstan and Our Lady of Worcester.[9] Readers of Ellis Peters' novels about Brother Cadfael will know how the monks of Shrewsbury Abbey stole the bones of St Winifred and brought them to the Abbey in order to attract more visitors. When Thomas à Becket was murdered, the Abbot of Shrewsbury rushed down to Canterbury and came back with the garment in which St Thomas was murdered, covered with his brains and his blood. This also became a tourist attraction.

But the religious communities had another function, which is often ignored. For many who entered them, the religious communities were centres of protest against the iniquities of the world. Those who wished to be committed to God were protesting against a Godless world. The communities, as we have seen, were vital points of economic growth and also provided a civilising effect on the world around them. Roger de Montgomery civilised Shropshire by establishing a string of abbeys and monasteries.

But things were changing and one factor, which has only been very briefly alluded to this weekend, was the Black Death. The Black Death was a deadly form of Bubonic plague which was carried all over Europe by black rats and arrived in England in 1348. It lasted for the rest of the century and carried on sporadically until the end of the seventeenth century. In the fourteenth century it wiped out a third of the population of England.

The effects of this were very profound. Armies were depleted and a scarcity of labour developed. Thus labour become more valuable. The working people began to gain power, hence the Peasants' Revolt of 1381. Another effect was the development of the English language. Until the end of the fourteenth century, the ruling classes spoke French. The Black Death led to a scarcity of French teachers and the Hundred Years War encouraged an anti-French feeling. So the English language came into its own, as we see in the writings of Chaucer, Langland, and Julian of Norwich.

Another development was the desire to pray for the dead. The early fifteenth century was the time when chantry chapels were endowed to say masses for the dead. The effects of pestilence, war and the short span of life impressed on people, who had a deep belief in the horrors of Hell, the need to prepare for death and pray for the dead. This made the religious communities even richer and more powerful. So powerful that many

[8] P. Brown, *The Cult of the Saints* (London, 1981).
[9] For a description of the Shrine see E. Duffy, *The Stripping of the Altars* (Yale, 1992), p. 403.

195

resented their wealth and power and so some endowed colleges of clergy and chantries at parish churches to avoid giving more money to monasteries. This is one factor in the decline of the influence of places like Coventry Priory.[10]

There is no doubt that the Reformation came as quite a shock, as Eamon Duffy has shown us.[11] But perhaps not as complete as some would think. If forms of devotion had met deep needs, people found other ways of expressing it. Let me give you two examples from the parish of Tong in Shropshire.[12] In the thirteenth century, under an agreement with the Lord of Tong, one Henry Hugefort, was granted some land to keep his pigs on. One of the conditions of this grant was that he presented to the Lord, 'a Chaplet of Roses upon the feast of St John the Baptist, if they be at Tong. If they be not at Tong the chaplet to be given to the Statue of Our Lady in Tong Church.' At the Reformation the Lady Chapel and the Statue were removed. Near the spot was the tomb of Dame Isabella de Pembrugge, who founded the church. What happened? The roses were given to her instead. They still are today. On the outside wall at the end of the south aisle of the church there are carved two rough crosses. These, says an old notebook, 'mark the place where the villagers prayed for their departed relatives'. On the other side of this wall had been the altar for requiem masses. So the praying continued outside. People will find means of meeting their needs in religious faith.

What strikes me most of all about this period before the Reformation is its restlessness and continual renewal and change. It is expressed in the way in which churches were continually rebuilt, adapted and changed. But it was happening in the faith as well. New religious orders emerged, like the Dominicans, not to preach the Gospel to unbelievers but to combat the teaching of heretics. New theologies emerged like that of Aquinas, following the importation of Aristotelian teaching from the Muslims. Prayer life changed through the growth of individualism and mysticism. It was a time of restless renewal and change.

That, of course, contrary to what many people think, is the essence of tradition. The way the faith is interpreted changes from age to age. This does not, however, mean that we have to reject what we receive from the past. If we do that we reject the benefits which people have received. We are always on the move. We bring with us the traditions of the past and we can examine them to see what we can learn from them. But we also have to ask questions and face new issues. We have to make new connections. We have to tell and make new stories. In so doing we make use of Scripture; we enter into the tradition of worship in the Church, which grows and changes within its

---

10 J. R. H. Moorman, *Ecclesiastical History of England* (London, 1954), pp. 115ff.
11 Duffy, *op. cit.*
12 See my forthcoming book *An Unexpected Discovery – Perspectives on a Shropshire Village.*

culture. We reflect on the Gospel, which comes out of our experiences. This includes our devotions and our moral and social considerations. All this is woven together. That is tradition; like a great unfolding tapestry. We all have to make our own contribution.[13]

So what conclusions do I draw from this for our own time?

Firstly, we have to make our own stories and not just live off and exploit the stories of the past. If we simply do that we shall become unrelated to the present and have nothing to pass on to the future.

Secondly, we should reflect more deeply on 'Mission as Presence' and see what it can achieve before we seek to be more activist.

Thirdly, we can see the need for simple spirituality, which can attract ordinary people. We have made it all too complicated and too intellectual.

Fourthly, we need to rediscover the way to be centres of protest in a world which exploits people to satisfy market forces, which is greedy for money and gain; a world where human life is too cheap and disposable.

Fifthly, we need to reflect on the significance of medieval patterns of worship. As I have already said, the medieval Church was seeking ways of expressing the Faith and communicating the Gospel in a non-literate world. The celebration of the Mass with lights, incense, music and ceremony was there to help people enter into an understanding of the mystery of God. In a world where the Church was dominant, much of Church life provided variety and excitement in a dull world. Liturgy was fun. Think of that event in the Sarum Rite on Palm Sunday, when at the end of a procession the choirboys mounted a platform and threw buns to the people. Liturgy contained much that was visual and festive.

What this teaches us is very profound. It is that worship is creative play.[14] We are so used to seeing leisure being exploited in a commercial way and debasing the significance of leisure which is, as Pieper put it:

> In leisure the truly human values are saved and preserved because leisure is the means whereby the sphere of the specific human can over and again be left behind.[15]

We need to discover ways of overcoming passive commercial leisure. What society needs is creative play. Play is the basic experience not just of children but of all of us.[16] Play is an essential means of learning and maturing. Worship is thus the way in which we share in God's creative play. In sacramental worship the full power of worship is realised as we are caught up into another dimension.

---

[13] R. L. Wilken, *The Myth of Christian Beginnings* (London, 1971).
[14] See note 7, above, for a development of this thesis.
[15] J. Huizinga, *Homo Ludens* (London, 1949).
[16] R. Alves, *Tomorrow's Child* (London, 1972).

This relates very much to the present state of the Church. The very fact that, unlike the Middle Ages, most of life has set itself free from the dominance of the Church means that the Church is set free to be itself. Thereby the Church is able to assert a different level of priorities to the world and be a centre of protest.

In the past we have used God to enable us to survive in the world. Now we can use the things of the world to enjoy God. We are free to enjoy God for God's sake. We have no need now to justify our existence. We need ourselves and to help others just to be. We need to affirm the value of being. Worship as play points to the transcendence of God among us and the possibility of real creativity. Thus when we look backwards, we can see that in our age liturgical revision has hardly begun. Such an attitude could have deep social implications as it did in the Middle Ages.

We cannot just celebrate the past. We have to face the problems of today's world, which calls us to a celebratory, protesting and simple way of life. R. S. Thomas puts it thus:

> Not the empty tomb
> but the uninhabited
> cross. Look long enough
> and you will see the arms
> put on leaves. Not a crown
> of thorns, but a crown of flowers
> haloing it, with a bird singing
> as though perched on paradise's threshold.
>
> We have over-furnished
> our faith. Our churches
> are as limousines in the procession
> towards heaven. But the verities
> remain: a denuclearised
> cross, uncontaminated
> by our coinage; the chalice's
> ichor, and one crumb of bread
> on the tongue for the bird-like
> intelligence to be made tame by.[17]

The Middle Ages are over. We have to make and tell our own stories, be our own centres of protest and rejoice in the God whose hand is over us all.

[17] See note 1, above.

GLOSSARY

abuttal	the immediate and adjoining property(ies)
actum, acta (pl)	an administrative document issued by, or in the name of, a bishop (or, rarely, a document to which his seal was attached)
almoner	the officer in a monastery responsible for distributing alms, clothing, food and drink to poor, old and sick
ambulatory	an aisle or 'walkway' around the back of the presbytery
aqueductor	monastic officer responsible for water supply and drainage
ashlar	masonry blocks with regular squared edges
aumbry	cupboard or recess
axial shaft	shaft in the centre of a group of shafts or mouldings, usually projecting forwards more than the others (see 'nook-shaft')
ball-flower moulding	carved globular flower of three leaves enclosing a small ball
bar tracery window	the decorative gridwork of stone which holds the glass, typical of Gothic windows in England from the late 13th century
bede (bead) roll	a list of deceased persons to be specially prayed for
bell moulding	a bell-shaped moulding, applied mainly to bases
bicephalous	literally, having two heads; in relation to the diocese of Coventry and Lichfield, the problematic relationship between the two cathedrals of Lichfield and Coventry
blind tracery	the stone gridwork of a Gothic window, applied to the surface of a wall (see 'bar tracery')
boss	carved knob at the intersection of vault ribs
cellarer	the officer in a monastery responsible for the provision of food, drink etc.
cellarium	the monastic food store or larder
censer	vessel in which incense is burnt
chamfered mitre moulding	moulding shaped like a wedge with a flattened point

199

chevet	French term for the east end of a church, taking the form of an ambulatory with chapels radiating from it
chrism dues/fee	payment made, usually to a cathedral, or especially in pre-Conquest times, to an ancient church, to obtain holy oils for sacraments
chrismatory	a vessel containing chrism or consecrated oil
cloister garth	a plot or garden enclosed by the cloister
comital	pertaining to a count or earl
correctional rights	power to impose disciplinary penalties
corrody	an allowance for maintenance or an annuity provided by a monastery to a lay person in return for a payment made earlier to the monastery by that person; also annuities paid to the former servants by the religious house or demanded from it for protégés by third parties (usually the crown)
cusping	spiky decorative edging in parts of Gothic windows and arches; each spike is a 'cusp'
demi-shaft	shaft or column of half circumference only, attached to a wall
donative	an ecclesiastical post in which the incumbent is appointed at the nomination of a patron, without institution or induction and without acquiring freehold rights in the office
dorter	the monastic dormitory
double-roll base	base shaped like two rings stacked up, the smaller ring on top of the larger
eigenkirche	'private church', a family foundation
enceinte	enclosure
escheat	the reversion, resulting from a failure of heirs, of any land of a lord's tenants, to the lord himself within his own manor, or to the crown in cases higher up the feudal hierarchy; also applicable to lands of religious houses and bishoprics which devolved to a patron or the crown during the vacancy
familia	entourage or staff
fane	church
filleted shaft	shaft with a narrow flat strip running up it

forma pauperum	literally 'in the form of the poor': papal provisions granted in considerable numbers to 'poor clerks' for benefices in the gift of named patrons (in England always religious institutions or bishops) without identifying a specific post
frater	the monastic dining hall
freestone	stone which can be cut easily in all directions (in contrast to an English 'marble' like Purbeck marble). Often a fine-grained sandstone, which comes in a variety of colours
frontal	covering of the front of an altar
galilee	porch or vestibule usually at the west end of a church
hanging pyx	see pyx
hospitaller	monastic officer responsible for receiving and attending upon visitors and pilgrims
houseling cloths	communion cloths
induction	the action of formally introducing a clergyman into possession of the church to which he has been presented and instituted together with all rights and profits
institution	the legal action prior to induction whereby a cleric's right to hold a benefice was recognised by the bishop
jambs	side piece or post of a door
keel moulding	shaft or rounded moulding with a sharp edge running up it
lancet	pointed-arched aperture, especially a single-light window
lierne vault	a later Gothic vault characterised by many short ribs ('liernes') to produce a decorative effect
mandate	a papal edict especially with reference to the preferment of a benefice
mediated fee	a money payment, paid through an intermediary
milites	knights, soldiers
multi-scallop capital	capital decorated with scalloped edges
nemus	woodland
nook-shaft	shaft set in an angle or corner of a wall, doorway, pier, etc.

obedientiary	a member of a monastery charged with any duty or 'obedience'; the holder of any office in a monastery under an abbot or superior
ogee keel moulding	variation of a keel moulding, with the edge more pronounced, like the keel of a ship's hull
parochia	a minster parish; a more extensive area of spiritual jurisdiction than that associated with a local or 'parish' church
pax	small tablet, having on it a representation of the Crucifixion or some other Christian symbol, which was offered to the congregation to be kissed during the Mass
paxbred	Same as pax.
penitentiary	monastic officer responsible for imposing penances in serious cases
pier	large masonry support, usually for an arch
pilaster buttress	buttress in the form of a vertical strip of shallow projection, attached to a wall
pittancer	monastic officer responsible for distributing and accounting for pittances, the small donations given to the monastery
porticus	a subsidiary cell or chapel opening off the main body of the church, particularly in Anglo-Saxon architecture
precentor	officer, in either a monastic foundation or secular cathedral, responsible for liturgy and leading the singing at choir
presbytery	the part of a church lying east of the choir, where the main altar is located
procuration	provision of entertainment for a bishop or other visitor by incumbent or religious institution, often commuted to a cash payment
pyx	ornamental casket in which the consecrated Host is preserved
questorial licences	licences granted by a bishop to representatives of worthy causes to collect alms, usually in exchange for indulgences
refectorer	officer in monastery responsible for furnishing and running of the refectory
reredorter	the building containing the latrines
respond	half of a pier bonded into a wall, and carrying one end of an arch

reversion	a tenurial arrangement by which lands held under lease revert, or are returned, to the grantor on completion of the agreed term
socle	shallow recess carved in the top surface of a base to receive a shaft
stipendiary curacy	the exercise of cure of souls in an identified territory by a cleric who was paid rather than holding a benefice
succentor	deputy to a precentor
trefoil-headed arcading	decorative arches applied to a wall surface, with the top of each arch decorated with two cusps (see 'cusping')
tricephalous	literally, having three heads; within the diocese of Coventry and Lichfield, the problematic relationship between the cathedrals of Lichfield and Coventry and the quasi-cathedral status of St John's, Chester
vesica shaped	oval shape, pointed at the head and foot

INDEX

This is an uncritical computer-generated index of the personal- and place-names encountered in the main text, with a few additions from select footnotes: 125 + n.46 means there are references in the main text as well as note 46 on that page; 125: n.46 means only the note is relevant. It was felt that it would not be practical to include ideas or analytical references to Coventry's religious institutions in the time available. The compiler was the publisher, Shaun Tyas.

Plate 1. 1920s photograph of the 'Spotted Dog'. *Courtesy of Local Studies, Coventry Central Library.*

Plate 2. St Mary's church, Gothic chevet, foundations of the north-east radiating chapel. *Courtesy HAG, CBP archive; photograph, P. Chatwin, 1955.*

Plate 3. St Mary's church, Gothic chevet, the north-east radiating chapel and loose stones. *Courtesy HAG, CBP archive; photograph, Arthur Cooper, 1955.* The figure in the foreground is J. B. Shelton, the well-known Coventry amateur archaeologist (d. 1958).

Plate 4. St Mary's church, Gothic chevet, foundations of the eastern radiating chapel.
Courtesy HAG, CBP archive; photograph, P. Chatwin, 1955.

Plate 5. St Mary's church, north choir aisle wall, exterior ground-course moulding.
Courtesy HAG, CBP archive; photograph, P. Chatwin, 1955.

Plate 7. St Mary's church, north choir aisle wall, socles of respond base. *Courtesy HAG, CBP archive; photograph, P. Chatwin, 1955.*

Plate 6. St Mary's church, north choir aisle wall, inside face looking from east to west. *Courtesy HAG, CBP archive; photograph, P. Chatwin, 1955.*

Plate 9. St Mary's church, north choir aisle wall, section of window sill. *Courtesy HAG, CBP archive; photograph, P. Chatwin, 1955.*

Plate 8. St Mary's church, north choir aisle wall, bases of the respond in pl. 7. *Courtesy HAG, CBP archive; photograph, P. Chatwin, 1955.*

Plate 10. Reconstruction elevation of the 13th-century west front
of St Mary's church, T. F. Tickner (n.d., *c*.1916-20).
Courtesy, Coventry City Council, Planning Services (location of original unknown).

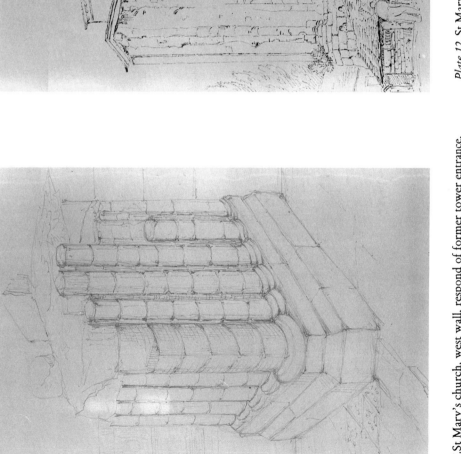

Plate 11. St Mary's church, west wall, respond of former tower entrance, Dr Troughton (n.d., c.1856). *Courtesy Coventry City Record Office, Troughton Sketches, IX 6.*

Plate 12. St Mary's church, north-west tower, from the north, Dr Troughton (n.d., before 1856). *Courtesy Coventry City Record Office, Troughton Sketches, IX 3B.*

Plate 13. St Mary's church, remains at the west end, looking north from Priory Row.
Courtesy History of Art Dept., Warwick University.

Plate 14. Vault boss in No. 9 Priory Row, rear cellar, *ex situ.*
Courtesy History of Art Dept., Warwick University.

Plate 15. Carved corbel in No. 9 Priory Row, front cellar (upper), *ex situ.*
Courtesy History of Art Dept., Warwick University.

Plate 16. Priory Row at Hill Top, from the south; No. 9 is on the right.
Courtesy History of Art Dept., Warwick University.

Plate 17. St Mary's church, the Gothic chevet foundations today.
Courtesy History of Art Dept., Warwick University.

Plate 18. Tewkesbury Abbey, interior of the choir and presbytery.
Courtesy History of Art Dept., Warwick University.

Plate 19. Peterborough Cathedral, interior of the nave.
Courtesy History of Art Dept., Warwick University.

Plate 20. Fragment of Saxon stonework found in Palmer Lane.
Courtesy Herbert Art Gallery and Museum.

Plate 21. General view of excavations with kitchen in foreground.
Courtesy Herbert Art Gallery and Museum.

Plate 22. Window and doorway in north dorter range. *Courtesy Herbert Art Gallery and Museum.*

Plate 23. Drain through kitchen court.
Courtesy Herbert Art Gallery and Museum.